THE REFORM OF BISMARCKIAN PENSION SYSTEMS

CHANGING WELFARE STATES

Processes of socio-economic change – individualising society and globalising economics and politics – cause large problems for modern welfare states. Welfare states, organised on the level of nation-states and built on one or the other form of national solidarity, are increasingly confronted with – for instance – fiscal problems, difficulties to control costs, and the unintended use of welfare programs. Such problems – generally speaking – raise the issue of sustainability because they tend to undermine the legitimacy of the programs of the welfare state and in the end induce the necessity of change, be it the complete abolishment of programs, retrenchment of programs, or attempts to preserve programs by modernising them.

This series of studies on welfare states focuses on the changing institutions and programs of modern welfare states. These changes are the product of external pressures on welfare states, for example because of the economic and political consequences of globalisation or individualisation, or result from the internal, political or institutional dynamics of welfare arrangements.

By studying the development of welfare state arrangements in different countries, in different institutional contexts, or by comparing developments between countries or different types of welfare states, this series hopes to enlarge the body of knowledge on the functioning and development of welfare states and their programs.

EDITORS OF THE SERIES

Gøsta Esping-Andersen, University of Pompeu Fabra, Barcelona, Spain
Anton Hemerijck, the Netherlands Scientific Council for Government Policy (Wetenschappelijke Raad voor het Regeringsbeleid – WRR)
Kees van Kersbergen, Free University Amsterdam, the Netherlands
Jelle Visser, University of Amsterdam, the Netherlands
Romke van der Veen, Erasmus University, Rotterdam, the Netherlands

PREVIOUSLY PUBLISHED

Jelle Visser and Anton Hemerijck, *A Dutch Miracle: Job Growth, Welfare Reform and Corporatism in the Netherlands*, 1997 (ISBN 90 5356 271 0)
Christoffer Green-Pedersen, *The Politics of Justification: Party Competition and Welfare-State Retrenchment in Denmark and the Netherlands from 1982 to 1998*, 2002 (ISBN 90 5356 590 6)
Jan Høgelund, *In Search of Effective Disability Policy: Comparing the Developments and Outcomes of the Dutch and Danish Disability Policies*, 2003 (ISBN 90 5356 644 9)
Maurizio Ferrera and Elisabetta Gualmini, *Rescued by Europe? Social and Labour Market Reforms from Maastricht to Berlusconi*, 2004 (ISBN 90 5356 651 1)
Uwe Becker and Herman Schwartz (eds.), *Employment 'Miracles': A Critical Comparison of the Dutch, Scandinavian, Swiss, Australian and Irish Cases versus Germany and the US*, 2005 (ISBN 90 5356 755 0)

The Reform of Bismarckian Pension Systems

A Comparison of Pension Politics in Austria, France, Germany, Italy and Sweden

Martin Schludi

AMSTERDAM UNIVERSITY PRESS

Cover illustration: Ferdinand Hart Nibbrig (1866-1915), 'Oude Zeeuwen', 1911

Cover design: Jaak Crasborn BNO, Valkenburg a/d Geul
Lay-out: Adriaan de Jonge, Amsterdam

ISBN 90 5356740 2
NUR 754

Table Of Contents

List of Tables

List of Figures

Acknowledgements

I am particularly grateful to Karen Anderson, Lucio Baccaro, Guiliano Bonoli, Agar Brugiavini, Bernhard Ebbinghaus, Maurizio Ferrera, Steffen Ganghof, Antonia Gohr, Christoffer Green-Pedersen, Miriam Hartlapp, Markus Haverland, Martin Hering, Karl Hinrichs, Ellen Immergut, Matteo Jessoula, Sven Jochem, Herbert Kitschelt, Bernhard Kittel, Anders Lindbom, Michael Littlewood, Margitta Mätzke, Bruno Palier, Edward Palmer, Birgitta Rabe, Anika Rasner, Bo Rothstein, Fritz Scharpf, Isabelle Schulze, Eric Seils, Christian Toft, Christine Trampusch, Axel West Pedersen and Harold Wilensky for their constructive criticism and useful hints.

June 2005
Martin Schludi

Introduction

The 1990s have been a decade of fundamental challenges to the European welfare states. Rising unemployment has put them under growing financial pressure, while unrestricted international capital mobility and intensified international competition have rendered existing welfare state commitments increasingly costly. Moreover, the legally binding criteria of the Maastricht Treaty have forced most European governments to adopt tight budgetary policies. The ageing of the population in virtually all European countries over the next decades will reinforce these pressures even further.

Due to these developments, the reform of the welfare state figures prominently on the political agenda of all European governments. As Bonoli (2000) has argued, welfare retrenchment is no longer an Anglo-Saxon idiosyncrasy. However, the process of welfare state restructuring has been accompanied by severe political and societal conflicts. Powerful pressures for cost containment collide with equally powerful forces defending existing welfare state arrangements. This struggle also left its imprint on the scholarly debate about the welfare state. One strand of current welfare state research emphasises the profound alteration of traditional social policy programmes in response to the above-mentioned pressures and points to the inevitability of welfare retrenchment under changed economic conditions. Another strand diagnoses a remarkable resilience of the welfare state and highlights the political difficulties of carrying out retrenchment policies.

This academic dispute is unlikely to be settled at a general level. In recent years, numerous authors have contributed to this debate and put forward a variety of theoretical propositions about the factors which facilitate or impede welfare retrenchment. While the empirical findings emerging from this body of literature are still rather inconclusive, a strong case can be made that the degree of social policy retrenchment and welfare restructuring appears to be highly contingent. In this respect, we can divide the existing explanatory approaches in the retrenchment literature into at least three broad categories. One strand of explanation focuses on the strength of adaptational pressures arising from external constraints on welfare state policy as the most important predictor for the degree of retrenchment. Another line of argumentation points to differences in the institutional design of social policy programmes which will determine the degree of political and societal resistance to retrenchment arising from the structure of affected interests in distinct social policy areas. Other scholars emphasise the importance of general political factors such as the partisan complexion of government or the role of political institutions as the crucial explanatory variables for the extent of social policy cutbacks.

Apparently these explanatory dimensions are not mutually exclusive. More often than not it will be difficult to assess the relative importance of these factors for retrenchment outcomes. By the same token, empirical studies on welfare retrenchment are frequently confronted with the problem of over-determination. In order to get a grip on this problem, I have chosen a "most-similar-case" design. This study investigates the reform of social insurance-based pension systems (henceforth referred to as "Bismarckian pension systems") in five West European countries (Austria, France, Germany, Italy, and Sweden) since the late 1980s. This case selection is suited to hold a number of potential explanatory variables for different degrees of retrenchment (relatively) constant. Most importantly, by focusing on Bismarckian pension systems I can control for a great deal of programme-specific variations. For a number of reasons these pension systems are more vulnerable to demographic and economic pressures than other pension arrangements. At the same time, the political resistance to retrenchment is particularly strong for this type of social policy programmes. I will discuss these aspects in more detail in the following chapter. Moreover, all of the countries studied had to cope with severe economic and fiscal crises in the early and mid-1990s. In addition, as (potential) candidates for the European Monetary Union, these countries were under extraordinarily strong pressure to consolidate their public budgets. Finally, they are subject to massive demographic changes arising from a rapidly ageing population over the next decades. In sum, pension policymakers in the countries studied have faced *relatively* similar challenges at least since the early 1990s. This study tries to answer the question whether these countries have been able to cope with these challenges and adjusted their national retirement systems accordingly. More specifically, it seeks to investigate the political conditions under which the national governments were able to carry out the necessary reforms of their pension systems and initiated measures that will prevent a spiraling of pension costs in the future.

The study is organised as follows. In chapter one, I provide a problem-oriented analysis of pension policy in the context of fiscal austerity and demographic ageing. The chapter briefly sketches the socio-economic pressures on European pension systems in general and on Bismarckian pension systems in particular. Moreover, it discusses the various options for pension policymakers to put these systems on a more sustainable basis. Finally, it seeks to empirically assess the differences in the types and magnitudes of challenges between the national pension arrangements analysed in this study. While these differences are less pronounced than the differences between Bismarckian and Beveridgian pension systems, they still must not be neglected.[1]

Chapter two provides an empirical account on the reforms of Bismarckian pension schemes since the late 1980s. While there have been a number of commonalties in the general direction of reform, we also observe substantial cross-national variation in the degree to which the pension systems under study have been transformed. For instance, among the five countries under investigation, only Italy and Sweden brought about a changeover from a defined-benefit to a defined-contribution scheme, and only Sweden implemented a new fully funded private pillar on a mandatory basis.

Chapter three develops a theoretical framework, which allows us to account for the variations in pension reform outcomes. In this chapter I first review the theoretical approaches dealing with social policymaking in an era of retrenchment. It then briefly portrays the theoretical concept of actor-centred institutionalism and seeks to adopt this concept to explain the politics of pensions in the Bismarckian countries. Starting from the assumption that pension reforms are politically risky as they impose tangible losses on large sections of the electorate I argue that governments have a fundamental interest in achieving the political support or at least the acquiescence of potential reform opponents, most notably of the parliamentary opposition and/or the trade unions. Subsequently, I analyse the conditions under which these actors are likely to co-operate with the government or not from a theoretical viewpoint.

On the basis of this theoretical framework, chapters four through eight provide national accounts of the political decision-making process in Sweden, Italy, Germany, Austria, and France. The sequence of the national case studies largely reflects the degree to which these countries have succeeded in adjusting their arrangements of old age provisions to the challenges described in chapter one. Within the individual country chapters, I will first sketch the key features of the national pension systems in the late 1980s. Thereafter, I will briefly summarise the country's recent achievements in pension policy. I will then turn to the description of the political reform process, which in principle will follow a chronological order, starting in the late 1980s and ending in 2001. At the end of each country chapter, I provide summaries of the national reform process, which try to assess more systematically the country's institutional capabilities to deal with the pension problem and at the same time highlight the factors which may explain possible differences in the country's reform success over time.

Chapter nine summarises the empirical findings that emerge from the comparison of the case studies and discusses them in the light of the theoretical approach outlined in chapter three.

1 The Need for Pension Reform: A Problem-Oriented Perspective

1.1 Public pension arrangements under adaptational pressures

Pension systems in virtually all advanced welfare states are exposed to a number of serious internal as well as external pressures, some of which will reveal their full effect only over the coming decades. Depending on the specific institutional set-up of retirement income policies, their relative impact is likely to differ from one country to another. Broadly speaking, we may distinguish between economic, fiscal, and demographic pressures, all of which challenge the sustainability of national pension arrangements. In the following section, I will briefly portray the variety of strains with which pension policymakers in advanced welfare states have to cope.

Economic and fiscal pressures

The economic slowdown since the mid-1970s and – related to that – sluggish wage growth and shrinking employment has significantly weakened the revenue base of public pension schemes in the EU (European Union). At the same time, public pension systems themselves were increasingly used as an instrument for an early exit from the labour market, especially in the Continental welfare states. In addition, regular jobs drifted increasingly toward the shadow economy in recent years or were crowded out by various forms of "atypical" employment, which were often not subject to social insurance contributions. As a consequence, public pension arrangements were faced with a growing gap between revenues and expenditures.

Initially, most governments closed this gap with an increase in pension contributions rates, which at the time was a politically more feasible strategy than cut-backs of pension entitlements (Palier 2002). However, in the context of growing economic internationalisation this option turned out to be increasingly costly. Within Europe, this development gained further momentum through the Single European Market dismantling the legal obstacles to the free movement of goods, workers, services and capital between

EU member states. Most importantly, intensified competition on product markets put a severe constraint on the capacity of domestic producers to shift any increase of labour costs on to domestic consumers. These pressures are reinforced by the fact that the post-socialist countries in central and Eastern Europe are increasingly important players on world markets. With their comparatively low social standards and with wage costs being only a fraction of those in Western Europe, these countries have emerged as serious competitors to the older EU member states. Due to these conditions and due to their geographical closeness they have also become increasingly attractive as locations of production for West European companies. In addition, a sizeable number of people from central and Eastern Europe are illegally employed in the richer West European countries such as Germany, especially in the construction industry and in gastronomy, thereby contributing to the growth of the black economy in these countries.

Against this background, the economic leeway for increases in social contribution rates has diminished considerably. At the same time, the globalisation of capital markets imposes tight constraints on fiscal policies and thereby limits the possibilities to bail out financial shortfalls in public pension schemes through higher state subsidies. Within the European Union, these fiscal constraints are greatly intensified by the European Growth and Stability Pact, according to which public deficits must not exceed 3% of national GDP while public debt should be kept below 60% of GDP. Thus, EU member states face strong economic and political pressures to contain the growth of public expenditures.

Not very surprisingly, fears were raised that these pressures may lead to a competitive "race to the bottom" within the EU and pave the way for a dismantling of European welfare states with their traditionally rather high level of social and employment protection. In order to prevent such a scenario and in order to maintain the basic features of the so-called "European Social Model", social policymakers both at the national and the European level sought to replace the predominating logic of economic integration with its primary focus on competitiveness and budget consolidation by a more balanced approach emphasising social and economic objectives alike. Against this background, they called for a deeper co-operation among member states not only in economic matters but also in the area of social protection including national pension systems. Hence, within the framework of the so-called "Open Method of Co-ordination", EU member states committed themselves to a number of common objectives in the area of pension policy. These objectives did not only concern the fiscal sustainability but also the adequacy of national pension systems. In particular, member states are expected to prevent old age poverty, to enable pensioners to maintain their previous standard of living and to promote solidarity within and between generations. In addition, member states committed themselves to adapting their pension systems to more flexible employment and career patterns while ensuring equal treatment between men and women (Council of the European Union 2001). However, due to the great institutional diversity of national pension systems within the European Union these objectives are formulated at a rather general level. Moreover, since these objectives are not legally binding their violation is not associated with any formal sanctions. Thus, the Open Method of Co-ordination is unlikely to form a significant counterweight against the strong competitive pressures triggered by economic internationalisation on the one hand and the tight legal constraints to public deficit spending imposed by the Maastricht Treaty on the other.

It should also be noted, that even the *political* costs of frequent increases in contribution rates or levels of taxation have become much higher than in the past. In a context of stagnant or even falling real wages, wage earners are increasingly unwilling to accept rising fiscal charges. As a consequence, governments nowadays take a substantial electoral risk if they increase the tax burden of wage earners.

Demographic pressures

The economic and fiscal strains on public pension schemes will become even more severe in the future, since demographic developments will lead to a massive ageing of the population from 2020 onwards. Two demographic trends are particularly important in that respect: increasing life expectancy and declining fertility rates. Due to both factors, the share of elderly people (65 years and over) will rise dramatically relative to the working-age population (15 to 64 years). Within the European Union, the age dependency ratio is projected to increase from a current level of 24% to 49% in 2045, an increase that is much stronger than for instance in the United States. Hence, the share of transfers that is channelled from the working age population to the elderly must double over the next decades if future pensioners are to maintain their living standard. However, for the reasons sketched above, it is rather unlikely that this increase of inter-generational transfers can be achieved by doubling contribution rates. Other measures have to be considered in order to come to grips with the consequences of demographic ageing for national pension schemes.

1.2   Specific vulnerabilities of Bismarckian pension systems

The above-mentioned pressures have particularly detrimental effects on the pension arrangements that exist in the countries studied. Austria, France, Germany, Italy, and – with some qualifications – Sweden belong to a cluster of countries whose pension systems are relatively similar in their basic structures. I will now sketch the common features of these pension schemes. And after that, I will explain the specific problems associated with this type of pension arrangements.

Pension arrangements in Western democracies differ greatly in their institutional design. Broadly speaking, we can identify two distinct models of pension provisions, often referred to as the Bismarck and the Beveridge model (Myles and Quadagno 1997; Bonoli 2000; Hinrichs 2000a; Myles and Pierson 2001). Pension systems of the Beveridgian type are typically aimed at poverty prevention and provide either universal flat-rate or means-tested benefits. Bismarckian pension schemes, by contrast, are based on the social insurance principle and provide for earnings-related benefits aimed at status maintenance during old age. Among the cluster of countries with a Beveridgian tradition in pension policy, a number of countries (such as Sweden, Finland, Norway, and Canada) moved towards the Bismarckian model in the late 1950s and 1960s by topping up their basic pension schemes with a second public pillar. This second pillar is typically financed out of social contributions, operates on a pay-as-you-go[1] basis and provides for income-related benefits. With the maturation of the supplementary pillar the relevance of the basic pension in these countries declined gradually (at least in relative terms). As a consequence, pension arrangements in these countries have become more similar to the Bismarck model, which prevails traditionally in countries such as Germany, Austria, France and Italy. At the same time, countries belonging to the Bismarckian tradition have broadened the coverage of their pension systems and – at least partly – established elements of minimum protection (Hinrichs 2000a). Hence, the countries studied nowadays display a number of strong similarities concerning the basic set-up of their pension edifice: the (quasi) universal character of social insurance pensions, the integration of the earnings-replacement function into the public pillar and hence an only limited significance of private and occupational pensions, the strong reliance on wage-based contributions and the relative dominance of pay-as-you-go financing within the overall system of old age provisions. The relative similarity of pension arrangements in the countries studied is also reflected in the level and in the structure of benefits. As table 1.1 shows, net pensions for an average earner amount to circa 80 to

Table 1.1   Replacement rate of public pension programmes

Country	Gross replacement rate		Net replacement rate	
% of avg. earnings	66	100	100	150
Austria	80%	80%	-	-
France	65%	65%	86%	84%
Germany	56%	54%	84%	74%
Italy	80%	80%	89%	90%
Sweden	69%	66%	79%	70%

Sources: Blöndal and Scarpetta 1998; Weaver 1998

90% of previous (net) earnings. At the same time, pensions are roughly proportional to previous earnings, although the replacement levels for high-wage earners are typically lower due to the existence of a benefit ceiling. In Beveridgian systems, by contrast, replacement levels are on average much lower and fall sharply with rising income levels.

Pension arrangements of the Bismarckian type are particularly vulnerable to the economic and demographic pressures sketched above (Hinrichs 2000a). By the same token, the national pension systems under study share at least four problematic features.

The first problem results from their mode of financing. As already noted, the public pension systems in Austria, France, Germany, Italy and Sweden provide relatively generous earnings-related benefits primarily financed out of social contributions. As a consequence, pension contribution rates are comparatively high by international standards, thereby boosting non-wage labour costs. This mode of financing has a particularly detrimental effect on employment at the lower end of the earnings scale, where social assistance arrangements set a reservation wage, below which net wages cannot fall (Scharpf 2000a). This effect is further aggravated by the fact that covered earnings are often limited to the bottom two-thirds of the earnings scale. As a result, rising pension costs fall disproportionately on middle and low wage earners (Myles and Pierson 2001). In addition, the strong reliance on *wage*-based social contributions renders Bismarckian pension systems particularly vulnerable to fluctuations in labour's share in national income.

Second, public pensions (making up the bulk of total retirement income in the Bismarckian countries) are traditionally of the defined-benefit type. Under a defined-benefit arrangement it is the benefit level rather than the contribution rate that is prescribed by a formula. This construction has at least two problematic effects. On the one hand, defined-benefit arrangements often imply only a loose connection between contributions and benefits and thus tend to distort the supply of labour. For instance, the pension systems under study typically used to allow for early retirement without actuarially fair benefit reductions. Hence, within these systems there may be an in-built incentive for the insured to withdraw early from the labour market. On the other hand, defined-benefit regulations impose a quasi-contractual obligation for policymakers to increase contribution rates, whenever pension outlays exceed revenues (Myles and Pierson 2001).[2] A growing share of pensioners will therefore automatically lead to higher contributions as long as pension policymakers are unwilling to renege on the benefit commitments entrenched in defined-benefit schemes.

Third, among the countries studied, the overall system of retirement income is predominantly based on the pay-as-you-go principle. In pay-as-you-go funded systems, current contributors are obliged to pay the pensions for the contemporary generation of retirees. Whenever the numerical relationship between contributors and beneficiaries declines, a pay-as-you-go system will come under fiscal strain. In order to restore the fiscal balance, either benefits have to be cut or more financial resources need to be diverted to the system. Thus, pay-as-you-go financed systems are highly vulnerable to demographic shocks. It has been argued that fully funded pension schemes are better suited to coping with the consequences of demographic ageing (Bovenberg 1996; Siebert 1998). In a fully funded scheme, current contributions are set aside and invested in order to finance the pensions of current contributors. In contrast to a pay-as-you go financed system, a fully funded scheme is not confined to the realm of a single national economy and thus may take advantage of the potentially higher growth rates in countries with a more favourable age structure. By investing capital in countries outside the OECD with relatively young populations and abundant labour, fully funded pension systems may exploit the phasing differential in the ageing process that exists between OECD and non-OECD countries (Bovenberg 1996). Moreover, pay-as-you-go systems are often considered to yield a lower rate of return than fully funded systems, as the latter tend to profit from the growing share of capital incomes in the national product (whereas the wage share has faced a commensurate decline due to the sluggish growth of real wages). Hence, throughout the 1980s and 1990s pay-as-you-go systems typically faced greater financial difficulties than fully funded systems (Scharpf 1997a). In addition, proponents of fully funded old age provisions have pointed to the potential growth effects for a national economy. Their (albeit contested) assumption is that fully funded systems lead to a higher level of national savings that would contribute to a higher investment ratio which again would result in a higher national income in the future. In this view, the level of contributions in a pay-as-you-go system that is needed to finance a given level of retirement income is higher than in a fully funded system. Additionally, the mere assumption of a lower "performance" of pay-as-you-go systems is likely to diminish public confidence in the system and reinforces the general perception of pension contributions as a kind of "implicit tax" with potentially detrimental consequences for the supply of labour.

But fully funded forms of retirement provisions are also afflicted with specific risks and problems. In particular, fully funded pensions are more vulnerable to investment risks on the capital market.[3] Following Krupp (1997), the investment risks associated with capitalised old age provisions are likely to grow in the context of demographic ageing. The internal rate of return that can be achieved in a fully funded system is likely to decrease, when a growing share of the population enters retirement age and therefore starts to clean out its savings while at the same time an ever smaller share of the population will accumulate capital. Several economists (Orszag and Stiglitz 1999; Barr 2000) even argued that in economic terms there is little difference between pay-as-you-go and fully funded schemes, as both are equally vulnerable to a shortage of economic output caused by demographic changes. However, as Barr (2000:98) points out, politicians are still likely to prefer funding over pay-as-you-go, *"since that way bad news would be seen to arise through the market outcomes rather than political decision"*. Capitalised systems also require higher administrative costs than publicly managed pensions on a pay-as-you-go basis.[4]

The bottom line is that both pay-as-you-go and fully funded schemes have specific strengths and weaknesses. Therefore, a more balanced mix between pay-as-you-go and fully-funding, as seen in countries with multi-pillar pension systems, is better suited to the diversification of the specific risks associated with either of these financing mechanisms than is true for the overly one-sided reliance on pay-as-you-go financing typical of Bismarckian pension systems.

A fourth design feature that has put Bismarckian pension arrangements under increasing fiscal pressure results from the fact that benefit entitlements are typically derived from an employment relationship. This has an expansionary effect on pension spending in the context of rising labour force participation. In virtually all of the advanced welfare states, female participation rates have risen considerably over the last decades. In an earnings-related pension system this trend translates into a gradual augmentation of accrued benefit entitlements among female retirees and thus into higher pension costs in the future. Hence, as long as the tendency towards rising female labour force participation persists, earnings-related pension systems have to serve growing pension claims among women. By contrast, a pension scheme that grants universal flat-rate benefits is immune to this development. A means-tested pension system may even profit from this development since a rising level of gainful employment among women is likely to reduce the number of potential beneficiaries.

1.3   Options for reform

The previous section highlighted the fact that public pension systems in advanced welfare states – in particular those of the Bismarckian type – are challenged by a variety of economic and demographic pressures to which national policymakers have to respond. This raises the question: from which options for reform can policymakers select in order to put their national pension systems on a more sustainable footing? This section briefly discusses the strengths and weaknesses of various reform options. In general, I will focus on four criteria of evaluation:

1 the economic consequences of certain reform approaches, in particular for the employment system;
2 the fiscal implications of various measures, both for the state budget and for the financial sustainability of the pension system itself;
3 the redistributive effects of specific reforms in particular with respect to aspects of intra- and inter-generational solidarity;
4 the political and legal feasibility of various reform options.

As suggested above, the strategy to address the fiscal problems of public pension schemes by raising contribution rates has turned out to be increasingly costly both in economic and in political terms. However, in recent years a number of alternative strategies have been employed in order to restore or to maintain the fiscal equilibrium of public pension schemes. These measures may apply either on the revenue or on the benefit side. I will first discuss those reform options which primarily concern the revenue side of public pension schemes (see table 1.2).

Table 1.2 Advantages and disadvantages of pension reform options on the revenue side

Reform option	Economic effects	Fiscal effects	Redistributive effects	Political/legal feasibility
Higher contribution rate	- increase in non-wage labour costs	+ higher revenues for the pension system	- regressive effect	- tax resistance
Inclusion of hitherto non-covered employment groups	+ revenue base of pension system broadened and made less vulnerable to changes in employment patterns - additional expenses during demographic peaks		+ improved old age protection for certain groups	- resistance by the affected groups
Shift towards more tax financing	+ reduction/stabilisation of non-wage labour costs	+ broadening of revenue base	(+) reduced tax burden for low income earners	- tax resistance - only feasible for non-contributory benefits
Replacement of contributory pension insurance by tax-financed basic pension + private pensions	+ strong reduction of non-wage labour costs - weaker work incentives as the link between contributions and benefits is dissolved	+ lower expenditures in the long-term + broader revenue base - higher expenditures in the short- and medium-term - greater pressure on public budget	+ prevention of old age poverty + reduced tax burden for low income -earners - rising income inequality among the elderly	- less protection against state intervention - political costs of changeover very high
Tax-financed basic pension + earnings-related pension	+ reduction of non-wage labour costs - weakening of work incentives	+ broader revenue base - higher expenditures - higher pressure on public budget	+ prevention of old age poverty and rising income inequality + reduced tax burden for low income earners	- strong tax resistance

Broadening the coverage of the pension system

In many cases, Bismarckian pension systems have excluded certain types of employment from compulsory coverage such as self- and low-paid employment. Their inclusion would broaden the revenue base of the public pension system and render it less vulnerable to changes in employment patterns (Schmähl 1999). Moreover, the level of old age protection for people with long records of atypical employment can be improved. Initially, the inclusion of new groups of contributors in a pay-as-you-go financed pension scheme will augment the level of contributions without increasing the level of expenditures. In the long term, however, these groups will become beneficiaries, too, and aggravate rather than mitigate the financial problems resulting from population ageing (Merten 1999). The same is true for an increase in the contribution ceiling, a measure which will improve the financial outlook of the system in the short run but typically create new benefit entitlements, which on their part will lead to higher pension expenditures in the long-term.

Shifting from contribution to tax financing

Another reform option consists of the (partial) refinancing of public pension schemes from wage-based contributions to general taxes. In general, a stronger shift towards tax-financing has a number of economic and distributive advantages. On the one hand, this move would imply a broadening of the revenue base and reduce non-wage labour costs. To the extent to which social contributions (which have a slightly regressive effect due to the existence of a contribution ceiling) are replaced by higher income taxes (which tend to be highly progressive), employment at the lower end of the income scale will be unburdened disproportionably, whereas the additional burden for high wage earners will likely increase. This may not only be justified via reference to the ability-to-pay principle but also with respect to the fact that taxes on labour have the most detrimental employment effects in the lower income brackets.

At the same time, however, a radical refinancing of contributory pension schemes towards more tax financing is likely to trigger fierce political resistance and will be extremely difficult to legitimise. In Bismarckian countries, pension coverage is typically not fully universal, i.e., the collectivity of potential beneficiaries is smaller than the collectivity of taxpayers. In this case, a pension system largely funded out of general revenues would lead to the consequence that some taxpayers (not necessarily belonging to the better-off stratum) would have to subsidise other peoples' earnings-related pensions (even those of highly paid employees) without having their own entitlements to the system. As Miegel and Wahl (1999) have correctly pointed out, this is not only questionable from a normative point of view but may also raise serious constitutional problems. Hence, the scope of tax-financing within a non-universal Bismarckian pension system is typically confined to the realm of non-contributory benefits (even though the definition of "non-contributory benefits" is far from clear-cut).

Replacement of the contribution-financed earnings-related pillar by a universal tax-financed basic pension

This dilemma could be solved through the introduction of a tax-financed and universal basic pension. In Germany, scholars such as Miegel (1999) have proposed a complete displacement of contributory social insurance pensions by a public basic pension providing flat-rate benefits for the whole population that is financed out of general taxes. Apart from its more employment-friendly revenue structure, a universal basic pension has been considered as an effective instrument in the prevention of old age poverty. Moreover, it has been argued that this solution is less costly than the retention of an earnings-related pension system and therefore better suited to weathering demographic shocks.

However, a number of serious objections have been raised against this approach (Müller and Tautz 1996; Krupp 1997; Maydell 1998; Rahn 1999). First, in a flat-rate system the link between individual payments and benefits no longer exists. Hence, economists like Krupp (1997) have argued that this may weaken work incentives and encourage dodging reactions such as a flight into clandestine employment.

Second, depending on the transitional arrangements, the expected savings associated with a system change from a contributory social insurance pension to a (typically less generous) universal basic pension may only accrue in the long run. When a universal flat-rate system is introduced, the overall costs of the pension system could initially be even higher than before. On the one hand, the inclusion of hitherto uncovered groups and the upgrading of very low pensions to the level of the new basic pension will cause additional expenditures. On the other hand, the pension claims built-up in the old contributory system that exceed the level of the basic pension still have to be served and will only decrease very gradually.[5]

Third, concerns are raised about the fiscal implications associated with such a system change. If pensions are entirely financed out of the state budget, governments may become more restrained in their capacity to deliver other essential public services (Krupp 1997). Conversely, in a tax-financed system pension benefits are not acquired as contributory entitlements and may thus more easily become the target of fiscal consolidation measures. In other words, tax-financed pensions will enjoy a lower degree of "legal safeguard" than pension claims acquired on the basis of individual contributions.

Fourth, the distributive superiority of a universal basic pension scheme providing flat-rate benefits has been questioned. By its very nature, such a system does not allow for a differentiation of benefits according to political priorities. For instance, flat-rate benefits do not offer the possibility for credit periods involving child rearing or elderly care (as can be easily done in a contributory pension system where activities of that kind may be honoured by additional benefit entitlements). Moreover, if the earnings-replacement function is completely left to market income, inequality among pensioners may even increase as low-income earners have only limited capacities to pursue individual old age provisions.

Fifth, a changeover from social insurance pensions basically covering dependent employees towards a universal pension system may require the inclusion of occupational groups (in particular, many of the self-employed) that had hitherto been covered by private mandatory schemes. In any case, the pension claims that have been built up within these schemes need to be honoured. By the same token, many of the self-employed have incurred sizeable financial obligations for the purpose of individual old age provisions (such as insurance contracts or the purchase of real estate). If these groups must also co-finance the public pension system through higher taxes, their overall financial burden may become unduly high. Hence, long-term transitory rules would have to be established for these groups (Merten 1999).

Sixth, it is politically difficult to master a changeover from a contribution-based to a tax-based system. In general, there will be a greater readiness to pay social contributions than to pay taxes and "tax" resistance will be lower in a system based on contributions for which people receive something in return. More importantly, people are keen to maintain their previous standard of living in their old age. As a consequence, they are likely to regard any shift from earnings-related social insurance to basic security with great skepticism. In Germany, for instance, opinion polls suggest that a broad majority of the citizens refuses the replacement of the existing pension system with a flat-rate basic pension.[6] Hence, the electoral costs of such a changeover will be in most cases prohibitive.

In addition, the introduction of a tax-financed basic pension may require a fundamental restructuring not only of the tax system but also of the public finance system in general. Arguably, this problem will be most pronounced in a federal state like Germany, where the bulk of the taxes consist of "shared taxes" (*Gemeinschaftssteuern),* most notably income and value added taxes. These taxes are decided upon at the federal level while the revenues are distributed between the central, regional, and local authorities. Moreover, any changes in this area require the approval of the *Länder* in the upper chamber (*Bundesrat*) in which the government parties at the federal level may lack a majority of their own. In addition, a changeover from a contribution- to a tax-financed pension system may also affect the financial relationships between the various branches of social insurance. In short, a radical alteration of the pension system will not only entail substantial reforms in pension policy itself but also require comprehensive and complex adjustments in neighbouring policy areas.

For all these reasons, it should not come as a great surprise that we cannot detect any empirical instance among OECD countries where a mature earnings-related pension system was replaced by a tax-financed basic pension.

Institutional separation between earnings-replacement and poverty alleviation

Some of the problems mentioned above may be avoided or at least alleviated if the earnings-related pillar was split into two functionally separate pillars. The first pillar would consist of a universal and tax-financed basic pension aimed at poverty alleviation. This pillar would be complemented by a second tier that serves the exclusive function of income replacement and that would be relieved of non-contributory benefits. This pillar would be exclusively financed out of social contributions. Hitherto, Bismarckian pension systems typically intermingle, in a rather unsystematic fashion, elements of redistribution (such as non-contributory benefits) with elements of insurance (i.e., income replacement). By contrast, due to the clear assignment of different redistributive functions to organisationally distinct pillars in a two-tier public pension system the redistributive rationality of the overall pension system would be enhanced. What is more, a sizeable share of total pension costs would be shifted away from wage-based contributions which would again contribute to a more employment-friendly financing structure.

However, the major problem associated with this changeover lies on the cost side. The necessary expenditures would most likely exceed those of the existing system. Total public pension outlays would inevitably grow if those people hitherto receiving no pensions or very low ones (such as housewives) drew a full basic pension and if at the same time earnings-related pension expenditures remained largely in place. To some extent, this might be refinanced by the abolition of non-contributory benefits. However, even if this was considered acceptable, it could only be implemented very gradually, as a radical reduction of these benefits for the current generation of pensioners would be politically unfeasible and legally problematic.

In sum, an expansion of the tax-financed share in order to cover non-contributory benefits appears to be a both economically efficient and politically feasible reform option. A tax-financed basic pension might also be considered an economically more robust arrangement than earnings-related social insurance. However, the *changeover* of the system may involve substantial transition costs and is likely to face virtually insurmountable political obstacles. Hence, changes in revenue levels alone will barely suffice in the maintenance of the fiscal equilibrium of public pension systems in the long-term and in avoiding harmful labour market effects (Pierson 1998). Therefore, pension policymakers also have to develop policy responses that effectively curb the growth of public pension outlays, promote the compensatory establishment of fully funded old age provisions and at the same time prevent a large increase in old age poverty.

With respect to cost containment reforms, we need to distinguish between measures aimed at achieving short-term budget relief on the one hand, and more structural reforms, on the other, designed to dampen the expected increase in contribution levels and to secure the fiscal sustainability of public pension schemes in the long term, in particular with respect to the challenge of demographic ageing. This analytical distinction appears necessary, although in practice the borderline between the two reform approaches may be blurred. Each type of retrenchment is likely to conform to a different political decision-making logic (Anderson 1998). Typically, short-term pension cuts are primarily inspired by acute budgetary crises. Their major objective is to achieve relatively modest but immediately effective savings for the public budget. By their nature these measures primarily affect current pensioners. Structural reforms, by contrast, typically become effective only over the long term, but may imply a radical reduction of benefit levels as well as a major restructuring of the contemporary design of the pension system, in particular with respect to the balance between public and private sources of retirement income. Moreover, in contrast to short-term cuts, long-term structural reforms typically affect future pensioners to a much greater extent than current retirees. Thus, pension policymakers are likely to pursue distinct purposes with either of these reform strategies. This needs to be kept in mind when we try to assess the scope of single-reform efforts in a comparative perspective. In the following section, I will discuss those reform options which may be deployed to curb the growth in public pension expenditures (see also table 1.3).[7]

Targeting of benefits

In countries relying on flat-rate public pensions, the introduction or the tightening of means, income, or affluence tests is a widely used instrument

Table 1.3   Advantages and disadvantages of various pension reform options on the expenditure side

	Economic effects	Fiscal effects	Redistributive effects	Political/Legal feasibility
Increased targeting	- weaker incentives to work and to pursue private retirement saving	+ lower expenditures + higher administrative costs	+ concentration on the truly needy - "violation" of actuarial fairness	- not feasible for contributory benefits
Increased retirement age	+ reduction of non-wage labour costs - higher pressure on the labour market in the short run	+ lower expenditures + higher revenues + lower pressure on public budget	- one-sided burden on the active population	- highly unpopular
Shift towards lifetime principle	+ reduction of non-wage labour costs + stronger work incentives	+ lower expenditures + lower pressure on public budget	+ greater actuarial fairness - rising poverty among groups with incomplete work careers or low income	- resistance by affected groups
Reduction of non-contributory benefits	+ reduction of non-wage labour costs + stronger work incentives	+ lower expenditures + lower pressure on public budget	+ greater actuarial fairness - potential hardships for groups with interrupted employment careers	+ political resistance limited + no major legal restrictions
Less generous indexation	+ reduction of non-wage labour costs	+ lower expenditures + lower pressure on public budget		- political resistance
Harmonisation of pension schemes	+ reduction of non-wage labour costs	+ lower expenditures + lower pressure on public budget	+ greater intra-generational equity	- resistance by affected groups - legal restrictions possible
Introduction of (means-tested) minimum pension	- weaker incentives to work and to pursue private retirement saving	+ higher expenditures + higher pressure on public budget	+ better prevention of old age poverty - "violation" of equivalence principle	- political resistance among the proponents of strictly contribution-related benefits

to curb pension spending. Typically, this strategy has been justified on the grounds that public social benefits should be confined to the "really needy" or at least exclude the rich. Such a strategy has also been applied in Sweden where the universal basic pension was transformed into a "guarantee pension" provided for those who receive no pension or only a small one from the supplementary scheme. However, as Bonoli (2000) and Myles/Pierson (2001) point out, this option is politically unfeasible or even legally restricted in contributory earnings-related schemes where pension entitlements are typically considered as "acquired rights". One important exception is survivors' pensions, which are typically derived from the beneficiary's family status rather than his/her own entitlements. This fact allows for arrangements in which eligibility for survivors' benefits is (at least) partly set off against one's own income. However, stronger means-testing may weaken individual work incentives as well as incentives for private retirement saving.

Increasing the retirement age

Pension policymakers in most OECD countries have in recent years also sought to raise the retirement age and to remove incentives for early retirement. The fiscal effect of this approach on public pension arrangements is two-fold. The revenue base of the pension system will be strengthened as people work longer. At the same time, expenditures will decrease as less people will be drawing pensions. In Bismarckian countries, in particular, the regular retirement age for women has been traditionally lower than for men. Hence, aligning the retirement age for women with those of men was an obvious starting point for cost containment reforms. This move was also enforced by a decision by the European Court of Justice, which demanded a gradual harmonisation of the retirement ages of men and women. In addition, generous access to various forms of early retirement especially in the Continental welfare states has become a key target for reform. In order to be effective, an increase in the pensionable age needs to be accompanied by actuarial reductions if an insured person retires prior to the regular retirement age. Conversely, an actuarial premium may be paid in order to encourage work beyond the normal retirement age. In other words, pension policymakers try to move the pension system closer towards actuarial neutrality, i.e., rendering the system neutral with respect to the retirement decision. A major difficulty associated with an increase in the retirement age concerns the effects of this strategy on the labour market. In national economies plagued by high levels of unemployment an increase in the retirement age may at least temporarily aggravate labour market problems. Moreover, steps to increase the retirement age are bound to be extremely unpopular, especially among those employees close to retirement.

Tightening the link between contributions and benefits

A frequently applied reform strategy in earnings-related pension systems is the reinforcement of the so-called equivalence principle. This principle suggests an approximate symmetry between individual contributions and individual benefits. However, as Myles and Pierson (2001) point out, even ostensibly earnings-related systems typically incorporate design features that deviate from this principle and entail significant inter-personal transfers. To the extent to which these features are considered to generate "inequitable" or even "perverse" distributive outcomes their abolition or reduction would not only help to contain pension spending but also "rationalise" the redistributive character of the pension system. Basically, strengthening the equivalence principle can take two forms. First, non-contributory benefits such as credits for periods of schooling or unemployment may be curtailed or eliminated completely. Arguably, these measures are unlikely to trigger major political controversies. Due to their selective nature, they will only affect a limited segment of the insured population. Moreover, these benefits are less likely to be perceived as "well-earned rights" and enjoy a lower level of "legal safeguard" than contribution-based entitlements. Hence, this form of retrenchment appears to be relatively unproblematic for pension policymakers. However, the limits of this strategy are also evident. Due to their relatively modest quantitative significance, a reduction of non-contributory benefits alone will hardly suffice to maintain the fiscal equilibrium of public pension schemes. Moreover, in most Bismarckian countries we also observe a countervailing tendency with respect to certain types of non-contributory benefits. In particular, many countries have introduced or increased pension credits for child and elderly care entailing an expansive effect on pension spending.[8]

However, a tighter link between contributions and benefits and thereby a potential for comprehensive expenditure cuts can also be achieved through changes in the pension formula. Traditionally, the pension formulas in all of the Bismarckian countries except Germany more or less deviate from the strict principle of lifetime earnings. Hence, changes in various parameters of the benefit formula may be employed to strengthen the equivalence between contributions and benefits. At the time of retirement, benefits in an earnings-related pension scheme are basically calculated on the basis of three variables: the reference salary, the period of assessed contributions, and the accrual factor.[9] Hence, the benefit formula for earnings-related old age pensions can be presented in a stylised form:

$B = y * t * c$
With
$B = Benefits$
$Y = Reference\ salary$
$T = Period\ of\ assessed\ contributions$
$C = Accrual\ factor$

All three parameters can be adjusted in order to strengthen or weaken the relationship between total lifetime contributions and pension benefits and thereby affect the level of aggregate pension expenditures. This is in so far as the distinction between defined benefit and defined contribution plans is seen as a continuum rather than a dichotomy. Many public pension schemes are in fact hybrid pension plans that combine some features of the defined-benefit approach and some aspect of the defined-contribution method (see box 1). The reference salary typically varies between total career earnings and earnings based on a number of "best" or last years. The shorter the period, on the basis of which the reference salary is assessed, the weaker the relation between contribution and benefits will be. Hence, in a system where the assessment period for the reference salary is short, employees with a steep earnings career will receive a higher pension than employees with a flat earnings history even if the overall amount of lifetime earnings is the same.

Once the reference salary is established, the result is then multiplied by the number of contribution years. However, the number of contribution years taken into account differs from one country to another. In general, the time required to reach a full pension (often referred to as the qualifying period) varies from 30 to 50 years. Shorter qualifying periods tend to favour individuals with fewer years of workforce participation.

The accrual factor determines the percentage of relevant earnings entered into the pension formula per contribution year. In most countries, the accrual factor for one additional year of contribution ranges from between 1% to 2% of assessed earnings that determines the replacement rate of the system. More often than not, the structure of this factor is proportional but it may also vary with the length of contributions or with the size of the assessed income.

The stronger these parameters deviate from the principle of lifetime earnings, the greater is the scope for austerity measures that can be justified with reference to the equivalence principle. Nevertheless, insured people with a

Box 1: Defined-benefit versus defined-contribution plans

In the classification of various pension arrangements, a distinction is often made between defined-benefit and defined-contribution plans. The bottom line is that in a defined-benefit plan the amount of benefits to be paid determines the level of contributions. By contrast, in a defined-contribution plan the amount of contributions that have been paid determines the level of benefits.

In defined-contribution plans, a system of contributions is set up in which members build up individual credits. When the pension is calculated, these credits are assigned a value based on the scheme's financial resources, which depend upon the flow of contributions collected. The total amount of contributions calculated under the scheme's rules is distributed to the beneficiaries in proportion to the credits they have acquired (thereby applying strict equivalence between contributions and benefits). Upon retirement, the balance in the account is converted into a life annuity based on estimates of the group's expected life expectancy. Thus, in a defined-contribution scheme the risk that contributions fall short of benefits (due to demographic or economic developments) is entirely imposed on beneficiaries since any shortfall will be made up by adjusting the value of pensions. By the same token, there is no element of redistribution in defined-contribution plans, neither within nor across generations.

By contrast, in a defined-benefit plan benefits are prescribed by a benefit formula. This formula may or may not imply a strict equivalence between contributions and benefits. As a rule, defined-benefit plans contain more or less strong elements of redistribution within and across generations. Depending on the benefit formula, shortfalls will be made up either by altering the contribution rate or by adjusting the value of pension or both.

Defined-contribution plans may be either fully funded or pay-as-you-go. In a fully funded defined-contribution plan, a periodic contribution is prescribed and the benefit depends on the contributions paid in plus the return on investment.

In a pay-as-you-go defined-contribution plan (often referred to as a *notional,* or "unallocated", defined-contribution plan) each participant has an individual account in which benefit rights are accounted for in a manner similar to that of a fully funded defined-contribution scheme. The worker's contributions are credited to his or her account but no funds are deposited in the account. The worker's account balance is periodically revalued upwards, just as if a funded account were being credited with

interest. In sum, a pension paid on the basis of a notional defined-contribution (NDC) plan
(a) bears an explicit relationship to contributions,
(b) is based on lifetime contributions,
(c) is adjusted for the life expectancy of the group, and
(d) economic developments. Moreover, it
(e) allows for a flexible retirement age with the pension being actuarially
adjusted.

Any of these features may to a greater or lesser extent also apply in a defined-benefit plan. In a notional-defined contribution (NDC) plan, however, all these parameters are constructed in a way that any shortfall will be
avoided in advance by an automatic adjustment of the value of pensions
(rather than by an increase in contribution rates). Insofar, the distinction
between defined-benefits and defined-contribution plans is a continuum,
not a dichotomy. An NDC plan can thus be regarded as a special case of a
pay-as-you-go defined-benefit system (Myles and Quadagno 1997; Barr
2000; Gillion et al. 2000; Settergren 2001).

long contribution record and a flat earnings career may still profit from a
tighter link between contributions and benefits. In countries where the period of assessed earnings is comparatively short, future benefits can be more
closely tied to contributions by bringing assessed earnings closer to lifetime
income, i.e., increasing the number of "best years". *Ceteris paribus*, this will
result in a sharp reduction in pension entitlements for workers with many
years of low earnings and a few years of high earnings. In addition, governments may also extend the qualifying period, i.e., raise the number of contribution years required to draw a full pension.[10] Finally, in those countries
where the accrual rate is differentiated according to the length of contribution or to the size of the assessed income, the unification of this rate at a lower average level may also yield substantial savings.[11]

Lowering the overall generosity of the pension system by reinforcing the
equivalence principle in the calculation of benefits appears to be a quite obvious route of adjustment in the Bismarck regimes. This may even take the
form of a complete changeover from a defined-benefit to a defined-contribution system, in which – broadly speaking – contribution rates are fixed and
benefits will be adjusted accordingly (see box 1). Most importantly, this
strategy reduces the "inequitable" redistribution between workers with a
flat earnings history and workers with a steep earnings career as well as be-

tween workers with a long employment record and workers with shorter periods of labour force participation. This does not necessarily imply that any gap in the work history of an insured person will automatically lead to lower pension entitlements. Instead, social protection may be targeted more specifically towards "legitimate" forms of labour market exiting. For instance, pension credits may be granted for periods such as parental leave, illness and unemployment (Myles and Pierson 2001).

A tighter link between contributions and benefits will also strengthen work incentives by reducing the negative impact of the "tax wedge" on labour supply (Schmähl 1999).[12] In particular, this approach may help to contain tendencies toward illegal employment and early labour market exits. However, there is less room for adjustments of this sort (and therefore less radical reforms) in countries such as Germany where benefits have traditionally been calculated on the basis of lifetime earnings. As a result, changes in the pension formula enacted in these countries are likely to take the form of lowered accrual rates, typically implying a general reduction of the replacement ratio. In many cases, this is achieved by shifting to a less generous indexation mechanism.

Changing the indexation mechanism

In recent years, most OECD countries have modified their indexation procedures to reduce the growth of pension outlays. For a number of reasons, changes in the indexation mechanism appear to be a quite powerful tool in curbing pension spending. First, this instrument can also be employed in the short term. As opposed to more fundamental changes in the pension formula such as a shift from "best years" to lifetime earnings, changed indexation procedures cannot be said to be a radical intervention in individual pension entitlements and thus do not require the implementation of lengthy interim regulations. Moreover, this kind of reform can in principle be applied to all types of pensions and to the population of pensioners in their entirety, hence allowing for larger savings than is true for cutbacks that affect only a limited segment of beneficiaries. In addition, once a less generous indexation mechanism is established on a permanent basis, this measure may yield ongoing and thereby very substantial long-term savings without repeated discretionary interventions by the government that are more likely to attract public displeasure.

The possibilities of switching to a less generous adjustment coefficient are manifold. Their effectiveness often depends not only on the indexation mechanism itself but also on the development of certain macro-economic factors which may change considerably over time. Many countries have switched from a wage to a price index (or a mixed wage/price index) as wages tend to grow faster than consumer prices. However, in periods of declining or stagnating real wages or severe economic and budgetary crises, even price indexation may be regarded as too costly. Under these circumstances, pension policymakers are likely to consider adhoc interventions into the indexation mechanism, such as a temporary or partial suspension (or a delay) of pension adjustment, as a necessary evil to avoid an imminent fiscal deficit or reduce an existing one in the pension system. Some countries have changed the indexing formula from gross to net wages in order to distribute the burden of higher taxes and social contributions more evenly between the gainfully employed and the retired. However, such a change may also turn out to be problematic as soon as tax reductions for the gainfully employed are implemented. In this case, indexation based on the development of net wages would lead to increased pension spending and perhaps to rising contribution rates. For this reason, Germany recently switched to a modified net wage indexation which no longer takes into account changes in income tax rates. Instead, a notional contribution to private old age provisions is subtracted from the assessment base (Schmähl 2001). In so doing, current pensioners automatically take a share in the financial burden that the gainfully employed are expected to shoulder through the necessity of increased private retirement provisions. An alternative but functionally equivalent strategy of dampening the yearly increases of pension payments was applied by the Kohl government, which integrated a "demographic factor" into the adjustment formula. In so doing, the (increasing) life expectancy of German citizens was at least partly taken into account in the calculation of benefits.

Harmonisation of different benefit regulations

As pointed out above, pension systems in the Bismarckian countries are typically fragmented along occupational lines. If this fragmentation goes along with differences in the generosity of benefits, "privileges" for certain groups of pensioners may be considered as a legitimate target for retrenchment. Typically, this concerns employees in the public sector who often enjoy more favourable benefit regulations than workers in the private sector. For instance, the calculation of the reference salary or the possibilities for early retirement without benefit deductions are often more advantageous for public employees.

From a budgetary perspective, the need to control pension spending is particularly pronounced for pension schemes covering employees in the public sector. Most countries massively expanded their share of public employment in the 1960s and 1970s. Hence, in the years to come a rapidly growing share of public employees will reach retirement age and impose an increasingly heavy burden on the public budget.[13] This makes a gradual downward adjustment of pension benefits for this group particularly urgent. However, a complete harmonisation of pension benefits between state employees and workers in the private sector is not an easily available policy option. In Germany, for instance, a changeover of civil servants pensions from "final salary" towards "lifetime earnings" would require a change of constitutional rules and thus a two-thirds majority in both the *Bundestag* and the *Bundesrat*. Therefore, savings in the German system of *Beamtenversorgung* typically take the form of across-the-board reductions in benefit levels rather than of fundamental changes in the principles of benefit calculations.

Establishing a stable system of means-tested minimum protection

The reform options discussed above are aimed at containing the increase of public pension expenditures. Hence, pension policymakers must develop strategies to ensure that (future) pensioners will not suffer serious losses in their living standard or sink into poverty as a consequence of benefit reductions. In a pension system where benefits are strictly tied to individual contribution records, pension cuts are likely to drive an increasing share of people with low incomes and/or incomplete working careers into old age poverty. Therefore, pension policymakers in the Bismarckian countries need to make sure that old age poverty is effectively prevented by a functioning system of means- or income-tested minimum protection. It is an open question, however whether such an arrangement should be established within the pension system itself or within the framework of social assistance. Among the countries studied, all have chosen the first option with the notable exception of Germany, which is the only OECD country lacking a (means-tested) minimum pension. In Germany, plans to establish a means-tested minimum protection within the statutory pension insurance have encountered strong criticism. In particular, fears were raised that such a measure would undermine the strictly earnings-related character of the pension system and in the long run favour a shift towards a basic pension (Ruland 1999). Hence, German pensioners lacking the resources to reach the subsistence level have to rely exclusively on social assistance benefits. There is some reason to believe that this construction may be ill-suited to protecting all pensioners effectively against the risk of income poverty. To the extent to which the combined effect of cuts in the generosity of the pension system and the growing share of atypical employment increases the number of very low pensions and thus the number of pensioners with a formal claim to social assistance, disguised old age poverty is likely to become more significant. The reason is that the receipt of social assistance benefits is often experienced as a stigmatising procedure, in particular by the elderly. Hence, a certain percentage of potential beneficiaries will likely refrain from making use of their claims. Germany has attempted to tackle this problem by improving the co-operation between pension insurance associations and social assistance agencies and by loosening the eligibility criteria for old age pensioners claiming social assistance. In particular, the liability of adult children vis-à-vis their needy parents was largely abolished. It remains to be seen, however, whether this approach will help to contain the problem of disguised old age poverty.

Shifting from pay-as-you-go toward fully-funding

If the living standard of old age pensioners is to be maintained in the future, the gap resulting from cuts in the public pension system needs to be filled by fully funded old age provisions either in the form of private or occupational pension plans. As pointed out above, a multi-pillar pension system that distributes the costs of an ageing population more evenly between pay-as-you-go and fully funded schemes is considered to be less vulnerable to demographic shocks than pension systems overwhelmingly based on pay-as-you-go financing. The macro-economic argument behind this assumption is that a higher share of capital funding in the pension system leads to a higher national savings ratio, which again entails higher investments and thus generates a positive effect on economic growth. It should be noted, however, that economists strongly disagree about the strength of this effect. In addition, increased capital funding is seen as a means of profiting from the potentially higher growth rates in countries where the problem of demographic ageing is less severe.

Another argument put forward in favour of multi-pillar systems is that payments to non-public forms of old age provisions are not part of the tax wedge and therefore have less detrimental effects on employment than wage-based social contributions. Hence, for pension policymakers in the Bismarckian countries the main challenge is to set in motion a process at the end of which the capitalised component of old age provisions is much more significant than today. Below I will briefly discuss the various options to bring this changeover about.

Table 1.4 Strengths (+) and weaknesses (-) of pay-as-you-go versus fully funded schemes

	Retention of a pure pay-as-you-go system	Combinations of pay-as-you-go and fully-funding		
		Pay-as-you-go with internal capital stock	Pay-as-you-go + occupational pensions	Pay-as-you-go + private pension plans
Protection against demographic risks	-	+	+	+
Protection against investment risks	+	-	-	-
Protection against political risks	-	- -	+	+
Administrative costs	++	+	o	- -
Redistributive capacity	+	+	o	-
Double payment problem	+	-	-	-

+ Beneficial impact; - Detrimental impact; o Neutral

It is debatable *how* large the fully funded component should be. On the one hand, a majority of economists advocates an expansion of capitalised elements within the overall system of old age provisions. On the other hand, there is broad agreement among pension policy experts that a complete changeover from a full-fledged pay-as-you-go system to a purely capitalised system is neither economically desirable nor politically feasible (DIA 1999). As suggested above, even a fully funded system is associated with certain risks, in particular as the future development of capital markets is concerned (see table 1.4). A complete replacement of a pay-as-you-go financed system by a fully funded system would aggravate these risks because such a dramatic shift is likely to have a depressive effect on the rate of return on financial capital. Moreover, a shift from a pay-as-you-go towards a fully funded system will always impose a serious double payment problem. In the transition period from the old to the new system, the gainfully employed would have to shoulder a sizeable additional financial burden. Throughout the transition phase they would still be obliged to pay the benefits for current pensioners in the pay-as-you-go system while at the same time saving for their own retirements. Hence, for both economic and political reasons there is neither the necessity nor the possibility for the radical abolition of the existing pay-as-you-go systems in the Bismarckian countries. As Myles and Pierson (2001) point out, the adoption of the World Bank's three-pillar model of old age income security is therefore largely irrelevant in countries with a mature pay-as-you-go system.[14] However, for politicians within democratic polities, typically oriented towards short-term election cycles, even a modest and incremental switch to a higher capitalisation of old age provisions may be politically costly, given that the costs of transition accrue immediately, while the (potential) benefits of a system change will only accrue over the long term.

In principle, a changeover from a pay-as-you-go to a (partially) capitalised system can be implemented both within the public and the private or occupational tiers of old age provisions. However, the economic, distributional, and political implications are different (see table 1.5).

Setting up a capital stock within the public pillar

One option to buttress the fully funded elements of old age provisions is to build up a capital stock within the public pension system. In this case, the contribution rate is set higher than would be necessary to cover current pension payments. A part of the accumulated capital reserves may be invested in high-yield instruments to exploit the potential of the capital market to the financial advantage of a basically pay-as-you-go based public pension system. What is more, a capital stock within the public pension system may also serve to distribute the fiscal burden resulting from the demographic shock more evenly over time and across generations. By gradually melting off the accumulated reserves at the time when the demographic burden hits its peak the future increase in contribution rates can be kept lower than would be necessary otherwise (Hinrichs 2000a). Moreover, as opposed to private or occupational pensions, a fully funded component within the public pension system enables pension policymakers to maintain the redistributive character of social policy. By the same token, public arrangements are better suited to dealing with the problem of adverse selection that is typical in the realm of private insurance. For instance, a public pension system, by its very nature, allows for a pooling of risks between people with different life expectancies. Hence, in a public pension system the higher average life expectancy of women (as compared to men) does not translate into lower pension payments (as would be typically the case within individual pension plans).

However, the creation of a state-controlled trust fund within the public pension system also entails a number of serious problems. In the short run,

Table 1.5   Strengths (+) and weaknesses (-) of various options to encourage supplementary
old age provisions

	Mandating		Tax incentives/subsidies to	
Impact on	occupational pensions	private pension plans	occupational pensions	private pension plans
Demand for labour	-	o	o	o
Savings ratio	++	++	+	+
Labour supply	-	-	o	o
Public budget	o	o	-	-
Coverage rate	++	++	+	+
Risk-sharing capacity	+	+	o	-
Political feasibility	-	-	+	+

+ Beneficial impact; - Detrimental impact; o Neutral

the creation of the capital stock would require additional resources and thus
lead to a higher tax wedge and increased budgetary pressures. Furthermore,
a state-controlled pension fund may be used for purposes other than augmenting the invested capital assets such as purchasing government or public
enterprise bonds or financing housing loans at low rates of return. As the
World Bank (1994) has pointed out, most publicly managed pension funds
have lost money in the 1980s, dissipating the accumulated reserves through
negative real interest rates. Even if the problem of public misinvestment
could be resolved, there is still a considerable political risk associated with
this option. Whenever a capital stock has been accumulated within the public pension system, governments may be tempted to grab at this money pre-
maturely in order to unburden their own budgets or to spend the money for
current pensioners in order to improve their electoral standing (Sinn
1999).[15] Even if the state has no direct access to these reserves, it may draw
on the capital stock in an indirect way by lowering the inflow of tax money
into the pension system without commensurate reductions in pension expenditures. The resulting deficiencies in receipts would thus lead to a
diminution of the capital stock.

Strengthening of occupational and private pension plans

The latter problems are of minor relevance if full funding takes the form of
private or occupational pension plans. These arrangements are less vulnerable to the political risks described above since the state has no legal power

and no fiscal incentives to cut non-public pension benefits. Moreover, contributions to private or occupational pensions do not amplify the tax wedge as long as they are paid on a voluntary basis. Hence, they have no distorting effects on the labour supply. Finally, they offer greater possibilities for individual choice than the uniform benefit regulations characteristic of the public pension system. For all these reasons most pension experts advocate an expansion of fully funded old age provisions outside rather than inside the public pillar.

However, the advantages of (semi-)private retirement provisions are at the same time its weaknesses. In contrast to public pension systems, private retirement schemes offer little possibilities for inter-personal redistribution, both horizontally, i.e., between groups with a different risk structure (e.g., people with different life expectancies) and vertically, i.e., between higher and lower income-strata. Private pension arrangements also require much higher administrative costs than public old age provisions. Moreover, they are exposed to the danger of private mismanagement. As the Enron scandal in the US has shown, private or occupational pension plans may be associated with enormous investment risks which may even lead to a total loss of the invested capital. However, by providing an appropriate regulatory framework that establishes a number of minimum standards with respect to the investment criteria, the state may be able to contain these kinds of problems.[16]

The specific strengths and weaknesses of private or occupational old age provisions also vary with the concrete design of these schemes. Concerning their organisational form, supplementary old age provisions may be pursued on a purely individual or on an occupational base. Occupational pensions may be further distinguished between employer-sponsored fringe benefits and collectively negotiated pensions on the one hand, and between defined-contribution and defined-benefit schemes on the other. Finally, a distinction can be made between mandatory and voluntary pension arrangements. In principle, these design features can be combined in various ways with one another, leading to a large pool of theoretically possible pension arrangements. Pension policymakers have to ponder carefully what the advantages and disadvantages of each arrangement are (see table 1.5).

In general, pension policymakers have two options to broaden the scope of supplementary retirement provisions. They can establish a legal obligation to insure, which is clearly the most effective strategy to ensure quasi-universal coverage. Alternatively, they can promote the development of supplementary old age provisions on a voluntary basis through financial incentives such as tax relief or direct state subsidies.[17] However, the coverage rates attainable on the basis of purely voluntary solutions may often be lower than intended by the government. First, there will be some shortsightedness especially among the younger generations with respect to the perceived necessity to pursue supplementary old age provisions as a means of maintaining a proper standard of living during one's old age. Secondly, low-income households have on average a lower savings ratio (and thereby a lower capacity to pursue private old age provisions) than middle- and high-income households. At the same time, the need for additional private old age provisions is most pronounced just for this group. To the extent to which public pensions are curtailed, low-income earners will have a hard time to build up pension entitlements that are sufficient to guarantee a decent standard of living. Hence, insufficient supplementary old age provisions among the low-income brackets may increase the demand for means-tested minimum pensions or social assistance benefits and thereby burden the public budget. Such problems will become less grave if supplementary old age provisions are made mandatory. In addition, this option is less costly for the public budget than a large-scale promotion through fiscal incentives. Finally, mandatory solutions allow – at least in principle – for a certain degree of cross-subsidisation between high- and low-risk individuals since the former cannot opt out from a compulsory system.

However, mandatory solutions are also associated with specific problems. From an economic point of view, the introduction of compulsory levies for private or occupational old age provisions entails some of the problems as they also occur in the case of statutory social contributions. Just as contributions for the public pension system contributions to private retirement schemes may have distorting effects on labour supply if these contribution payments are mandatory. For instance, any kind of wage-based levies (regardless whether they are public or private) may render illicit employment more attractive for individuals displaying a high discount rate on future consumption. However, to the extent to which mandatory levies for private old age provisions yield a higher rate of return and imply a higher degree of *actuarial fairness* than contributions to the statutory pension insurance, these distorting effects will be limited.

The key problem of mandatory occupational pensions is the potential impact on overall labour costs. In this case, employers will be legally obliged to offer and to (co)finance occupational pensions for their employees. In Switzerland, all employers are required by law to top up state pensions by occupational pension benefits. In the Netherlands and Denmark, a broad coverage by occupational pensions has been achieved by collective agreements between the social partners often made mandatory by the legislator via extension clauses. However, both approaches may have a negative impact on overall labour costs as long as employers are unable to shift the expenses for occupational pension schemes entirely on to employees.

Mandatory solutions also entail substantial political risks. Rendering individual old age provisions mandatory will reduce workers' disposable income and may therefore trigger resistance among workers and their representatives. By contrast, the introduction of compulsory occupational pensions is likely to evoke conflicts with employers, who fear a general increase of overall labour costs. By contrast, mobilising political support for an expansion of supplementary old age provisions will be much easier if this takes place on a voluntary basis, in particular if the state provides for generous financial aids.

Another crucial issue is the question whether the promotion of supplementary old age provisions should focus on occupational or on private pension plans. In principle, both tiers may either complement or replace public pensions. Depending on the concrete design of the respective arrangement, each tier has specific advantages and disadvantages in economic, distributional and political terms. While it is beyond the scope of this study to discuss this issue in detail, I will briefly highlight three crucial aspects:

1 Occupational pension arrangements based on industry-wide agreements may be better suited for achieving high rates of coverage among dependent workers than private pension plans, especially if workers are legally entitled to convert part of their salaries into occupational pensions. This is particularly true for low-income earners whose individual capacity for private retirement saving is often very limited and those who may profit from the collective establishment of occupational pension plans. However, occupational or collective solutions are not applicable to occupational groups outside an employment relationship such as the self-employed. For these groups, private retirement provisions will remain indispensable.

2 Occupational pensions on a collective basis allow for the integration of "bad risks" without actuarial surcharges. This is not possible with private pension plans. For instance, private life insurance policies typically take into account the individual risk of longevity. Hence, due to their higher average life expectancy, women will end up paying higher insurance contributions than men. Thus, if individuals can freely choose their own pension packages, adverse selection will undermine intra- and inter-generational risk sharing and redistribution. Under a collective arrangement the problem of adverse selection can be handled more easily (Bovenberg 1996).

3 The costs for the administration of collective pension plans are much lower than those of private pension plans. Although the latter are able to offer pension packages attuned to specific individual needs and hence allow for greater individual choice,[18] they cannot take advantage of the economies of scale characteristic of uniform pension plans based on collective agreements. This again will substantially reduce the rate of return of private pension schemes.

1.4   Varying degrees in the need for adjustment

In the previous section I discussed the most important reform options available to pension policymakers in dealing with economic and demographic challenges. As argued above, these challenges are more severe in the Bismarckian countries than in countries with a multi-pillar pension system. Nevertheless, even within the cluster of Bismarckian countries, the magnitude of pressures and challenges differs significantly. Hence, even among the countries studied, pension policymakers have different starting points for their reform efforts. In the following section I will try to assess how great the need for adjustment is for each country with regard to the various kinds of challenges. To this end, I will present a number of empirical indicators that will allow for a comparison of reform pressures between the countries (for an overview see table 1.6 at the end of this chapter). Only on this basis can we judge whether the reforms enacted in these countries are sufficient to put their pension systems on a more sustainable path. By the same token, the relative "progress" of pension reform policies within a country cannot be judged primarily by the absolute magnitude of changes associated with legislative actions. Instead, I will take the magnitude of legislated changes relative to the respective size of challenges (at a certain point in time) as the crucial yardstick to assess in how far the measures adopted in pension policy can be considered as successful. For instance, a reform reducing the projected increase in pension outlays by, say, 5% of GDP may be considered sufficient in a situation where the projected increase in pension spending prior to legislation was relatively modest while the same reform will be regarded as insufficient if pension expenditures had grown dramatically without this reform. Here again, we should distinguish between short-term pressures largely driven by acute budgetary crises and long-term challenges primarily resulting from the problem of demographic ageing. A reform might be appropriate to cope with short-term pressures on the public pension system without really addressing the long-term challenges. Conversely, pension reforms may turn out to be very effective in the long run, but may not address the acute fiscal problems of the pension system.

Variations in short-term pressures

The most immediate pressure for changes in pension policy emerges from acute or imminent financial deficits within a social insurance-based pension system. Social security schemes outside the general government cannot borrow to finance current expenditures. Hence, differences between revenues and outlays must be (temporarily) covered by government money (Bonoli 2000). Therefore, any fiscal shortfall in a public pension scheme lacking a buffer fund to iron out short-term imbalances will immediately affect the public budget. This problem has been the most severe in France and Italy. Both countries displayed huge (and in the Italian case chronic) deficits in their public pension schemes in the early 1990s, which imposed an increasing burden on the state budget.[19] However, the other countries also frequently faced situations in which pension outlays exceeded revenues, which again created a need for repeated short-term adjustments.

Short-term pressures towards the reduction of pension costs are also the result of large deficits in the state budget. The reason is that a sizeable share of public pension expenditures is financed out of the state budget, even in contribution-based pension systems. Hence, public pension schemes are a privileged target of governments' attempts to consolidate the public budget. Fiscal pressures have been strongest in Italy, which suffered from chronically huge (often two-digit) public deficits up to the early 1990s. This again jeopardised Italy's compliance with the convergence criteria of the Maastricht Treaty. Budgetary pressures were similarly strong in Sweden during the first half of the 1990s, when the public budget surplus of 4.2% in 1990 became a deficit of 12.3% of GDP in 1993. Hence, substantial spending cuts in the public pension system were necessary to balance the public budget. Public deficits were also quite large, albeit somewhat less dramatic, in Austria with a peak of 5.1% (in 1995) and in France with a peak of 6.1% of GDP (in 1993). Among the countries studied, budgetary pressures were comparatively modest (albeit by no ways absent) in Germany. Despite the costs of unification, fiscal deficits never did exceed 3.5% of national income in the 1990s. It should be noted, that high public deficits are at least ambivalent in their effects on the capacity of national policymakers to reform the pension system. While high public deficits increase the economic and fiscal pressure to cut public pension benefits, they also restrict the fiscal leeway for side payments to potential reform opponents and thereby endanger the political feasibility of pension reforms. In particular, large fiscal deficits narrow the scope for a large-scale promotion of fully funded old age provisions through tax incentives and direct state subsidies.

As noted above the high level of non-wage labour costs in Bismarckian countries requires a stabilisation of pension contributions. In the face of steeply rising unemployment rates, this goal gained increasing priority among governments in the 1990s. However, the current contribution rates differ significantly from one country to another, indicating varying degrees of problem load: With a level of about 30%, the pension contribution rate is clearly highest in Italy, followed by Austria with a contribution level of 22.8%. In France, Germany, and Sweden contribution rates are more modest and oscillated around 20% in the 1990s. Looking at aggregate spending figures we obtain a relatively similar ranking. In 1993, pension spending peaked out in most European countries. Again, Italy stood out as the highest spender with pension outlays amounting to 14.9% of national income followed by Austria (14.2%), Sweden (13.7%), France (13.4%) and Germany (12.5%). Irrespective of these differences all five countries display pension contribution rates and expenditure levels far above the OECD average. Therefore, these countries have to cope with disproportionably high levels of non-wage labour costs. In sum, the countries studied were under acute adaptational pressures in the 1990s with respect to the financial position of their public pension systems. These pressures were most pronounced in Italy, somewhat less severe in Austria, France, and Sweden and – compared to *these* countries – least dramatic in Germany.

Variations in long-term challenges

We can also identify significant cross-country variations in the long-term challenges for public pension arrangements. The most severe challenges result from the impact of demographic ageing. As noted above, the overall trend is relatively similar across the OECD countries. However, there is significant variation around the general trend line even among the countries studied. In 2000, all of the countries studied displayed old age ratios[20] of around 25%. According to EU projections, this ratio will increase to 62% in Italy (2045), 54% in Austria (2040), 50% in Germany (2035), 46% in France (2050), and 42% in Sweden (2045).

The demographic shock is also reflected in gloomy scenarios concerning the long-term growth of pension expenditures. OECD calculations (1988) based on the legal status quo of the mid-1980s (reflecting the situation prior to the period analysed) projected dramatic increases in pension expenditure ratios as a result of these demographic changes. Pension spending levels were projected to reach more than 35% of GDP in Italy, more than 30% in Austria and Germany,[21] about 27% in France, and about 18% in Sweden until 2040. Although these figures need to be treated with great caution, they give some indication of the extent of policy changes that at the time were required in order to make the public pension systems in these countries more sustainable.

Thus, there was a strong need to reduce the huge implicit debt accrued in these pension systems (corresponding to the value of outstanding pension claims minus accumulated capital reserves). This pressure is further amplified by the fact that the countries studied have also accumulated a sizeable explicit public debt, which hit its peak in the 1990s. From an economic point of view both the implicit pension debt and the explicit state debt constitute a liability that needs to be served in the future and therefore restricts the budgetary leeway of future governments. Here again, Italy is in the most unfavourable position as the level of explicit state debt is considerably higher than in the other countries studied.

The above indicators illustrate the long-term need for adjustment primarily with respect to the containment of aggregate spending levels in the face of rapidly graying societies. With respect to this challenge, Italy appeared to be under the greatest pressure for reform at least until the mid-1990s, followed by Austria, Germany, and France. In Sweden, by contrast, the magnitude of these pressures was more modest. However, apart from the need to contain aggregate pension spending in the long-term, pension policymakers in the Bismarckian countries must also deal with a number of structural deficiencies in the overall system of old age provisions in order to improve its distributive and economic efficiency.

Among those deficiencies, the extensive misuse of early retirement options has become a major concern for pension policymakers. Here, the challenge consists of increasing the effective retirement age and thereby enhancing employment rates for elderly workers. In that respect, the need for adjustment was (and still is) the greatest in Austria and Italy. In both countries, the effective retirement age and the employment levels among elderly workers is very low compared to international standards. This is primarily due to a generous system of seniority pensions allowing for early labour market exiting at a very low age, or as in Italy, with no age limit (provided a contribution record of at least 35 years or 15 to 25 years for public sector employees). France and Germany also have to cope with a serious problem of early labour market exiting even though the situation appears to be less dramatic than in Austria or Italy. In Sweden, by contrast, the effective retirement age and the average employment ratio for older workers are comparatively high by international standards.[22] Nevertheless, even in Sweden, employment ratios among older workers fell substantially in the early- to mid-1990s. Hence, as Wadensjö (2002) points out, in Sweden it is the decline rather than the remaining high level of labour market participation among the elderly that has been a matter of major political concern.

Another major challenge to the reform of Bismarckian pension systems is the need to create a stronger link between contributions and benefits. This primarily implies a tighter link between pension benefits and lifetime earnings. As mentioned previously, this reform approach would not only dampen the growth of pension expenditures and strengthen work incentives but also remove distributional deficiencies resulting from different earning careers. Traditionally, only Germany has a benefit formula entirely based on lifetime earnings. In the other countries, benefits are traditionally based on a number of "best" or last years and on a limited number of contribution-years required for a full pension. Thus, in Austria, France, Italy, and Sweden pension policymakers sought to modify the benefit formula towards a closer link to lifetime earnings.

As suggested above, the categorical fragmentation of public pension schemes in the Bismarckian countries is often associated with marked differences in the generosity of benefits among these schemes (in particular between the public and private sector). This fragmentation is most pronounced in France and Italy where a multitude of pension schemes with strongly diverging benefit regulations exist side by side (Bonoli 2000; Ferrera and Gualmini 2000a). To a lesser extent, distributive disparities resulting from an institutionally fragmented pension system also exist in Austria and Germany where civil servants are covered in separate pension schemes and enjoy a number of privileges concerning their benefit entitlements. By contrast, there is no need for a harmonisation or alignment of pension schemes in Sweden, because it already has a universal pension system covering the entire population.

Finally, as suggested above, the reduction of public pensions needs to be accompanied by the promotion of supplementary retirement provisions. Thus far, the overall system of retirement income provisions in the countries studied is for the most considered as undercapitalised. This problem is particularly pronounced in Austria, France, Italy, and Germany where the volume of pension fund assets (relative to GDP) is virtually negligible. Sweden is in a somewhat more favourable position due to the existence of quasi-universal and fully funded occupational pensions and to its higher share of funding within the public system. Combined, these assets amounted to roughly 43% of GDP in 1999.

Table 1.6   Selected indicators for the magnitude of challenges in pension policy in the 1990s

Larger challenge ▉   Moderate challenge ▓   Smaller challenge ▒   No challenge ☐

A) Short-term pressures

Reform goals/ Challenges	Indicators for the size of challenges	Austria	France	Germ.	Italy	Sweden
Lower the burden on the public budget	Budget surplus/deficit as % of GDP (avg. for 1990s)	-3.0	-3.5	-2.2	-6.5	-3.1
Stabilisation/Reduction of social contributions	Pension contribution rate as % of wages (1995)	22.8%	19.8%	18.6%	29.6%	19.8%
Containing the growth of pension outlays	Pension expenditures as % of GDP (1993)	14.2	13.4	12.5	14.9	13.7

For definitions and sources see page 49

B) Medium- and long-term challenges

Reform goals/ Challenges	Indicators for the size of challenges	Austria	France	Germ.	Italy	Sweden
Coping with the impact of demographic ageing	Projected change in old age ratio (65+/15-64 years): 2000 –> peak year (in %)	23-54	24-46	24-50	27-62	24-42
Containing the growth of pension outlays	Peak in future pension outlays (as % of GDP) based on 1988 OECD projections	31.7	27	31.1	35.7	18
Lowering the burden on the public budget	Gross public debt as % of GDP (peak in the 1990s)	69.7	65.2	63.3	124.0	78.3
Raising the effective retirement age	Effective retirement age (avg. for men and women, 1995)	57.6	58.8	59.5	58.9	62.7
Raising the effective retirement age	Employment rates for workers aged 55 to 64 years (1995)	29.0	33.5	37.5	27.0	61.9
Changing the benefit calculation to career earnings	Number of "best years" on which reference salary is based (1990)	10	10	Career earn-ings	5	15
Changing the benefit calculation to career earnings	Number of contribution-years required for full pension entitlement (1990)	45	37.5		40	30
Harmonisation of benefit regulations	Percentage of insured people covered by the largest single scheme	80 to 90% (?)	ca. 65%	82%	ca. 54%	100%
Promotion of fully funded pensions	Pension fund assets as % of GDP (1999)	3.3	5.1	6.8	6.7	42.7

Definitions for table 1.6

Reform goals	Indicators for problem load/ need of adjustment	Definition of the size of challenge
Lower the burden on the public budget	Budget surplus/deficit as % of GDP (average for the 1990s)	Relatively large challenge: 5% or over Relatively moderate challenge: 3% to 5% Relatively small challenge: under 3%
Stabilisation/Reduction of social contributions	Contribution rate (1995)	Relatively large challenge: 20% or higher Relatively moderate challenge: 15% to 25% Relatively small challenge: under 15%
Containment the growth of pension outlays	Pension expenditures as % of GDP (1993)	Relatively large challenge: 14% or higher Relatively moderate challenge: 12% to 14% Relatively small challenge: under 12%
Containing the growth of pension outlays	Peak in future pension outlays (as % of GDP) ac-cording to OECD projections from 1988	Relatively large challenge: 30% or more Relatively moderate challenge: 20% to 30% Relatively small challenge: under 20%
Containing the growth of pension outlays	Projected peak in old age ratio (65+/15-64 years) up to 2050	Relatively large challenge: 60% or more Relatively moderate challenge: 50% to 60% Relatively small challenge: under 50%
Lower the burden on the public budget	Gross public debt as % of GDP (peak in 1990s)	Relatively large challenge: 100% or more Relatively moderate challenge: 50% to 100% Relatively small challenge: under 50%
Changing the benefit calculation to career earnings	Number of "best years" on which reference salary is based (1990)	Relatively large challenge: under 5 years Relatively moderate challenge: 5 to 20 years Relatively small challenge: more than 20 years No challenge: life-time principle
Changing the benefit calculation to career earnings	Number of contribution-years required for full pension entitlement (1990)	Relatively large challenge: under 35 years Relatively moderate challenge: 35 to 40 years Relatively small challenge: 40 years and over No challenge: life-time earnings
Harmonisation of pension benefits	Percentage of population covered by the largest single scheme	Relatively large challenge: under 70% Relatively moderate challenge: 70% to 80% Relatively small challenge: more than 80% No challenge: 100%
Promotion of fully funded pensions	Pension fund assets as % of GDP (1999)	Relatively large challenge: under 10% Relatively moderate challenge: 10% to 20% Relatively small challenge: more than 20%

Sources: Abramovici 2002; Blöndal and Scarpetta 1998; Economic Policy Committee 2000; Gern 1998; Klammer 1997; Mantel 2001; Neumann 1999; OECD (1988; 2000a)

In sum, the structural deficiencies of the pension system were the most pronounced in Italy. The pension systems in Austria and France also featured a high degree of dysfunction in virtually all of the relevant reform dimensions. The structural deficiencies were somewhat less pronounced in the German and Swedish pension systems, since both systems are traditionally characterised by a number of features that appear to be relatively unproblematic with respect to some of the above-mentioned challenges. Germany is unique because the principle of lifetime earnings is traditionally established in the benefit formula. Sweden has also been in a more favourable starting position, due to its higher effective retirement age, its higher share of funding, and the presence of a unified pension system with no systematic disparities across different occupational groups.

2 An Empirical Overview of Policy Change in Bismarckian Pension Regimes

In this section I will briefly analyse to what degree the countries studied have adjusted their pension systems along the lines sketched above. I will begin by presenting a number of empirical indicators measuring the degree to which national pension policymakers have successfully addressed the short-term problems of public pension schemes. As pointed out above, governmental actors typically pursue at least three short-term goals in pension policy: the elimination or avoidance of fiscal imbalances within the public pension system, relief of the fiscal pressure on the state budget, and the stabilision of pension contributions in order to contain the growth of non-wage labour costs. Thus, in the short run, governments are primarily concerned with curbing the growth of pension outlays and – albeit to a lesser extent – stabilising or augmenting the revenue bases of the pension system.

To what degree have Austria, France, Germany, Italy, and Sweden accomplished the goal of containing pension costs in the 1990s? Due to the economic recession and the concomitant expansion of early retirement, pension outlays increased relative to GDP in the early 1990s. Thereafter, the pension expenditure ratio remained relatively stable in Austria, France, and Italy (see table 2.1). In Germany, pension expenditures increased by about 0.5% of GDP, whereas they fell by 1.5% of GDP in Sweden. At first sight, these figures suggest that governments have done relatively little to curb the growth of pension expenditures in the 1990s. This impression is quite misleading, however. A number of intervening factors have to be taken into account in order to assess the "real" magnitude of pension cutbacks on the basis of aggregate spending data. First, due to their increasing labour force participation, women have accumulated ever higher pension entitlements in recent years. Moreover, the share of people above 65 (and thereby the number of pension beneficiaries) increased between 1993 and 1999 by 1.1% in Sweden, 4% in Austria, 7% in Germany, 8.2% in France, and 12.3% in Italy. Obviously these trends had an expansionary effect on total pension outlays. Without this effect, the share of national income devoted to public pension benefits would have declined significantly in all of the five countries.

Table 2.1   Change in public pension expenditures between 1993 and 1999

	Austria	France	Germany	Italy	Sweden
As % of GDP (1993/1999)	14.2 / 14.0	13.4 / 13.5	12.5 / 13.0	14.9 / 15.1	13.7 / 12.2
Standardised expenditure ratio* (1993/1999)	95 / 90%	91 / 85%	80 / 77%	96 / 87%	78 / 69%

* = Expenditures in % of GDP / share of people aged 65+ (100% = GDP per head of population)

Source: Calculations by the author, based on Abramovici (2002) and OECD, Labour Force Statistics 2001

Table 2.1 also displays a standardised pension expenditure ratio. This indicator clearly demonstrates that pension payments per head of the older population has (at least in relative terms) decreased by about 9% in Italy and Sweden, 6% in France, 5% in Austria, and 3% in Germany. Note, however, that the only modest decrease in German spending figures was also caused by the gradual upgrading of pensions in former-East Germany towards the levels in West Germany. Thus, empirical evidence suggests that the countries studied have been relatively successful in recent years in stabilising the level of pension expenditures despite significant countervailing pressures.

The quantification of the long-term savings effects of recent pension reforms on a comparative basis runs into even greater difficulties than the quantitative assessment of pension cuts, which have already gone into effect. This is because highly speculative projections about future growth rates, wages, and rates of workforce participation and a host of behavioural responses to these reforms would have to be made. Predictions about the long-term development of these parameters include large uncertainties. Moreover, due to the enormous complexity of pension systems, accurate projections about the financial impact of single pension reforms have to be based on a multitude of data and institutional knowledge, which thus far can only be provided by national institutions (European Commission 1996; Myles and Pierson 2001). However, recently published reports by the European Commission (Economic Policy Committee 2000; Economic Policy Committee 2001) provide empirical data about the projected growth of pension expenditures that are based on broadly similar macro-economic and demographic assumptions and thus at least partly allow for comparisons across countries. While these figures do not reveal the assessment of the magnitude of *single* reform measures on a quantitative-comparative basis, they do offer some indication of whether the legal actions taken in pension policy have been sufficient in stabilising future pension outlays (see table 2.2).

Table 2.2 Estimated change in pension expenditures according to different projections (in % of GDP)

Country	Spending level in 2000	Estimated change from 2000 to peak year (1)				
		EPC Standard scenario (2)	EPC Optimistic scenario (3)	CSIS Projection (4)	Avg.	Projections made in 1988 (5)
Austria	14.5	+4.2	+1.4	+6.2	+3.9	+14.1
France (6)	12.1	+4	+2.8	+7.3	+4.7	+10.5
Germany (6)	11.8	+4.9	+2.8	+6.8	+4.8	+14.7
Italy	13.8	+2.1	+0.9	+5.1	+2.7	+18.8
Sweden (6)	9.0	+2.6	+1.6	+4.2	+2.8	+5.9

(1) Between 2000 and 2050
(2) Economic Policy Committee baseline scenario
(3) Economic Policy Committee "Lisbon" scenario
(4) Centre for Strategic and International Studies (based on "pessimistic" assumptions)
(5) Figures display the expenditure increases projected by the OECD in 1988.
(6) Please note that the figures for France, Germany, and Sweden do not fully reflect total pension outlays (such as disability pensions). The percentage covered in the simulation models is 95% in France, 91% in Germany and 83% in Sweden.

Sources: Economic Policy Committee 2001; Werding 2001; Jackson 2002

Table 2.2 displays the level of public pension spending in 2000 as well as the peak increases in pension outlays as a share of GDP[1] according to different simulation scenarios taking into account the effects of the reforms adopted until 2001. The share of public pension expenditures is most likely to increase in all five countries studied. The expenditure peak will be reached somewhere between 2030 and 2050. Even in the most optimistic scenario, the increase in pension outlays ranges from 0.9% (Italy) to 2.8% of GDP (France, Germany). The projected increases are significantly higher under the assumptions of the EPC baseline scenario, ranging between 2.1% in Italy and 4.9% in Germany. A more pessimistic scenario calculated by the Centre for Strategic and International Studies predicts increases that vary between 4.2% of GDP in Sweden and 7.3% in France (Jackson 2002). However, even in the worst-case scenario, the expected growth in pension outlays will be far more modest than had been predicted in the mid- and late-1980s by the OECD under the assumption of an unchanged legal status quo. Hence, there is clear empirical evidence that the pension reforms undertaken in the late-1980s and 1990s have effectively curbed the imminent escalation of pension costs in the face of an increasingly ageing population. For the time being, the strongest expenditure dynamics is predicted for France and Germany. For these countries, the projected growth rates vary from between 2.8% in the optimistic scenario and 6.8 and 7.3%, respectively, in the CSIS scenario and may therefore reach a total of well above 15% of GDP. For Austria, prospects are only slightly less gloomy as the projected bandwidth of spending increases ranges between 1.4 and 6.2% of GDP. Hence, due to its high starting level, Austria may end up in a position where it will spend about one fifth of its national income or even more on public pensions if further reforms are not undertaken. Italy, by contrast, albeit starting at a roughly similar level, will most likely keep the expenditure ratio below 20% of GDP even under unfavourable economic and demographic conditions. Sweden will also experience only a comparatively modest growth in pension expense ranging between 1.6 and 4.2% of GDP and is therefore unlikely to reach an expenditure ratio above 15%.

The countries studied also differ in the degree to which they have addressed the structural deficiencies of their pension systems. As pointed out in the previous section, a major weakness of these systems involves the rather loose and unsystematic connection between contributions and benefits. Until 2001, only Italy and Sweden have engineered a complete changeover from a defined-benefit to a (notional) defined-contribution scheme. Once in place, such an arrangement effectively ensures that contribution rates can be maintained at a stable rate into the future, as benefits will be adjusted downwards if contributions fall short of pension outlays. However, Italy in particular will institute very long transition periods to implement the change towards the new system. In Germany, benefits are traditionally based on lifetime earnings. However, German pension policymakers have thus far avoided a clear move towards a defined-contribution system as the pension formula still entails a target replacement ratio.[2] In Austria and France, the link between contributions and benefits has been tightened somewhat, however, without mastering a complete changeover to lifetime earnings. In France, the qualifying period for a full pension has been extended from 37.5 to 40 years, while the period over which the reference salary is calculated has been increased from the best 10 to the best 25 years. In Austria, the reference salary calculation has only been increased to the best 18 years. At the same time, a higher (rather a lower!) accrual rate has been established effectively lowering the qualifying period for a full pension from 45 to 40 years.[3]

The countries studied also differ in the extent to which they have raised the retirement age in order to improve the numerical relation between contributors and pensioners. France stands out as the only country in the study that left the formal retirement age untouched. The rest have all increased the retirement age, especially for women. However, only Sweden and Italy will gradually introduce a pension system in which incentives for early retirement will be completely abolished. The reason is that in both countries the change from a defined-benefit to a defined-contribution system is associated with the introduction of a flexible retirement age based on actuarial principles. By its nature, such a system is fiscally immune to premature exiting from the labour market since the additional costs of early retirement will be completely individualised. It should be noted, however, that the implementation of these changes is extremely slow in the Italian case and will only become fully effective in the distant future.[4]

As pointed out above, pension policymakers in the Bismarckian countries also have to deal with the problems resulting from the categorical fragmentation of the pension system, in particular, as the pension privileges for public sector employees are concerned.[5] In that respect, Austria and Italy were the most successful. Both countries will largely harmonise the different benefit regulations between the private and the public sector albeit with long transition periods. In Germany, no serious efforts were undertaken to arrive at more uniform benefit provisions between the public and the private sector. Nevertheless, pension cuts in the general scheme were typically applied to civil servants' pensions as well. However, while the overall volume of cutbacks was largely similar in both systems, these measures will not challenge civil servants' pension privileges. In France, the benefit gap between public and private sector employees has, in fact, widened due to a failed attempt to reform public sector pensions (Jolivet 2002).

Finally, national pension reform records vary in the degree to which they have strengthened elements of capital funding (Leinert and Esche 2000). In that respect, Germany, Italy, and Sweden have implemented the most far-reaching reforms. In Germany and Italy, recent reforms have encouraged the development of private or occupational pension plans on a voluntary basis by means of (relatively generous) state subsidies and tax advantages. In Germany, an albeit very modest public reserve fund will be developed in order to smooth out the fiscal burden resulting from the imminent cost explosion in the area of civil servants' pensions (Färber 1998).[6] In Sweden, a new fully funded pillar was recently established, whereby the insured people are obliged to invest 2.5% of their income into a pension fund at their option (which can be either private or public). In Austria and France, by contrast, the promotion of fully funded pension plans has thus far only proceeded very slowly, albeit there is a growing consensus among pension policymakers in these countries that major steps in this direction are necessary or at least desirable.

Table 2.3 Private pension benefits as a percentage of GDP*

	2000	2010	2020	2030	2040
Austria	n.a.	n.a.	n.a.	n.a.	n.a.
France	0.1%	0.1%	0.2%	0.2%	0.3%
Germany	0.9%	1.2%	1.8%	2.9%	3.4%
Italy	1.3%	1.7%	2.1%	3.2%	4.3%
Sweden	2.2%	2.7%	3.5%	4.5%	5.3%

* Includes all funded employer pensions, personal pensions, and severance pay schemes

Source: Jackson and Howe 2002

France confined itself to establishing a small buffer fund within the public pension system. Austria introduced only very modest tax incentives to promote private or occupational pension schemes. In short, among the countries studied, only Germany, Italy and Sweden have taken substantial steps to promote supplementary old age provisions, whereas Austria and France lag behind in this regard. This is also reflected in recent projections about the future growth of private pension benefits (see table 2.3).

Below I will try to summarise the major empirical findings emerging from this brief account of pension reforms in the Bismarckian countries. To begin with, a radical change of these pension systems towards the three-pillar model advocated by the World Bank (in particular a full privatisation of the earnings-related pillar) has never been a serious policy option in these countries. As Myles and Pierson (2001) correctly point out, the inherited pension policy profile, in particular the presence or absence of a mature earnings-related public pension scheme on a pay-as-you-go basis, represents the single best predictor of the basic direction of national pension reforms. These policy legacies constitute powerful political constraints, which are extremely difficult to overcome in democratic polities.

However, while radical reform is unlikely for precisely this reason, we can detect remarkable examples of "transformative" (Brooks 2000) or "path-departing" (Hering 2000) changes even within the cluster of Bismarckian pension systems. In all of the countries studied the benefit commitments made under the conditions of economic prosperity have been considerably downgraded since the late 1980s. More importantly, a number of structural innovations have been inserted into the pension edifice of Bismarckian countries, such as the gradual switch to a defined-contribution design in Sweden and Italy, the establishment of a fully funded pension pillar in Germany, Italy, and Sweden or the large-scale harmonisation of benefit regulations between public and private employees in Austria and Italy. Even if these changes are not considered radical, it appears that welfare state reform even in continental Europe may well go beyond "marginal adjustments" (Esping-Andersen 1996:82). By the same token, the capacity for effective policy responses in these countries may not be as restricted as authors such as Scharpf (2000a:124) have suggested. This study highlights a major shortcoming of the contemporary literature on welfare state retrenchment. As Green-Pedersen/Haverland (2002) and Palier (2002) have correctly argued, most scholars (Pierson and Weaver 1993; Pierson 1994; Pierson 1996; Pierson 1998; Weaver 1998; Myles and Pierson 2001) have thus far directed their attention primarily to the relative stability rather than the changeability of welfare state arrangements. This study also presents a more dynamic perspective and seeks to explore the conditions under which welfare reform is possible.

The empirical account of pension policy changes in the Bismarckian countries also suggests that the reform capabilities seem to differ substantially among the countries studied. By and large, Sweden has been the most successful in making its pension system more sustainable. To some extent, this also holds true for Italy, albeit the reforms will only become fully effective in the distant future. Germany and Austria have made less progress in pension reform than Italy and Sweden although they still rank above France, which thus far has adopted only marginal adjustments.

However, the degree of adjustment also varies within countries. As shown above, pension policymakers in the Bismarckian countries have to tackle different tasks at the same time and they may be more successful in one reform dimension than in another. Moreover, a country's overall record in adjusting its pension system is typically the result of successive reform efforts that may differ considerably among one another in their ambitions and in their effective scope. As we will see, in most of the countries studied we find legislative decisions that have been quite successful and relatively far-reaching. We also find reform efforts that clearly missed their target or even failed completely. In other words, the conditions for successful adjustment in pension policy are likely to vary over time. Hence, the relative progress of a country in reforming its pension system can only be explained with reference to single decision periods and with respect to specific dimensions of reform. In the following section, I will therefore put forward a theoretical framework that tries to set out systematically the conditions which facilitate or impede the implementation of effective pension policy responses in concrete decision situations.

3   The Politics of Pension Reform: An Actor-Centred Explanatory Framework

In the previous sections I have shown that the interplay between economic, demographic, and political pressures on Bismarckian pension schemes has triggered a multitude of reform measures throughout the 1990s, which were primarily but not exclusively aimed at curbing the growth of pension spending. This development has also left its mark on the scholarly debate about the welfare state. In recent years, welfare state research has gradually shifted from studying welfare state expansion to studying the retrenchment of welfare state arrangements (Green-Pedersen and Haverland 2002). In this chapter, I will first provide a brief survey of the most important theoretical approaches to welfare state retrenchment and discuss their usefulness for the explanation of pension policy outcomes. I will then develop a distinct theoretical framework based on the concept of actor-centred institutionalism. This framework establishes a number of heuristic hypotheses that allow us to identify the political and institutional conditions facilitating or impeding the problem solving capacity of national pension policymakers.

3.1   Social policymaking in an era of retrenchment: A review of theoretical approaches[1]

The new politics of the welfare state

In his seminal 1994 work, the *Politics of Retrenchment*, Paul Pierson has pointed to the remarkable resilience of welfare state arrangements in spite of an increasingly fierce climate of fiscal austerity. Following Pierson, the politics of retrenchment is qualitatively different from the politics of expansion. While the "old politics" of welfare expansion is seen as a strategy of "credit claiming" for highly popular initiatives, the "new politics of the welfare state" is regarded as an attempt to avoid blame for unpopular policies. Once social policies have become established in a society, a powerful network of interests is likely to evolve around these arrangements, which will try to avert any efforts aimed at rolling back the welfare state. As Pierson has argued in his earlier work (1994; 1996), these client-based policy interest groups have to a large extent replaced leftist parties and trade unions as upholders of welfare objectives. Their impact on the success of governmental retrenchment efforts will primarily depend on the specific structure of welfare programmes. According to Pierson, the inherited profile of social policy programmes is the most important predictor for the relative resilience of welfare arrangements. From that point of view, welfare state trajectories appear to be highly path-dependent rendering radical institutional change and sweeping retrenchment extremely unlikely. This holds particularly true for mature pay-as-you-go financed pension systems in which benefits are earnings-related, cover a large section of the population, and are perceived as "acquired rights" by the (potential) beneficiaries. Hence, under the conditions of democratic party competition, benefit cutbacks tend to be very incremental and will only be brought about if governments are able to devise strategies that reduce the political costs of welfare retrenchment. According to Pierson, organised labour has lost a great deal of its explanatory power with respect to welfare state developments as the advocates of the power resources approach had argued in their studies investigating welfare state expansion (Stephens 1979; Korpi 1983; Esping-Andersen 1990).

Partly in reaction to Pierson's work, a large number of studies have been published in recent years that try to improve our empirical and theoretical knowledge about the factors that explain different degrees of retrenchment in advanced welfare states.[2] These scholars have emphasised alternative or at least additional explanatory factors relating to the socio-economic, partisan, and institutional context in which retrenchment efforts take place.

Some authors (Castles 2001; Huber and Stephens 2001) have stressed the impact of macro-economic pressures, especially of rising unemployment and increasing public deficits, as the major driving force behind welfare state retrenchment. Another strand of the literature emphasises the importance of economic internationalisation as an influence on recent welfare state developments. For instance, Scharpf (2000a) has argued that increased competition on product markets constrains the ability of national policy-makers to increase non-wage labour costs, thereby limiting the scope for an expansion of welfare programmes financed out of wage-based social contributions. Pierson (1998) himself has drawn our attention to other socio-economic developments that are at least equally important as push factors for welfare retrenchment such as the relative growth of the service sector and population ageing. However, there is a growing consensus within the retrenchment literature that economic and demographic pressures are not automatically translated into commensurate cutbacks. Hence, most studies of welfare state retrenchment emphasise political factors. These approaches stress the role of political parties and political institutions.

The role of political parties in welfare retrenchment

With respect to the influence of political parties on welfare state development in the context of fiscal austerity, various scholars have arrived at strikingly contradictory findings. In accordance with Pierson, a number of welfare state researchers (Wagschal 2000; Castles 2001; Huber and Stephens 2001; Kittel and Obinger 2001) have diagnosed a declining importance of partisan politics or even the absence of any significant partisan effects on welfare spending in recent years. Theoretically, this empirical finding is typically explained by referring to the growing economic and political constraints to which governments of all stripes are exposed. Economic constraints have increasingly curtailed the capacity of leftist governments to expand social policies, whereas political constraints have also seriously hampered the abilities of market-liberal governments to cut back on welfare entitlements.

Other authors (Hicks 1999; Siegel 2002), by contrast, have found empirical evidence that the positive correlation between leftist party incumbency and changes in social expenditure ratios, which was characteristic of the 1960s and 1970s, is still confirmed in the 1980s and 1990s. Yet another group of scholars has suggested a completely opposing logic. In electoral terms, it may appear easier for leftist governments to curtail welfare entitlements than for bourgeois ones, as the latter are unlikely to represent a serious alternative for voters seeking to express their dissatisfaction with welfare cutbacks enacted by a leftist government. Conversely, a leftist opposition party may find it relatively easy to accuse a right-wing government of dismantling the welfare state. Hence, a bourgeois government cutting back popular social benefits will run a great risk of triggering an exodus of voters to the leftist camp. As the Nixon-goes-to-China thesis[3] this argument has found its way into recent welfare state research (Haverland 2000; Ross 2000; Kitschelt 2001).

As Kitschelt (2001) has suggested, the relevance of this mechanism is contingent on the configuration of a particular nation's party system. In a constellation where the major parties on both sides of the political centre are equally acknowledged as supporters of existing welfare arrangements, even a bourgeois opposition party may successfully exploit the issue of social policy cutbacks in the electoral arena. Thus, Christian Democratic parties can more credibly denounce welfare cuts adopted by leftist governments as "socially unfair" than can the bourgeois parties with a distinctly market-liberal ideology. Following Kitschelt, the latter cannot exploit the issue of pension cutbacks electorally since voters alienated by benefit cuts will not turn to a party known as critical of a large welfare state. From this perspective, we would expect the political costs of retrenchment, and thereby the obstacles to social policy reform, to be highest in countries with weaker market-liberal parties and stronger centrist (e.g., Christian Democratic) and Social Democratic parties.

The institutional structures of welfare state arrangements

Another broad strand in the retrenchment literature emphasises the role of institutions as a crucial factor in mediating adaptational pressures on the welfare state. Here, a clear distinction needs to be made between the institutional structures of welfare state arrangements themselves and the institutional set-up of the political system. With respect to the institutional legacies of welfare state programmes, authors such as Swank (2000) have found empirical evidence that liberal welfare states appear to be more vulnerable to downward pressures than Social Democratic or conservative welfare regimes. Governments in liberal welfare states can cut more easily since they have a higher discretionary power over social policy programmes if these are based on the criterion of need (rather than contributory entitlements) and funded out of general taxation (rather than earmarked as social contributions).[4] As far as pension systems are concerned, Siegel (2002) developed an institutional index of reform elasticity in order to assess the degrees of freedom for policymakers to embark on retrenchment policies. According to this index, pension systems providing for means-tested minimum protection (as in Australia or in New Zealand until 1985) display the lowest legal and political barriers against governmental interventions. Pension arrangements granting universal flat-rate benefits appear to be somewhat less vulnerable to governmental retrenchment strategies since their political support base is much broader. However, they lack the high degree of legal safeguards entrenched in earnings-related social insurance pensions where contributory entitlements constitute quasi-property rights.

Myles and Pierson (2001) pointed to an additional factor accounting for the strong resilience of Bismarckian pension arrangements. The higher the degree of system maturation the higher will be the number of people who have built up substantial benefit entitlements and who are therefore likely to oppose benefit cuts. In this study, I have deliberately selected countries where public pension schemes are organised around the social insurance principle and display a high degree of system maturation, and thereby countries in which the legal and political reform constraints embedded in the pension system itself are particularly tight.

In the retrenchment literature, two further programme variables are thought to have an impact on the resilience of welfare arrangements: the degree to which social policy programmes are split along occupational lines and the extent to which administrative and regulative competencies are delegated to quasi-public institutions managed by the social partners (Palier 2002; Siegel 2002). As Swank (2000) has pointed out, conservative welfare states tend to fragment programme constituencies on the basis of occupational status. Compared to a universal programme-design, this institutional feature may allow for a more targeted retrenchment strategy that excludes occupational groups with a high potential for political conflict. Thus, while corporatist conservative welfare states accord both working and middle class groups relatively generous social insurance benefits (and therefore generate a very broad political support base) the political division of constituencies in these countries may narrow the number and strength of potential reform opponents. This again may amplify the possibilities for policymakers to tailor politically feasible reform packages.

Another characteristic feature of corporatist conservative welfare states is a partial decentralisation of authority to quasi-public administrative bodies often controlled by labour and business representatives. As several authors (Swank 2000; Palier 2002; Siegel 2002) have suggested, this organisational structure increases the number of key players in the realm of social policy and provides them with notable opportunities to slow down or to block adverse policy change. In a similar vein, Palier (2002) has argued that union involvement in the management of social security grants unions a de facto veto power against welfare state reforms.

The institutional structures of the political system

As mentioned above, a second strand of institutional analysis focuses on the specific institutional structure of democratic polities as the crucial factor determining government capabilities of pursuing welfare reform. These structures vary considerably across countries providing governments with different degrees of control over the policymaking process. It has been suggested that a government's ability to achieve its preferred policy outcome is primarily dependent on the existence or absence of veto points in the political system (Immergut 1990; Immergut 1992; Bonoli 2000). To a varying degree these veto points allow interest groups to gain access to the political de-cision-making process.[5] By forging (ad-hoc) alliances with actors that occu-py formal veto positions in the political process or by influencing the policy preferences of formal veto players,[6] various interest groups may be able to block legislation that runs contrary to their interests. The higher the num-ber of veto points, the more restricted the political leeway for governments to influence policy outcomes will be. For a government trying to expand so-cial benefits the presence of multiple veto points is most likely to retard poli-cy change. It is less clear, however, whether the same logic also applies when welfare retrenchment is on the political agenda. As a number of authors have suggested, a high degree of power concentration resulting from the ab-sence of major veto points, is a two-edged sword for governments commit-ted to curtailing welfare spending (Pierson and Weaver 1993; Pierson 1994; Bonoli 2000). While potential reform opponents cannot formally block leg-islative decisions if policymaking authority is concentrated in the hands of government, the concentration of power will also enhance government's ac-countability for unpopular measures and thereby increase its electoral vul-nerability. As Bonoli (2000) has argued, the relative importance of these two countervailing effects is dependent on at least three distinct factors:

1 The strength of the accountability effect hinges on the intensity of party competition in a certain political context. The fear of electoral retribution will only be of subordinate importance to the strategic calculus of govern-ments, if the likelihood of a change of government is comparatively low. For instance, the risk of electoral punishment is less pronounced for a gov-ernment facing a weak and internally divided opposition.
2 Policymakers are likely to attach greater importance to the accountability effect in a first-past-the post electoral system, where even modest losses in votes may be transformed into dramatic losses of parliamentary seats.[7] By contrast, this amplifying effect is more or less absent in electoral systems with proportional representation. Nevertheless, in the face of increasingly volatile voting behaviour even parties in a proportional electoral system run the risk of a massive deterioration of their parliamentary representa-tion.
3 The intensity of the accountability factor will also reflect the electoral cy-cle. At the beginning of an electoral term, politicians are more likely to adopt unpopular measures than in the run up to an election. By the same token, the electoral costs of such measures are likely to be higher in coun-tries with a higher frequency of elections.

This list could also include a fourth factor, namely trade union strength. As Scarbrough (2000) points out, labour unions in most West European countries still play a key role as defenders of existing welfare arrangements. In a number of countries, their mobilisation capacity remains considerable. In many cases, the organised labour movement has taken a leading role in organising popular protest against programmatic cutbacks including mass demonstrations and large-scale strikes. Thus, the presence of powerful trade unions is likely to amplify the accountability of governments for unpopular cuts in social benefits.

As Tsebelis (1995; 1999) has argued, the potential for policy change will not only depend on the number of veto players but also on the dissimilarity of policy positions among veto players. Therefore, the presence of a veto player strongly committed to defending the current status quo in social policy will mostly suffice in preventing major benefit cutbacks.

3.2   The concept of actor-centred institutionalism

The previous section discussed numerous theoretical approaches that are frequently applied in the analysis of welfare state developments involving economic and fiscal crises. Each approach highlights important aspects of the political economy of welfare retrenchment. However, each of them quickly reaches its limits when the remarkable variation of pension reform outcomes across time and space needs to be explained. Typically, the traditional explanation in comparative welfare state research – regardless of whether they are institutionalist, functionalist or party-based – argue at a rather general level and tend to neglect the fact that policy-specific outcomes are caused by the *interaction* of different factors rather than by a single dominating driving force. An appropriate analysis of pension policy therefore requires a conceptual framework that combines and integrates various theoretical perspectives and at the same time allows us to highlight the specific contextual factors that appear to be relevant in an individual decision period. The framework applied in this study largely draws on the heuristics of actor-centred institutionalism, which combines actor-centred and institution-centred approaches and thereby seeks to overcome the prevailing analytical dichotomy between the two theoretical strands. As Scharpf (1997b:36) notes:

> What is gained by this fusion of paradigms is a better "goodness of fit"
> between theoretical perspectives and the observed reality of political in-
> teraction that is driven by the interactive strategies of purposive actors

operating within institutional settings that, at the same time enable and constrain these strategies.

Thus far, only a few scholars have explicitly applied the concept of actor-centred institutionalism to analyse political decision-making processes in pension policy.[8] As I will try to show, it has greater explanatory power with respect to pension policy outcomes than the theoretical approaches sketched in the previous section.

The basic explanatory framework of actor-centred institutionalism is depicted in figure 3.1. As Scharpf (1997b) points out, the starting point of analysis consists of identifying the set of interactions that produces the policy outcomes that need to be explained. In the next step, we need to identify the *actors* who are involved in the policy process and whose choices will ultimately generate specific policy outcomes. These actors are characterised by specific *capabilities* (such as legal competencies defined by institutional rules), specific *perceptions*, and specific *preferences* (including both institutional self-interests and normative orientations). These actors face specific policy problems and operate in a specific socio-economic and institutional context. In most cases, policy outcomes are not determined by a single actor. These outcomes are typically generated by a plurality of actors which interact in specific ways. Hence, we need to analyse the *actor constellations*, describing the actors involved, the actors' strategic options, the policy outcomes generated by strategic combinations and the preferences of the players over these policy outcomes. A certain constellation may then allow for different *modes of interaction*, denoted as "unilateral action", "negotiated agreement", "majority vote", and "hierarchical direction". These interaction modes are again shaped by institutional rules. In the following section, I will draw on these theoretical categories in order to explain the political context in which pension policy outcomes are produced.

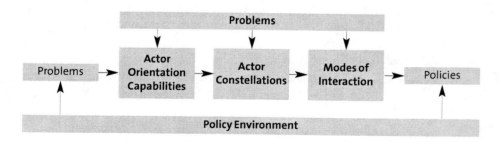

Figure 3.1 The theoretical framework of actor-centred institutionalism

As a first step in our analysis we have to specify the key actors in pension politics and their preferences. To begin with we can plausibly assume that the government is the most important actor in pension policy (at least this is true for the Bismarckian countries where income security in old age is largely provided by the state). After all, it is the government that decides whether the issue of pension reform is put on the political agenda or not. I assume that the parties in government (as well as political parties in general) have multi-dimensional preferences. Typically, parties within democratic polities are policy seekers and political entrepreneurs at the same time. In the first dimension, political parties represent the interests of their core constituencies (in particular, of specific socio-economic groups) and pursue appropriate policy goals irrespective of their organisational self-interests (Lipset and Rokkan 1967). To a certain degree, the policy goals of political parties (particularly of large catch-all parties) may also be inspired by the notion of "public interest", at least at the level of public discourse. As Scharpf (1997b) points out, party politicians are more likely to argue in categories of "public interest" or "social justice' in order to justify their actions than are representatives of interest groups whose legitimation is primarily based on its representation of the collective interest of their members. In the second dimension, typically emphasised by rational choice theorists, party leaders strive first and foremost to maximise their individual gains. From this perspective, party leaders seek to maximise their chances of holding on to their positions and winning votes (Downs 1957). In addition, they must ensure the long-term continuity of the party and hence a minimum of internal cohesion within the party organisation (Bergmann 1999). As Mulé (2000) points out, these goal dimensions are not mutually exclusive. Party leaders typically must pursue *each* of these aims. However, their relative weight is likely to depend on specific institutional context factors (Strøm and Müller 1999) (see figure 3.2).

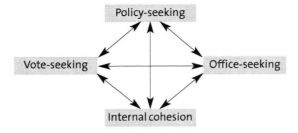

Figure 3.2 Goals of political parties

3.3 The politics of pension reform

The convergence of pension policy positions

I will first attempt to discuss the policy interests that governments are likely to pursue with respect to pension policy. As argued before, economic, demographic, and political factors have put public pension schemes under increasing adaptational pressure. Against this background, pension retrenchment has become a major political issue in practically all of the advanced welfare states throughout the 1990s. policymakers have become increasingly aware of the necessity to curb the growth of pension spending. Basically this holds true for governments irrespective of their general ideological orientation. At the same time, however, market-liberal governments face severe political and legal constraints to the radical dismantling of mature social insurance-based pension systems, which grant contribution-related benefits that are perceived as "acquired rights" on the part of the (potential) beneficiaries. Thus, the viable space for reform in pension policy is tightly constrained in the contemporary policy environment. Pension policy positions of both left- and right-wing parties have therefore converged considerably in recent years (Bonoli 2000). In other words, neither an increase nor a radical dismantling of pension benefits appears to be a politically feasible option for pension policymakers in Bismarckian countries. This constellation is depicted in figure 3.3, which displays a continuum stretching from a leftist agenda of benefit expansion to a neo-liberal agenda of radical retrenchment.[9] To simplify matters, I assume that the retention of the status quo in pension policy is identical to the preservation of current benefit levels and more or less rapidly rising contribution rates. This assumption is justified by the fact that the traditional defined-benefit design of public pension schemes requires an increase in contribution levels, whenever outlays exceed revenues (as will be most likely the case in the context of a sharp increase in old age dependency ratios). On that basis, we can establish the following theoretical propositions (see Figure 3.3):

First, due to the demographic, economic, and fiscal strains, pension policy positions have generally gravitated increasingly towards cost containment rather than benefit expansion.

Second, the constituencies of most political parties have an age structure that does not deviate dramatically from the general age distribution within the electorate.[10] This is especially true for catch-all parties, which cannot afford to disregard the interests of certain age groups to the benefit of others. By the same token, these parties need to adopt pension policy positions that

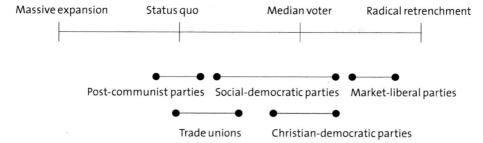

Figure 3.3 Policy positions towards pension reform in the context of demographic ageing and fiscal austerity

can be presented as a fair compromise between the interests of young, middle-aged, and older voters (and thereby between contributors and pensioners). This compromise will come relatively close to the pension policy positions of the average voter, who in most Western democracies is roughly in his or her mid-forties.[11] Most people in this age group have built-up substantial benefit entitlements in the public pension system, but must continue to pay pension contributions for another 10 to 20 years. In line with Pierson (1998), I expect the average voter to be considerably distant from both the status quo and from a position of radical retrenchment. This is because neither the retention of the status quo (possibly leading to exorbitant increases in contribution rates) nor a dismantling of pension entitlements will be acceptable to the median voter (all the more so since the time to compensate these cuts by an increase in private savings is relatively limited). If faced with a tragic choice between exploding contributions on the one hand, and sharp pension cuts on the other, voters in this age group are likely to regard a mixed solution (somewhat higher contributions *and* somewhat lower public pensions) as the lesser evil, as this allows the smoothing over of the financial burden during the individual's life-cycle. This middle position is reinforced by the fact that the median voter is typically middle class with no clear socio-economic preferences. It is important to note, however, that this policy position reflects the "theoretical" interest of the median voter. In practice, the median voter may ignore the inevitability of adjustment measures and react negatively to benefit cuts and higher contributions alike. Nevertheless, a strong deviation from this policy position both to the left and to the right will be even less attractive to the median voter. Therefore, the parties of the political centre (in particular Social and Christian Democratic parties) have a strong interest in approaching a "medium" policy position in order to optimise their electoral standing and to occupy the pivotal position in the party system.

Third, radical retrenchment of pension entitlements (let alone a complete privatisation of the pension system) is neither a politically nor a legally feasible reform option, even for parties with a market-liberal orientation (which in principle may prefer private over public old age provisions). However, for ideological reasons market-liberal parties are likely to reject any increases in taxes or social contributions, the more so as their core clientele usually is usually found among the higher income strata. Hence, they will advocate for stronger pension cuts than centrist parties. Thus, liberal parties are most likely to place themselves at some distance from both the average voter and from the position of radical retrenchment.

Fourth, communist or post-communist parties position themselves far to the left of Social Democratic parties. Typically, these parties do not aim to appeal to the average voter but try to represent the interests of the low-income strata. At the same time, even these parties would not advocate a large increase in pension benefits, which would unduly shift the burden of adjustment to the working-age population. At best, they may present themselves as defenders of the status quo in pension policy.

Finally, political parties cannot be assumed to be unitary actors and thus represent a certain bandwidth of policy interests rather than a fixed point on the left-right spectrum. For communist as well as market-liberal parties, this bandwidth will be comparatively narrow, as these parties are typically characterised by a relatively coherent ideological profile and represent only a relatively small constituency with comparatively homogeneous social policy interests. Hence, the leadership of these parties will have little problem in organising an intraparty consensus on the party's overall view on pension policy. By contrast, centrist catch-all parties such as Social or Christian Democratic parties must aggregate relatively heterogeneous (or even diverging) social policy interests, since their constituency is composed of quite different socio-economic groups. Typically, these parties comprise different ideological wings with respect to their profile in social and economic policies. Christian Democratic parties, for instance, must incorporate wage earner and employer interests alike. In Social Democratic parties we can diagnose tendencies of increasing conflicts between an ideological membership with a traditionally leftist orientation in social policy (including many trade unionists) and a more pragmatic, office-seeking leadership trying to move the party towards the political centre so that it will occupy a more pivotal position in the party system. Thus, in both cases, the party leadership will have a hard time in generating intraparty consensus on a well-defined position in pension policy.[12] These intra-party tensions will become particularly severe as soon as the party takes governmental responsibilities. In this case, budgetary constraints will force the party leadership to accept the necessity of cost containment reforms in pension policy and to adopt a policy that is at odds with the policy preferences of the traditionalists within the party. By contrast, an opposition party can more easily ignore "factual constraints" in pension policy and is thus likely to maintain more "leftist" or "populist" positions.

The political risks of pension reform

Welfare retrenchment, even if justified with reference to fiscal or economic "factual constraints", is a highly unpopular undertaking. This holds especially true for public pensions, in particular those based on individual contribution payments. However, there is no unanimous opinion among welfare state scholars about the underlying reasons for the unpopularity of social benefit cutbacks. For instance, Pierson and Weaver (Pierson and Weaver 1993; Pierson 1994) have attributed the unpopularity of benefit cutbacks to their high visibility and their concentration on specific groups. By contrast, the benefits of welfare retrenchment are considered as rather diffuse as they affect all taxpayers.

As Anderson (2001) points out, however, this argument is only applicable to tax-financed programmes for a relatively small group of beneficiaries.[13] In this case, the average voter argument needs to be modified. Welfare beneficiaries will not face any trade-off between contributions and benefits if the latter are completely financed by the taxpayer. However, this reasoning does not apply to contribution-financed pension systems. In this case, an increase in contributions is not necessarily less unpopular than a reduction of benefits. Opinion surveys indicate little popular support for cuts in social benefits, but an equally low level of willingness to pay the extra taxes and social contributions required to maintain current welfare standards in the face of rising demographic and economic pressures on the welfare state[14] (Taylor-Gooby 2001). The same holds true for increases in the retirement age. Thus, in the context of fiscal crisis and population ageing, pension reform basically boils down to the highly unpopular imposition of welfare losses. In recent years pension cuts have been enacted on a large scale, whereas pension contribution rates remained at a high level or even increased. Similarly, a rapidly ageing population will require benefit cuts which will, however, only result in a *slower increase* rather than in *declining* contributions levels. By the same token, a delay of pension reform may stabilise benefit levels for a short while, but may also result in a sharper rise of contribution rates and/or levels of taxation. This may have been politically acceptable in an era of high economic growth and rising post-tax salaries. However, voters are unlikely to accept a growing contribution burden in the context of stagnant or even falling real wages. Hence, governments cannot avoid unpopular and perhaps electorally detrimental choices in pension policy even if they opt for the retention of the status quo. They are likely to be punished for whatever they do (Scharpf and Schmidt 2000:334).[15] This may also hold true if a government is able to convince a majority of voters about the inevitability of loss-imposing reforms. It is rather unlikely, however, that most of these voters will vote for the government parties *because* of its pension cuts or because of its decision to increase contributions. The best the government can hope for is that pension cuts will not play a significant role in their voting decisions. In other words, governments will have a hard time trying to take electoral credit for those measures even if most voters accept them. By contrast, even if only a limited percentage of the electorate is fiercely opposed to pension cuts and thus likely to express its displeasure at the ballot box, this may be just enough to vote a government out of office.

The political salience of pension policy is enhanced by the fact that an overwhelming majority of the citizens still considers old age provisions to be primarily a government task. This is revealed by attitude surveys from the International Social Survey Project (ISSP). According to the most recent ISSP figures (1996), about 97% of respondents in Germany and about 98% of respondents in Sweden shared the opinion that it is the government's responsibility to provide a decent standard of living for the old. By contrast, there is less support for public provisions for the unemployed (84% and 90%, respectively) or the reduction of income differences between rich and poor by the state (69% and 71%, respectively) (Taylor-Gooby 2001). By the same token, the acceptance of benefit cuts is significantly lower in the area of pensions than it is for other social policy programmes. For instance, according to a German opinion survey conducted in 1993 (Roller 1999), only 3% of German citizens would approve cuts in old age pensions, while for other social policy programmes, the share of respondents favouring cutbacks is higher. For instance, 30% of respondents regarded unemployment benefits as the main target for social spending cuts (for comparison: benefits for asylum seekers 21%, health services and child benefits 13%).[16] In electoral terms, the salience of the pension issue is amplified by the clear over-representation of middle-aged and older groups among the active voters.[17] This is why pension policy implies considerable electoral risks for democratic governments operating in the context of tight fiscal and demographic pressures.[18]

The political advantages of concerted pension reform

Despite the general unpopularity of pension cuts, governments do not necessarily become the subject of electoral retribution when they opt for pension retrenchment. This is because voters will only react to government actions regarding pension policy if political actors outside the government successfully mobilise the public against it. In line with Scharpf (1997b), this process can be seen as a sequential game between three players (see figure 3.4). The government has to decide whether it launches a major legislative initiative in pension policy or not. If significant cost containment measures are not taken, the government will often be forced to increase contributions or taxes in order to avoid financial deficits in the pension system. Given the government's choices, the opposition must then decide whether to ignore the issue, support the proposal, or use its limited resources to oppose the initiative and mobilise voters on a large scale.[19] In the former case, we can assume that voters will largely ignore the issue. In the latter case, swing voters may either ignore the issue or agree with opposition criticism and vote against the government in the next election.

To be sure, this kind of game is largely irrelevant in consociational democracies where all of the major political parties are represented in government and where party competition is therefore largely disabled as a mechanism of democratic accountability. As a rule, however, most democratic polities display a more or less strong element of party competition (Lijphart 1984; Scharpf 1997b). In this case, there will always be the risk for the government that pension reform will emerge as a major electoral issue. Moreover, given the extraordinary significance of pension policy for the incomes of large elements of the population, there is a great chance that voters will respond to this issue. Hence, faced with the threat of electoral retribution, governments tend to seek a consensus with the very political actors who are most capable of mobilising large sections of the electorate against its pension reform plans.

Typically, this applies not only to parliamentary opposition parties but also to trade unions. At least in continental Europe, trade unions still play a crucial role as defenders of earnings-based social insurance schemes and may have the capacity to mobilise their members against adverse welfare reforms. Conversely, unions' approval or at least their acquiescence is likely to reduce the general political resistance against unpopular pension reforms (Anderson 2001; Palier 2002).

However, governments may have additional reasons to seek consensus with these actors in pension policy. First, both the opposition and the trade

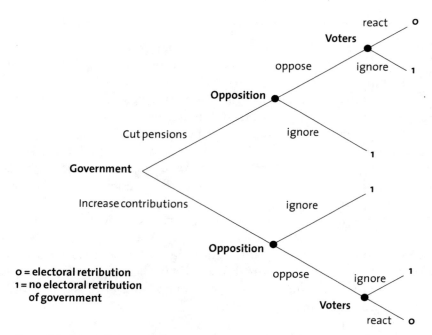

Figure 3.4 Sequential game between government, opposition and voters

unions may – at least indirectly – occupy veto positions in the decision-making process allowing them to block governmental pension reform initiatives.
Second, policy-oriented governments must have an interest in sustaining the
durability of enacted reforms by assuring that these are not overturned after
the next election.[20] Third, predictability and reliability of pension policy (as
opposed to frequent and unexpected ad-hoc interventions by the government) constitutes its own a value. By their very nature, pension reforms imply more or less profound changes in the retirement income packages, particularly for future pensioners. As current contributors have to adjust their
employment biographies and their savings behaviour long in advance, they
have a genuine interest in the long-term predictability of pension policy and
thus in a broad political and societal consensus on pension reform. Finally,
by striking agreements with external political actors, the government may
effectively neutralise internal reform opponents. For instance, a broad
cross-party agreement will generate broad parliamentary majorities and
thereby disable the potential veto power of reform adversaries within the
government factions. By contrast, a pension consensus between government and trade unions will facilitate the acquiescence of left-wing deputies

in Social and Christian Democratic parties, who otherwise may have resisted governmental plans to curtail pension benefits.

For these reasons, it should not come as a surprise that successfully implemented pension reforms are mostly concerted reforms (Pierson 1998; Baccaro 2000; Hinrichs 2000a; Hinrichs 2000b; Council of the European Union 2001a; Myles and Pierson 2001). By the same token, the efforts of governments to form a broad pension consensus typically go above and beyond the search for a simple parliamentary majority (Hinrichs 2000a). The government has an interest in ensuring the acquiescence of trade unions and in trying to avoid a situation in which the opposition parties mobilise against its pension reform initiatives. If governments attempt to impose pension reforms unilaterally or fail in their effort to bring unions and opposition parties on board they run the risk of being voted out of office or being forced to withdraw their reform plans.

I will therefore now focus on two crucial arenas of pension politics: the partisan arena as a potential platform for a pension consensus between government and opposition, and the corporatist arena as a potential platform for a pension consensus between government and trade unions (possibly including the employer organisations). In most cases, each concerted effort is potentially enough to generate a stable political support base for pension reform. With a broad partisan consensus, pension reform becomes politically feasible even if unions oppose the reform. First, a consensus backed by the major political parties provides a stable parliamentary majority, which trade unions could not effectively oppose. By contrast, if the ruling parties can only manage a slim majority and do not win the parliamentary support of the opposition, even a comparatively small trade union opposition along with other internal opponents may have enough power to stop the government. Second, a broad cross-party agreement would deprive unions of the ability to exploit the electoral division between the government and the opposition.

Conversely, the parliamentary opposition faces greater difficulties in blaming the government for unpopular pension cuts, if the reform is supported by the trade unions which enjoy great credibility as defenders of the welfare state. Moreover, support by the unions would make it easier especially for a left-wing government to organise a consensus within its own ranks. To be sure, in cases where the opposition party has institutional veto power (e.g., by controlling a second chamber whose agreement is necessary to adopt pension legislation) trade unions' support will not be enough to overcome the opposition.

As Pierson (1998) has pointed out, we still know relatively little about the circumstances that facilitate or impede the negotiation of substantial adjustments. Therefore, we need to ascertain more systematically the positive and negative incentives for both trade unions and opposition parties to arrive at a consensus with the government. I will deal with this question in the following sections.

First, the opposition not only has a substantive interest in pursuing its own policy goals through favourable compromises but also a competitive interest in defeating government initiatives in order to undermine the government's political reputation (Scharpf 2000b). Opposition parties may therefore be tempted to denounce the government for "unfair" pension cuts or "breached election promises" in order to improve their own electoral standing, even if they do not deviate very much from the government's position in substantive terms (Kitschelt 2001). However, opposition parties have to mediate between their substantive policy interests on the one hand, and their interest to maximise their election chances on the other hand. In principle, the opposition has three strategic options in its reactions to the government's pension reform plan:

1 It may try to negotiate a pension compromise with the government in order to move the reform output as close to its ideal point as possible. In this case, however, the opposition would forego the opportunity to exploit the pension issue in the electoral arena (as it can no longer attack the government on this issue).
2 Alternatively, the opposition may refuse its support though without promising to reverse the cutbacks after a change of government. In this case, the opposition would profit from the potential long-term economic benefits resulting from reform (such as higher economic growth and higher employment). On the other hand, it would be unable to influence the content of the reform and foregoes the possibility of fully exploiting the potential electoral gains that may accrue by the promise of a reversal of the government's benefit cuts. To be sure, this strategy would only be available if the opposition has no veto power in the decision-making process.
3 Finally, an opposition party may conduct a large-scale election campaign against a government's pension reform including the promise to reverse the cutbacks after a change of government. In the short term, this strategy may be the most promising for those seeking a change in government. However, if it does not remain true to its election promise after taking of-

Table 3.1 Likelihood of a partisan consensus on pension reform

		Policy distance between government and opposition		
		Large	Significant	Small
Positional conflict	High	-	-	-
	Medium	-	(+)	+
	Low	(-)	+	+

+ Emergence of consensus likely; - Emergence of consensus unlikely

fice, it will seriously damage its credibility in the eyes of the electorate. If it sticks to its promise by reversing the preceding government's cutbacks, it still has to resolve the issue of rising pension costs and may then find it even more difficult to legitimise pension cuts.

How does an opposition party solve this strategic dilemma? Table 3.1, in a highly stylised manner, depicts the constellations under which an opposition party would likely co-operate with the government.

As I argue, the opposition's willingness to enter into a pension consensus with the government depends on the interaction of two factors, denoted as "policy distance" and "positional conflict". This conceptualisation is different from Tsebelis' (1995; 1999) veto player model in which both dimensions are not treated separately. Within my theoretical framework, I define the "policy distance" between two actors as the distance between their "true" normative policy preferences, i.e., the policy positions they would adopt as mere policy seekers (and thus without considering the policy positions of other actors). By contrast, Tsebelis' notion of "policy position" describes the position of an actor's ideal point in the policy space regardless of the extent to which the location of the ideal point reflects its normative policy preferences or its (institutional) self-interest. Based on the former definition, I distinguish three possible gradations of policy distance (see also figure 3.3):

1 We may define the policy distance between government and opposition as *large,* if these actors position themselves at opposite sides of the status quo. As argued before, this constellation has become the exception to the rule. Under conditions of fiscal austerity and demographic ageing, both Social Democratic and bourgeois parties no longer deny the necessity of cost containment reforms. Within the spectrum of democratic parties, at the most (post)communist parties will continue to defend the pension policy status quo.

2 The policy distance between two actors is denoted as *significant*, if the respective ideal points are at some distance from one another, but are still located on the same side of the status quo.
3 The policy distance is defined as *small*, if two actors occupy relatively similar positions on the continuum.

The second dimension of "positional conflict" tries to measure the degree to which an opposition party is able and willing to improve its electoral position at the expense of the governing parties. In other words, the degree of "positional conflict" determines the extent to which co-operative or conflictual strategies improve or diminish a party's chances of maximising its electoral possibilities. For analytical purposes, I distinguish three levels of positional conflict (albeit in practice a smooth transition between them exists):

1 As a rule, the degree of positional conflict between government and opposition will be quite high in a party system where political majorities are narrow and where elections typically have a strong impact on the composition of the government.[21] This may be reinforced when elections are frequent or when a majority-based electoral system exists.
2 However, even in a highly competitive party system, situational and policy-specific factors may (temporarily) lead to a reduced level of positional conflict on certain issues. For instance, if opinion polls indicate that an opposition party is going to return to power after the elections, its incentives to exploit unpopular issues such as pension reform in the electoral arena may be substantially lowered. By the same token, the willingness of an opposition party to co-operate with the government might be greater if there are no major elections in the near future. With respect to social policy issues, positional conflict is moderated if an opposition party has great difficulties in presenting itself as a credible defender of the welfare state. A market-liberal opposition party, for instance, will have a hard time presenting itself as a reasonable alternative to voters dissatisfied with welfare cutbacks implemented by a left-wing government.
3 Finally, positional conflict can be characterised as low, if government and opposition parties are competing for votes but not for office. Under certain conditions, an opposition party might even have an interest in keeping rather than replacing an existing government. For instance, it cannot be in a communist opposition party's interest to have a Social Democratic government replaced by a bourgeois one. Alternatively, an opposition party may co-operate with the government to present itself as a potential coalition partner of the ruling party.

I argue that the degree of an opposition party's co-operation is the combined function of its policy distance to and its positional conflict with the parties in government. The opposition is unlikely to co-operate with the government if both its policy distance to and the degree of positional conflict with the government is high, hence a cross-party pension consensus will not emerge. Conversely, a constellation of "low positional conflict" and "small policy distance" will be highly conducive to a pension consensus.

However, the opposition is faced with a strategic dilemma if policy interests and competitive incentives operate in opposite directions. For instance, a small distance between the policy positions would allow for a cross-party consensus, although this could be countervailed by strong competitive incentives for the opposition not to co-operate. To the extent that disagreement with the government strengthens not only its electoral prospects but also its chance to replace the government, an opposition party would probably not support a government's pension reform. Thus, in a situation of strong positional conflict, I predict that an opposition party will thwart a pension consensus with the government irrespective of its material policy goals.[22] Hence, even a negligible policy distance is not a sufficient condition for the emergence of a cross-party pension consensus in the context of fierce party competition. In this situation, opposition parties are likely to opt for *strategic disagreement* (Gilmour 1995).

Conversely, a low level of positional conflict between government and opposition clearly facilitates negotiated adjustment. In this constellation, strategic considerations do not only enable but *reinforce* the search for consensual policies. For instance, an opposition party may try to demonstrate its co-operativeness by supporting the government's enactment of unpopular welfare reform. In doing so, it positions itself as a potential coalition partner.[23] Nevertheless, even in the context of low positional conflict between the government and an opposition party, we cannot generally assume that the latter will be prepared to support government policies that are diametrically opposed to its own policy interests, as this may drastically harm its chances to maximise votes.

Finally, in configurations of medium-level positional conflicts, strategic considerations enable a relatively policy-oriented bargaining process. Here the likelihood of a pension consensus is largely dependent on the policy distance between government and opposition. I predict that a policy-oriented opposition party would not join forces with the government, if the policy distance between the two is large. If it is confronted with a policy outcome that is (from its own perspective) inferior to the status quo, an opposition party will either try to block the reform or try to reverse it after the government constellation has changed. If a medium level of positional conflict is not combined with a large policy distance, a negotiated solution is basically within reach. That is because this constellation allows for policy outcomes that are superior to the status quo for both sides, while the absence of strong competitive incentives facilitates policy-oriented bargaining. Moreover, if government and opposition parties reach a pension reform agreement, it may be relatively far-reaching given the fact that the general necessity of cost-cutting measures is more or less uncontested even among the leadership of Social Democratic parties.

Pension politics in the corporatist arena

As suggested above, a consensus between government and trade unions will in many cases create a stable political support base for pension reform even if the reform is not backed by the parliamentary opposition. Unlike the opposition parties, trade unions have basically no competitive incentives vis-à-vis the government. Their primary interest revolves around substantive policy solutions not electoral competition (Scharpf 2000b). Given that trade unions and governments do not compete in the electoral arena, neither has any interest in engaging in conflicts with the other side. In general, both the government and the trade unions probably prefer a joint solution to social conflict, which may be costly to both sides. This is particularly true for the government, because a massive conflict with the unions may harm its electoral prospects.

Although this may favour a pension consensus between these actors, the pension policy goals of government and trade unions often diverge considerably. In principle, this is also true for left-wing governments. Under conditions of fiscal austerity, unions can no longer count on the uncompromising political support of labour governments (Ney 2001a). Trade unions, by contrast, tend to adopt a pension policy position that is much closer to the status quo. In particular, trade unions often resist major pension cuts even if this means higher contribution rates. Given the common ideological roots of trade unions and Social Democracy, the increasing divergence of their pension policy positions is remarkable. We can identify a number of reasons which may help account for this phenomenon.

– First, the membership of most trade unions is characterised by a relatively pronounced seniority bias. As a consequence, union leaders often end up defending the interests of elderly workers. In principle, unions face a trade-off between the interests of contributors and beneficiaries when they develop their own approach to pension reform. However, this trade-off is moderated by the fact, that current contributors are also future pensioners. With increasing age, public pension insurance contributors become increasingly less likely to accept the scaling down of their own pension claims. Hence, it is mostly elderly workers who resist pension cuts. By the same token, elderly workers are more likely to reject efforts to increase the retirement age (for the same reason that elderly workers are even more sensitive to changes in pension laws than current pensioners).[24] At the same time, it is precisely this age group that is the most influential among trade unions' rank and file (Brugiavini et al. 2001).[25] What is more, in some countries pensioners account for a sizeable share of union membership. In Italy, for instance, approximately half of the union members are pensioners (Fargion 2000). Thus, the trade unions' rank and file typically displays a stronger age-bias than the general electorate. One reason may be that trade unions have a hard time recruiting new members (in particular among the younger generation), which leads to a disproportionately higher share of older members.

– Second, trade unions by their very nature represent the interest of wage earners (or in the case of a specific union, only of a certain segment of wage earners) rather than the general society as a whole. At the same time, they tend to regard contributory pension entitlements as a form of "deferred wage". Hence, from the union's point of view, pension politics primarily reflects a distributive conflict between capital and labour rather than between older and younger generations. This is also why trade unions strongly encourage the participation of employers in the financing of old age provisions. Trade unions also typically call for stronger state involvement in the financing of public pensions, which would mitigate the potential conflict of goals between contributors and pensioners. By contrast, even left-wing governments cannot confine themselves to representing the "narrow" interests of wage earners and pensioners. Political parties must also pay attention to the interests of other social groups like the unemployed, students, single mothers, and self-employed people. To the extent, that an increasing share of public resources is devoted to the payment of pensions, tight budgetary constraints forces governments to cut expenditures in other areas of public services such as family benefits, education, and public infrastructure. This again would seriously violate the interests of groups not represented by trade unions but which may nevertheless be crucial for the electoral prospects of political parties.

– Third, trade unions also tend to defend existing pension arrangements as an instrument that offers relatively attractive pre-retirement options to older workers at the expense of the general tax-paying population. The accessibility of this "exit option" also increases unions' bargaining power vis-à-vis the employers. In other words, the access to generous soft landing options via the public pension system will reduce the pressure on unions to moderate their wage demands (Brugiavini et al. 2001). Governments have instead become increasingly aware of the fact that continuing generous pre-retirement options will mean unbearable burdens on the public budget.

Thus, as a rule, governments tend to favour larger and quicker pension cuts than trade unions. The latter are therefore interested in moderating or even impeding such reform efforts. In principle, trade unions have at least three strategies at their disposal to achieve this goal:

1 They may try to change the reform outcome by *bargaining* to win a package deal with the government. In exchange for their political support of the reform package, they may obtain significant government concessions or side-payments.
2 Unions may try to influence reform content by *lobbying,* mainly through party channels. If unions manage to organise a critical mass of supporters within political parties (and especially in parliament) they may have the power to block the reforms they do not like. In this case, governments may end up abstaining from initiating corresponding reform proposals.
3 Trade unions may try to *mobilise* their members or even the general public against the reforms. This may take the form of public declarations, demonstrations, or even strikes. This strategy may increase the political (especially the electoral) costs of reform to the government. This is especially true for strike actions that may have drastic consequences on the entire national economy.

These strategies are not necessarily mutually exclusive. Quite the contrary, union success may occur when they combine these strategies. For instance, the unions' bargaining power may increase when they exert additional pressure on the government by intensifying their lobbying activities or by mobilising (or at least threatening to mobilise) protests against the government's plans in the public arena. Nevertheless, the relative significance of these strategies may differ considerably. Most importantly, however, the final outcomes of these interactive processes may be radically different. Unions and the government may arrive at a specific agreement but may also end up in a head-to-head confrontation, at the end of which one side must give in.

Moreover, both an agreement and a non-agreement may offer a broad range of possible outcomes regarding reform content depending on how far the government is willing to – or forced to – accommodate union demands.

Despite differences in pension policy positions between governments and trade unions, the latter are more likely to prefer negotiated reform (which may offer them a voice in its implementation) over a reform that is unilaterally imposed by the government (or by a "grand coalition" of government and opposition parties). The government typically prefers a negotiated reform, in which trade unions offer a "green light" to unpopular welfare cutbacks. However, the government has to balance its desire to obtain union consent with its desire to implement real changes. If union consensus is its primary goal (rather than reform implementation), it ends up handing unions a de facto veto power (Wijnbergen 2000).

To summarise, the unions' main interest is in attaining a reform outcome that is as close to their position (somewhere between the status quo and the government's position). The government also seeks to influence the status quo toward its position, but must also simultaneously try to obtain union approval in order to lower the political costs of reform. This raises two questions: Under what conditions will both actors agree on pension reform and where will the final agreement be situated? Figure 3.5, in a highly stylised manner, depicts the possible bargaining constellations between the government and the unions, assuming that the pension policy preferences of the relevant actors can be depicted on a one-dimensional policy space (indicating the degree to which a reduction in pension spending is seen as necessary).

The bottom line is that three factors determine the policy outcome:

1 the location of the government's preferred policy outcome, i.e., its ideal point in a given policy space;
2 the location of trade unions' ideal point;
3 the location of the non-agreement point, i.e., the location of the policy outcome when no agreement is achieved. Non-agreement between the two means maintenance of the status quo if the government is either unwilling or incapable of imposing the reform on the trade unions. Conversely, non-agreement may also lead to a policy outcome that is identical to (or at least similar to) the government's position, if the government is both willing and capable of imposing this reform even without unions' approval.

Thus, in order to assess the final position of the policy outcome we have to proceed in two stages. First, we need to localise the ideal points of the government and of the trade unions. Here we can identify a number of factors

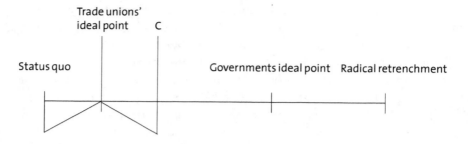

Figure 3.5   Bargaining constellation between government and trade unions

that influence the preference formations of these actors in pension policy. Once their ideal points have been established, we must assess the position of the non-agreement point.

The government's ideal point in pension policy is likely to reflect the strength of adaptational pressures. The stronger these pressures are and the more vulnerable a pension system is to these pressures, the more necessary cost containment reforms become and the more the government's ideal point will diverge from the status quo. As was argued in the previous section, cost containment pressures vary significantly across countries (even within the cluster of Bismarckian countries) but they will also vary over time.

The intensity of adaptational pressures will also have an impact on the pension policy outcome preferred by the trade unions. The reason is that trade unions must also have a fundamental interest in the long-term sustainability of public pension arrangements. However, specific trade union features such as their traditional ideological orientation, the share of elderly workers and pensioners in the rank and file or the degree of their organisational fragmentation may also have a considerable impact on their pension policy preferences. Finally, the unions' ideal point cannot be assumed as fixed because it varies considerably across countries and over time as well as from one union to another. This aspect will be explored in greater detail in the individual country sections. The bottom line is, however, that in the vast majority of cases, trade unions have a more leftist position concerning pension policy than the government.

Finally, the policy outcome resulting from government and trade union negotiations will depend on the location of the non-agreement point. As mentioned above, this position indicates whether or not a government is willing and capable of enforcing a reform even without trade union support.

Hence, the location of the non-agreement point reflects the relative balance of power between these two actors. In that regard, two crucial aspects need to be distinguished: First, the unions may be able to block or at least mitigate pension reform bills via lobbying efforts, especially if the government is institutionally weak and ideologically fragmented and also if trade union functionaries and their allies control important executive and legislative party offices (Kitschelt 1994). Alternatively, trade unions may to some degree be able to mobilise large-scale protests among their members or even among a large section of the general public against the government's reform plans. This will again increase the political costs of pension reform especially for governments that display a high degree of electoral vulnerability. Thus, trade unions may have varying capacities to pressure the government in both the legislative and electoral arenas, which dramatically affects their relative bargaining power and thus their power to defend the status quo.

In a constellation where they have an actual chance to defend the status quo, unions will not accept an outcome that is (from their point of view) inferior to the status quo. Given its agenda-setting power, the government, in this case, proposes a reform located at C (see figure 3.5). C is to the right of the unions' ideal point and equidistant from the unions' ideal point and that of the status quo. Provided that the unions are capable of impeding the reform, unions will oppose any outcome to the right of C. Thus, within this power constellation the location of the final bargaining outcome can be directly derived from the unions' ideal point and its distance from the status quo. This also means that even a "weak" government can achieve far greater pension cuts if a trade union is relatively reform-oriented and acknowledges the need for cost containment measures.

The bargaining constellation looks different, if the non-agreement point is identical with the government's ideal point. Here we assume that an institutionally strong government with a low degree of electoral vulnerability can convincingly impose painful pension cuts despite union resistance. This means that a policy-oriented union is always prepared to accept an outcome inferior to the status quo (to the right of C) as long as the government is willing to make at least some concessions. In doing so, the unions avoid an even worse outcome if the government had acted unilaterally.

Strategic choices of the government concerning the sequencing of negotiations

While government leaders desire support for their pension reform initiatives from other political parties and trade unions, they must also achieve an internal consensus on pension reform, both between the government coalition partners and within party organisations. Hence, the leaders of the various government parties have to negotiate the content of pension reform in several arenas and with different actors. This may have important implications for the government's strategic course of action with respect to the sequence of negotiations best suited to producing an outcome as close as possible to its own ideal point. As Tsebelis (1995) has pointed out, party leaders can basically choose between three different bargaining strategies.

First, the leaders of a ruling party may try to hammer out an agreement with the leadership of other parties (which may be inside or outside the government) without referring to their own party. Second, the party may discuss the issues first, reach an agreement close to the party's ideal point, and then negotiates with the other parties. Third, the leaders of the various parties meet, arrive at an agreement, and then submit it as a whole to their own parties. The number of potential bargaining strategies will increase further, if the trade unions are also considered an important negotiating partner. Party leaders will try to achieve the *first* agreement with an actor whose policy position is closest to their own ideal point. For instance, Social Democratic party leaders would probably choose the third method of negotiation. By firstly negotiating with a bourgeois party located at the centre of the policy space, they may hammer out an agreement that is relatively close to their own ideal point, which can be presented as a more or less accomplished fact vis-à-vis their own rank and file and vis-à-vis the trade unions. Similarly, a bourgeois government would probably first seek a consensus with the leadership of the Social Democratic opposition before contacting the trade unions (provided that this option is available).

3.4   Summary of the theoretical framework

In this section, I have presented a stylised theoretical framework to analyse the strategic context in which pension politics takes place. In summarising the theoretical arguments, I will now formulate a number of heuristic hypotheses, which will later be discussed in the light of the empirical findings presented in the individual country chapters:

– Neither the retention of the status quo nor a radical dismantling of existing pension entitlements appears to be a politically feasible option for contemporary pension policymakers in the Bismarckian countries. As a consequence, the pension policy positions of both Social Democratic and bourgeois parties are increasingly converging towards cost containment. Thus, I expect few systematic differences in the cost containment efforts between left- and right-wing governments.

– Pension reform under the conditions of fiscal austerity and demographic ageing is inevitably unpopular. In order to reduce the associated electoral risks governments seek to obtain the political support (or at least the acquiescence) of those actors who are capable of mobilising large groups of voters against possible pension cutbacks. This primarily concerns the parliamentary opposition parties and the trade unions. Hence, I expect governments to try to bring at least one of these actors on board.

– Whether or not an opposition party is willing to arrive at a pension consensus with the government will depend primarily on its strategic calculus. An opposition party is unlikely to support the government's pension plans if this seriously damages its electoral prospects and, specifically, its chances to regain power. Thus, in the context of fierce party competition, the emergence of a broad cross-party consensus appears to be rather unrealistic.

– If a broad cross-party agreement on pension reform is negotiated, we can expect relatively far-reaching adjustments since both Social Democratic and bourgeois parties in principle acknowledge the necessity of substantial cost-cutting measures. Moreover, a broad party consensus could prevent unions from erecting a parliamentary majority against the reform or from exploiting the pension issue in the electoral arena.

– The emergence of a pension consensus between the government and trade unions is likely to be hampered by disagreement over the scope of necessary pension cuts. Union pension policy positions are much closer to the status quo than the government's irrespective of the latter's general political orientation. Thus, I expect pension policy to cause serious conflicts between these two actors.

– Regardless of their substantial disagreements over reform content, it is fairly likely that the government and the unions have a mutual interest in reaching a compromise. If they receive at least something in return and if they lack the power to prevent the government from imposing a reform unilaterally, trade unions will accept an agreement even if they consider it less attractive than the status quo (because a unilateral reform outcome might be even worse). By contrast, if unions are capable of blocking the reform, the government will be obligated to win union approval by offering more or less far-reaching concessions.

– The bargaining agreement between government and the unions will be the result of two factors: the policy distance between government and trade unions (which again will largely depend on the unions' willingness to reform); and the balance of power between these two actors. This balance depends on among other things the institutional strength and the electoral vulnerability of the government as well as on the unions' mobilising capacity. Because these factors vary from country to country as well as over time, the scope of the agreement between government and trade unions will vary as well.

– Unilateral attempts at pension reform entail a large potential risk of political failure. If both the parliamentary opposition and the trade unions object to government pension reform initiatives, these initiatives may lack a parliamentary majority. Moreover, if governments seek to impose pension reforms single-handedly they may trigger massive public protests or even large-scale strikes, which may in turn prompt the government to cave in. Finally, even if a government succeeds in getting its pension plans passed, it still runs the risk that future governments may (partly) overturn the reform.

In the following individual country chapters, I will not only describe various instances of the political reform process in the area of pension policy but try to locate the individual decision-making processes in the broader theoretical context outlined above. The sequence of the country chapters loosely reflects the relative success of a particular country in making its pension system more sustainable.

A further remark must be added. The countries studied have each adopted a multiplicity of legislative measures in pension policy since the late 1980s. It would go beyond the scope of this study to exhaustively analyse the political decision-making process of all the changes relevant to pension policy. I will focus instead on selected instances of pension reform efforts for each country. I will concentrate on reform attempts that have produced (or which were supposed to produce) major changes and which have been important sources of conflict among the political actors.

4   Sweden: Policy-Oriented Bargaining

Traditionally, the Swedish pension system differs from pension arrangements in the other countries studied, in so far as it provides for a basic pension covering all residents in Sweden over 16 years of age (including most foreigners).[2] The National Pension System includes three schemes:

1 the basic pension (*folkspension*), which consists of a universal flat-rate pension, supplemented by various partially income-tested benefits (such as housing allowances);
2 the earnings-related supplementary pension (*allmän tilläggspension, ATP*);
3 the partial pension (*delpension*) consisting of a part-time early retirement pension.

Both the basic and the supplementary pension schemes provide for old age, invalidity, and survivors' pensions.

All pension benefits are indexed in accordance with the so called "base amount" which is typically linked to the consumer price index.[3] A single pensioner is entitled to a guaranteed "minimum pension" which amounts to 144% of the base amount (consisting of a basic pension which equals 96% of the base amount, and a pension supplement which equals 48% of the base amount).

The old age basic pension is normally payable from the age of 65. However, it may also be drawn from the age of 60, in which case the pension is reduced by 0.5% for every month under the age of 65. The basic pension scheme is financed by contributions from employers, central government, and local governments.[4] The employer contributions are not earmarked for the pension but are in fact a payroll tax.

The general supplementary pension scheme (ATP) covers all economically active people over age 16. Self-employed people have the right to contract-out of the scheme. The supplementary pension is earnings-related, and is payable to anyone who has earned more than the "base amount"' for at least three years. The amount of the supplementary pension scheme depends on the "average pensionable income" earned in previous years and on the number of years of gainful activity. For each year, a ratio is calculated by dividing the individual income (up to 7.5 times the base amount) by the general base amount for the respective year ("pension points"). The average number of pension points for all one's years of gainful activity (for a period of more than 15 years, the average is calculated for the 15 best years) is then multiplied by the base amount for the month/year in which a person retires resulting in the average pensionable income. A full supplementary old age pension amounts to 60% of the average pensionable income and requires a record of 30 years of accumulated pension points. For each missing year the pension is reduced by 1/30 or 2%. For the supplementary old age pension, the normal retirement age is 65, with the same possibilities for early or deferred retirement as in the case of the basic pension. The ATP scheme is financed by contributions from employers (about 10% of wages without any ceiling) and, to a lesser extent, from the self-employed (Olsson 1987). In principle, the ATP system works on a pay-as-you-go basis. In addition, however, the ATP scheme relies on five trust funds (AP funds) separate from the state budget and invested in stocks and bonds that were built up during the first 30 years of the system's operation because the revenues from contributions exceeded pension outlays (in the beginning, contribution rates were deliberately set up to 3% higher than would have been necessary to cover current pension payments). In the short run, these funds were designed as a buffer fund that would offset temporary deficits in the ATP system. In the long-term perspective, the AP funds should also cover the expected increase in ATP expenditures (Finansdepartement 1998). At the same time, the AP funds were supposed to increase public savings in order to compensate for the expected decline of private savings triggered by the establishment of the ATP system. In 1986, the value of these funds corresponded to six times the yearly expenditures of the ATP system (Anderson 1998).

Employees between the ages of 60 to 65 can combine part-time work with a partial pension (*delpension*). After July 1987, this scheme compensated for 65% of the loss of income resulting from the reduction of working hours. It is financed by employer contributions equalling 0.5% of the wage total.

In addition to the major public schemes, there are four important occupational pension schemes established by collective agreements covering all public employees and the majority of workers in the private sector. These schemes compensate about 10% of earnings up to the benefit ceiling in the ATP system and a higher share for those parts of income exceeding this ceiling (Wadensjö 2002).

Sweden's pension reform record in the 1990s

Among the five countries studied, Sweden adopted the most far-reaching measures in pension policy. In the 1990s, Sweden was extraordinarily successful in restoring the fiscal soundness of its public pension system, which had come under massive cost containment pressures due to the severe recession of the early 1990s and the concomitant deterioration of public finances. More importantly, apart from Italy, Sweden was the only country among those studied in which the public pension system will gradually be converted from a defined-benefit into a defined-contribution scheme. In the process, the long-term growth of public pension outlays will be contained effectively. Moreover, most recently a private and fully funded pillar was introduced on a mandatory basis. In this chapter, I will attempt to identify the political conditions under which Swedish pension policymakers were able to carve out a fundamental restructuring of the pension system.

In order to flesh out the general course of Swedish pension policy in recent years, we need to recall an important distinction made in the first chapter. On the one hand, we can identify instances of pension retrenchment primarily geared towards short-term budget relief and towards a stabilisation of non-wage labour costs in the face of acute economic and fiscal crisis. A different type of pension retrenchment is "long-term structural reform" typically aimed at addressing the problems emerging from the dramatic change in the population's age structure that will loom large in the decades to come. As opposed to short-term cuts, this type of reform is as a rule not exclusively geared towards cost containment but is comprised of measures to remove inefficiencies in the overall design of the pension system. Structural reform may also include steps towards reinforcing second and third pillar arrangements. Such reforms typically require extraordinarily long time horizons and a stable and sustainable political support base in order to become fully implemented. In the Swedish case, the distinction between the two reform approaches appears to be particularly applicable. Both types of pension reform were pursued simultaneously, but relatively independent of one another. By the same token, the decision-making logic of the two approaches differed greatly. Hence, despite their temporal coincidence, I will discuss both strands of pension reform separately in this chapter.

Short-term cuts

Throughout the 1980s, changes in Swedish pension policy remained very modest. A first attempt at retrenchment in pension policy was made by the bourgeois government in the early 1980s. In the face of high inflation (exceeding wage increases) and a severe budgetary crisis, the government decided to change the indexation of pensions temporarily so that pensioners would only be partly compensated for rising prices (by disregarding changes in energy prices). This measure caused a public outcry, and the Social Democratic opposition promised to restore the full value of pensions after the 1982 elections.[5] However, the SAP only partly fulfilled its promise, as pensioners were not fully compensated for the loss in purchasing power resulting from the strong currency devaluation that had been enacted by the new government. As a consequence, the bourgeois press fiercely accused the Social Democrats of having stolen the election by making false promises to pensioners. In the late 1980s, however, most of the effects of the devaluation cut had been restored. The powerful LO, the blue-collar union federation, and the Left Party Communists, on whom the SAP depended for support in parliament, effectively blocked any attempts at retrenchment by the Social Democratic government (Pierson and Weaver 1993; Anderson 1998; Lundberg 2001).[6] In the 1985 and 1988 elections, the SAP even sought to present itself as the defender of the existing pension system vis-à-vis the bourgeois parties, which had suggested moderate welfare cuts in pensions and other places. This strategy clearly made it possible for the SAP to maintain its strong electoral position in the Swedish party system. At the same time, however, the Social Democratic government increased the rate of contributions only modestly in order to cover the explosion of ATP expenditures in the 1980s. Instead, the SAP opted to make the AP funds bear some of the burden of pension payments in order to contain increases in labour costs for employers.[7] As Pontusson (1997) points out, this policy may have reflected a growing recognition within the Swedish labour movement that the AP funds served as an inadequate instrument to influence industrial restructuring.

In striking contrast to the mid- and late-1980s, a multitude of pension cuts were enacted in the 1990s. These cuts were first and foremost triggered by the severe economic recession in the early 1990s. From 1991 to 1993, the Swedish economy suffered three consecutive years of negative growth rates. This had a disastrous effect on public finances. The state budget, still displaying a sizeable surplus of 4.2% of GDP in 1990, turned into a deficit of 12.3% in 1993. By the same token, two major currency crises in 1992 and

1995 put the Swedish Crown under enormous pressure. Thus, Swedish governments had no choice but to adopt a policy of fiscal austerity in order to restore sound public finances. As the largest single item of public social spending, the pension system became an important target for retrenchment both for the SAP and bourgeois governments.[8]

Between 1991 and 1997, the so-called base amount (used to calculate most social transfer payments including pensions) was repeatedly not adjusted for increases in consumer prices. As part of the tax reform negotiated between the Social Democratic government and the Liberals in 1990, the base amount for 1991 and 1992 did not take into account various price increases. Nevertheless, until 1992, net pensions were still increasing significantly in real terms (Socialdepartementet 1996). While the recipients of middle and high pensions profited from lower taxes, people with low incomes from pensions were compensated with a higher pension supplement (only paid to people with ATP pensions below a certain ceiling) and higher (means-tested) housing benefits. From 1993 onwards, however, direct pension cuts as well as higher taxes for pensioners led to a decrease in real benefit levels. Most importantly, during the currency crisis of November 1992, the bourgeois government came at an agreement with the Social Democratic opposition concerning a consolidation package which also included tangible cuts in pension benefits. For one, a reduced base amount was introduced (corresponding to 98% of the "normal" base amount) that applied to both the basic and the ATP pension. As a consequence, pensioners were virtually uncompensated for the strong devaluation of the krona in the wake of the 1992 currency crisis. Recipients of low pensions received compensation, however, by increases in means-tested benefits. In addition, it was decided to increase the retirement age from 65 to 66 years (to be phased in between 1994 and 1997).[9] The crisis package had been negotiated behind closed doors by party leaders in a desperate (albeit unsuccessful) effort to avert a devaluation of the Swedish krona. As Anderson (1998) points out, the crisis atmosphere as well as the cross-party agreement allowed politicians to withstand the inevitable protests from unions and pensioner associations.

The bourgeois minority government also enacted significant cutbacks in the partial pension system. However, in this case it proved much more difficult for the government of Premier Carl Bildt to orchestrate a parliamentary majority for its retrenchment ambitions. In the face of severe budgetary constraints, the government proposed eliminating the programme in the spring of 1992. The employer contribution of 0.5% of payroll was to be shifted to work injury insurance, which was running a deficit. Thus, the government's intention was to keep employer contributions stable while at the same time not burdening its own budget. However, the initiative met with fierce criticism from the SAP and the Left Party. At the same time, New Democracy (a right-wing populist party in the opposition) opted against eliminating the partial pension scheme, arguing that this measure would primarily shift the costs to long-term sick pay and disability pensions. Hence, the government only achieved support for a reduction in the partial pension contribution from 0.5% to 0.2% with the difference being transferred to work injury insurance (Anderson 1998).

Another attempt to cut partial pensions was made the following year (1993). The proposal sought an increase in the qualifying age from 60 to 62 years and a reduction in the replacement level from 65 to 50%. Again, this proposal did not win a majority in the Riksdag, because both the leftist opposition and New Democracy (which initially had agreed to the cuts in the committee) opposed it. However, gradually the Social Democrats shifted course and signalled their readiness to support savings measures in the partial pension system. Their key concern was to retain a fairly low age limit of 61 years (rather than 62 years as sought by the government). In return, the SAP offered far-reaching concessions with respect to the replacement level which was reduced from 65 to 55% (the government had aspired to a level of 50%). Thus, after two failed attempts, the bourgeois party leaders managed to hammer out a compromise solution with the Social Democratic opposition (Anderson 1998).

Another important change in pension legislation adopted during the Bildt government's tenure refers to tighter eligibility criteria for the basic pension. Prior to 1993, everybody with at least 5 years residency in Sweden was entitled to a full basic pension. After 1993, new rules were gradually introduced, that stated that a full basic pension could only be drawn after 40 years of residence or after 30 contribution years in the ATP system. This move was motivated by Sweden's entry into the European Union in 1995. Based on previous regulations, EU foreigners moving to Sweden would have become immediately entitled to a full basic pension. The same would have been true for people who had been residents in Sweden for five years, even if they had long ago left the country. Under these conditions, retaining previous regulations might have induced considerable additional expenditures for the public budget. Thus, faced with the potential threat of growing "welfare tourism", Sweden felt compelled to partly dissociate itself from the traditional model of a universal welfare state.

The reform of partial pensions highlights the fact that the SAP had a crucial impact on social policy outcomes even in opposition. This can be attributed to three factors. First, without the support of the New Democracy party the bourgeois minority government inevitably became dependent on the Social Democrats in seeking a parliamentary majority. Second, the Bildt government strove for SAP support in order to contain the political costs of welfare retrenchment. With the backing of the Social Democratic opposition, the government could more easily withstand vigorous protests from the LO and TCO (confederation of white-collar unions) against the reduction of partial pensions. Third, collaboration with the SAP was necessary if the cuts were to be sustained even after a change of government. This again became the likely scenario, given the strong electoral position of the SAP in the Swedish party system. This was accented by the fact that the SAP was predicted to regain power in the 1994 elections and could ill afford to allow the bourgeois government to leave public finances in disorder.

After their re-election in 1994, the Social Democrats launched a series of measures in order to restore sound public finances as quickly as possible. In contrast to the previous government, they adopted a two-pronged strategy of fiscal consolidation which also included substantial increases in taxes and social security contributions for the insured. To win parliamentary support for these tax increases, the SAP minority government relied on the support of the Left Party. On the expenditure side, the Social Democrats forcefully adopted the policy of benefit cutbacks pursued by its predecessor. This was also true when it came to pension policy. Most importantly, a temporary change in indexation rules in 1995 was established, which meant that the adjustment of the base amount would only take into account 60% of the changes in consumer prices as long as the public budget deficit exceeded a certain amount. Quite remarkably, the pension cuts by the leftist government also affected low income pensioners. Hitherto, this group had had its general pension cuts largely compensated for via an expansion of means-tested benefits (such as a higher pension supplement and improved housing benefits). The SAP government, instead, opted for a noticeable *reduction* of pensioners' housing supplements in 1997. Other changes involved reducing the basic pension for people married to non-pensioners and the introduction of an income test for widow pensions paid to people under the normal retirement age, a measure that triggered a heated public debate. In sum, between 1994 and 1998, the SAP government enacted a number of substantial savings measures in pension policy on top of the cutbacks adopted by the previous bourgeois government. These cuts were primarily implemented with the parliamentary backing of the bourgeois Centre Party, which – in exchange for its support – was given a say in the decommissioning of the country's nuclear power industry (Palme and Wennemo 1997; Schludi 1997).

It is interesting to note the electoral repercussions of the harsh austerity policy adopted between 1994 and 1998. In the 1998 election, both the SAP and the Centre Party suffered an extraordinarily sharp decline. The SAP's vote share fell from 45.3% in 1994 to 36.6% in 1998, which was its worst showing in 77 years, whereas the Centre Party declined from 7.7% to 5.1%, its worst showing in its history. Most of the electorate that the Social Democrats lost – particularly LO trade union members – turned to the Communists, which almost doubled their vote share to 12% (the best election showing ever by this party). About 30% of the party's voters – most notably LO members – had come from the SAP. As well, a sizeable share of the electorate did not vote – voter turnout dropped from 86.8% to 78.6% (the lowest since 1958). Among the bourgeois parties, only the Christian Democrats managed to emerge as big winners by tripling their share (from 4.1% in 1994 to 11.8% in 1998). In contrast to the (market-liberal) Moderates, which only managed to stabilise their relative electoral position,[10] the Christian Democrats had repeatedly emphasised the need for *increased* social spending, including on pensions. This may also explain why older voters turned to the Christian Democrats. In 1994, only 3% of those aged 65 or older voted for them, whereas 17% did so in the 1998 elections (Arter 1999; Madeley 1999; Möller 1999).

Despite their overwhelming defeat in the 1998 elections, the result has not altered the SAP's pivotal position within the Swedish party system. Because there was a strong party to the left of the SAP, many disappointed Social Democratic core voters turned to the partisan alternative. Thus, the leftist camp lost less dramatically than the SAP by itself. If there had been no far leftist alternative, even more leftist voters would have chosen not to vote (or even turned to the bourgeois parties), which in turn would have paved the way for a bourgeois government. This indicates that the presence of a powerful leftist alternative may actually facilitate rather than hamper retrenchment efforts by a Social Democratic government.

In their 1998 election campaign, the Social Democrats promised improvements in pensions and other social benefits. For the most part they kept this promise. From 1999 onwards, pensions were again calculated on the basis of a full base amount (rather than 98% of it, as had been the case after 1993). Moreover, the disappearance of budget deficits meant that pension benefits could again be fully linked to inflation (by contrast, they were automatically adjusted by a lower rate from 1995 to 1998). Finally, housing supplements for needy pensioners, which had been lowered from 85% to 83% of housing costs in 1997, were raised to 90% in 1999. To a large extent, the return to an expansionary social and pension policy became possible due to a drastically improved economic environment and a concomitant recovery of public finances.[11] Moreover, in the face of the dramatic decline among its core constituencies in the previous election and pressured by a strong Communist party, the SAP really needed to restore its reputation as the guarantor of the Swedish welfare state model.

The "big" Swedish pension reform

Besides the short-term pension cutbacks, which were largely enacted as a response to the dramatic economic and fiscal crisis in the early- to mid-1990s, Swedish pension policymakers also launched a comprehensive structural reform of the country's overall pension system, aimed at rendering the system less vulnerable to economic and demographic changes and enhancing its redistributive efficiency. In a nutshell, this reform means a shift from a defined-benefit towards a (notional) defined-contribution design as well as the creation of an additional private mandatory pillar on a fully funded basis ("premium reserve system"). The key features of the new Swedish pension system can be summarised as follows (Finansdepartement 1998; Ministry of Health and Social Affairs 1998)[12]:

– The new system will be based on lifetime income. Previously, pensions were based on the best 15 years and a full pension was archieved after 30 years of contributions (15/30 rule).
– Basic security for those with low or no income-related pensions is provided by a tax-financed guaranteed pension (thereby replacing the universal basic pension, which until the late 1980s was predominantly financed by employer contributions, as well as the pension supplements for those with no or low ATP pensions). For a single pensioner who has earned between 1.26 to 3 base amounts, the guaranteed pension is only partly offset against the earnings-related pension (leading to a transfer withdrawal rate below 100%). No deductions are made in the case of capital income, occupational pensions, private pension insurance, or care allowances. A full guaranteed pension requires 40 years of residency in Sweden.
– 18.5% of income is paid to the new system, equally split between employers and the insured (hitherto the ATP system has been financed exclusively and the basic pension largely by employer contributions). 16% will be used to finance current pension payments, 2.5% is diverted into pre-funded individual pension accounts ("premium reserve system").
– The new pay-as-you-go system is linked to economic growth and is responsive to demographic variations. The value of the pension rights grows along with general income development. Upon retirement, the accumulat-

ed pension rights are divided by a factor reflecting the average remaining life span of the respective age group as well as the assumed future growth in real wages (for the time being, the assumed growth rate is 1.6% per year). Payable pensions are pegged to an economic adjustment index according to which pensions will be fully compensated for inflation if real average income growth is 1.6%, whereas they will increase/decrease in real value if real wage growth is higher/less than 1.6%.

– In contrast to the old rules, periods of child rearing, military service, and – to a lesser extent – higher education are credited under the new system. The respective pension entitlements will be financed completely out of the state budget. The same is true for periods in which income replacement benefits (such as sickness benefits, parental benefits, or unemployment compensation) were drawn.

– A flexible retirement age as of 61 years was introduced on a strict actuarial basis.

– 2.5% of income is channelled into a mandatory premium reserve system which is administered by a new authority. The individual can choose whether his/her money is invested into a private or a public fund.

– The new system is phased in gradually with transition rules on a pro-rata basis for those born between 1938 and 1954.

In sum, the state assumed greater financial responsibility under the new system, as all non-contributory benefits as well as pension contributions on social transfers are henceforth financed out of the public budget. This also holds true for early retirement and survivors' pensions, which are to be phased out gradually, but are still a significant expenditure item. In return, the state withdraws from the co-financing of the gradually phased-out universal basic pension (yet finances the new "guarantee pension" which tops low ATP pensions up to a certain minimum level). Nevertheless, a higher fiscal burden will be imposed on the state budget especially during the transition period. In return, however, a sizeable share of money from the AP funds is channelled into the public budget to limit the strains on public finances. Conversely, the size of the AP funds will eventually decrease substantially which will in turn restrict their role largely to a buffer function for the new pension system (Finansdepartement 1998).

As this review of the new Swedish pension system shows, Swedish policymakers have addressed many of the critical issues and implemented a host of structural changes to existing pension arrangements, which also helped contain future pension costs. As a consequence, the contribution rate under the new system in 2040, is likely to be between 3.1% and 9.4% lower than it would have been without reform (Palmer 2000). As measured by the changes adopted in other Bismarckian pension regimes, the Swedish pension reform is unique with respect to the degree and scope of the changes enacted. This is all the more surprising because the long-term challenges to the Swedish pension system were less dramatic than in some of the other countries studied. For instance, the need for reform was – and still is – far more pronounced in Austria or Italy, where public pay-as-you-go financed pensions absorb a substantially higher share of GDP. To be sure, the technical difficulties as well as the political resistance associated with such a large-scale reconstruction of the Swedish pension system could not be overcome easily. Hence, the political reform process was bound to be protracted. In fact, the reform process was initiated by the appointment of a pension commission in 1984, while the final legislation on the pension reform was only finally settled in 2001 (see table 4.1). Various governments of different political orientations were involved in the decision-making process. Which factors were responsible for the eventual success of this reform package?

Before I attempt to answer this question, I will briefly sketch the chronology of the political reform process.[13] Basically, we can identify three distinct time periods within this process (see also table 4.1). The first period runs from 1984 to 1991, a time of Social Democratic minority governments. In October 1984, the government hired a commission of parliamentary experts to develop recommendations for reforms of the Swedish pension system. This was primarily motivated by the need to get a grip on the growing shortfalls in the ATP system and to address the problems resulting from the expected steep increase in the share of the elderly. The commission of roughly 30 members included representatives of all of the political parties, trade unions, employer organisations, and pensioner organisations. Moreover, experts from the social insurance administration, various ministries, and academic experts were represented as well. The final report (SOU 1990:76), published in November 1990, did not contain concrete proposals for reform but confined itself to pinpointing some of the weaknesses of the existing pension system (i.e., the weak link between contributions and benefits) and to proposing various alternatives for reform. Given its sheer size and its heterogeneous composition, the commission proved unable to agree on a common viewpoint. By the same token, the Social Democratic government showed only limited interest in pushing the pension issue in the run-up to the 1991 elections. Hence, the government opted for a long period of discussion on the report that would only be completed after the elections (Haag 2000).

Table 4.1   Chronology of the "big" Swedish pension reform

Reform phase I: 1984-1991 (Social Democratic governments)

October 1984	Government creates a pension reform commission (*pensionsberedningen*) consisting of representatives of all of the major parties, social interest groups, and pension experts.
November 1990	The commission presents its final report (SOU 1990:76, "Allmän pension. Huvudbetänkande av pensionsberedningen") suggesting various reform alternatives. However, no agreement is reached within the commission and no political decisions are made.

Reform phase II: 1991-1994 (Bourgeois government)

November 1991	A pension working group (*pensionsarbetsgruppen*), chaired by the Minister of Social Affairs, is nominated, in which all parties in Parliament (but no interest groups) are represented.
August 1992	Pension working group report presents the major reform principles ("Ett reformerat pensionssystem – bakgrund, principier, skiss", Ds 1992:89).
End of 1993	A new pension working group is established from which the Left Party and New Democracy are excluded.
January 1994	Agreement among five parties (SAP, Moderates, Christian Democrats, Centre Party, Liberals) concerning key features of the new pension system (The Left Party and New Democracy vote against). Agreement set up to survive future elections.
February 1994	Pension working group presents its final report ("Reformerat pensionssystem", SOU 1994:20). Concerned interest groups had until 15 April 1994 to comment on it.
28 April 1994	Government presents "Reform of the general pension system" bill (Prop. 1993/94:250: "Reformering av det allmänna pensionssystemet") to Parliament, which includes underlying principles of the new pension system.
8 June 1994	Proposal is adopted by the Riksdag with coalition of SAP and four bourgeois parties.
23 June 1994	Government nominates an implementation group (*Genomförandegruppen*), consisting only of the five parties in favour of the reform. Group is commissioned to work out concrete reforms based on principles adopted by the Riksdag.

Reform phase III: 1994-2001 (Social Democratic governments)

1 January 1995	Individual contributions of 1% to the old age pension system introduced. Contributions start being transferred to premium reserve system.

28 June 1995	Ministry memorandum "A Reformed Pension System – Income-Related old age pension Act" ("Lag om inkomstgrundad ålderspension", Ds 1995:41).
1995 Budget Bill	Implementation of the reform deferred until 1 January 1997.
1997 Budget Bill	Implementation of the reform deferred until 1 January 1999.
March 1996	Emergency SAP party conference where leadership is heavily criticised for content and its adoption of five-party-agreement. As a consequence, a broad intra-party reform consultation is launched. Some 500 written and mostly very critical reform comments from party rank and file are collected.
December 1996	In response to strong party criticism, SAP demands a re-negotiation of the five-party-agreement particularly with respect to the change from employer contributions to parity financing between employers and employees and the establishment of a premium reserve system. While this resolution is welcomed by LO, the bourgeois parties react angrily and insist on its enactment. Five-party-agreement is seriously threatened.
September 1997	SAP Party congress discusses pension issue again. Congress resolves to denounce five-party-agreement. But party leadership continues to work with implementation group.
Beginning of 1998	The controversy about the fee swap comes to a head and is resolved with compromise. Employees to be compensated for higher pension contributions due to abolition of employees' sickness insurance fees and lower taxes rather than by an increase of gross wages. In exchange, bourgeois parties insist on need to increase contributions to individual account system from 2 to 2.5%.
8 June 1998	New pension system is adopted by Parliament. Some financial questions remain unresolved.
May 2001	Final pension reform legislation (Automatic balance mechanism) adopted by Riksdag.

Sources: Ministry of Health and Social Affairs 1998; Haag 2000; Settergren 2001

The reform process gained momentum during the bourgeois minority government's time in office (1991-1994). As early as November 1991, the Bildt government appointed a parliamentary working group to be chaired by the Minister of Health and Social Affairs. The group included members of all of the parties represented in the Riksdag as well as experts from the National Social Security Board and from the Ministries of Finance and Social Affairs. The working group was expected to develop concrete proposals for a new pension system. In a remarkable break with earlier traditions, however, representatives of the social partners were not included in the working group. In August 1992, this working group issued its first report, in which some of the key principles of the new pension system were already sketched (Ds 1992:89). Among other things, the report suggested a tighter link between contributions and benefits by calculating pensions on the basis of lifetime earnings. However, both the Left Party and New Democracy were opposed to the report's proposals. As a consequence, at a certain stage, their representatives were excluded from the working group, which henceforth only included representatives of the four bourgeois coalition parties and the SAP (plus the experts from the above-mentioned institutions). However, there were also dramatic disputes between the SAP and the bourgeois parties on a number of issues. Serious disagreements emerged specifically on the issue of whether to insert an individualised premium reserve system into the ATP system and on whether contributions should be levied on income above the benefit ceiling in the ATP system. Other contentious points included the demand by the bourgeois parties for an even split of pension contributions between employees and employers and the procedure with which this fee swap should be organised in order to secure the full compensation of wage earners. After protracted negotiations a compromise was reached and a final report was issued in February 1994 (SOU 1994:20). On the one hand, the bourgeois parties achieved the introduction of a premium reserve system. Of the total 18.5% in pension contributions, 2% were to be diverted into this scheme. On the other hand, the SAP successfully promoted the retention of pension levies above the benefit ceiling, albeit only at a rate of 50%. As a pure "tax" this money was to be transferred to the state budget. Moreover, the SAP grudgingly accepted the parity financing of pension contributions. Other elements of the proposed reform package remained relatively uncontested among the five parties, such as the introduction of real wage indexation and the switch to lifetime earnings. The Pension Working Group stipulated a comment period on its final report issued in February 1994, which only lasted until April 15, 1994.[14] The motive behind this provision was to present the proposal to the Riksdag in the spring in order to keep the issue out of the election campaign, which would peak in the fall of 1994 (Anderson 1998; Haag 2000).

The reactions to the report were mixed. The unions' responses to the proposed changes ranged from cautious approval to fierce criticism. In general, Swedish trade unions accepted the need for reform. All of the unions specifically embraced the idea that pensions should be indexed to changes in wages rather than to changes in consumer prices in order to enhance inter-generational equity. At the same time, these unions also welcomed the fact that even the future Swedish pension system would be largely based on a public and earnings-related pillar. By the same token, unions generally agreed with the proposal to raise the hitherto fixed benefit ceiling within the ATP system in line with wage developments, in order to retain the earnings-related character of the pension system. Conversely, Swedish trade unions also jointly criticised their exclusion from the working group and the short period for reactions as well as the planned split of contributions between employers and employees. Trade unions specifically feared that a gradual transition from employer contributions to parity financing by employers *and* employees (as proposed in the final report) would mean a risk that wage earners would receive insufficient compensation from employers.[15] In other respects, however, the various Swedish trade unions had different reactions to the reform proposals outlined in the report. LO, the organisation of blue-collar unions, for instance, basically favoured the proposed shift towards lifetime earnings (and even of a changeover from a defined-benefit to a defined-contribution scheme), as many LO members displayed a contribution record of more than 30 years, for which no pension rights are granted under the old system. By contrast, the TCO and SACO white-collar unions were more critical of the move toward lifetime earnings, since their members spent more time in higher education, relatively less time in the labour market participation and had steeper earning profiles during their careers and thus profited from the existing 15/30 rule. A shift to the lifetime principle for the calculation of benefits would only have been acceptable to white-collar unions, if periods of education were credited much more solidly than recommended in the proposal. By contrast, the LO strongly opposed the idea of a privatised premium reserve system, whereas the TCO (Confederation of White Collar Employees) and in particular SACO (Confederation of Academics) were less critical of this reform element (LO 1994; SACO 1994; TCO 1994). In summary, the reform package contained both elements that were favoured or at least accepted and elements that were fiercely rejected by the various unions. Hence, the Swedish trade union movement (as well as the LO itself) was internally split in their reactions and proved unable to sustain a unified front against the proposal (Anderson 1998; Haag 2000).

A few elements of the proposal were modified, however, in response to the criticisms raised by the trade unions. Most importantly, in the subsequent bill presented to the Riksdag in April 1994, a procedural change concerning the sought-after fee swap was recommended. Rather than phasing in the shift to parity financing gradually, the fee swap was supposed to be implemented completely in one step. In doing so, employers would arguably find it more difficult to withhold full compensation from wage earners (Anderson 1998).

In June 1994 (i.e., before the elections), the bill including the major reform principles was adopted by Parliament (opposed by New Democracy and the Left Party). However, a number of issues remained unresolved such as the fee swap, the economic adjustment index (used to calculate yearly adjustments), and pension entitlements for years spent in higher education. Moreover, the issues of how the premium reserve system should be administered and whether income from collectively agreed pensions should be offset against the new guarantee pension remained unresolved. A vast array of technical questions also needed to be addressed. In order to handle these problems, an implementation group consisting of representatives of the same five parties that had supported the proposal in the Riksdag was created. (Anderson 1998).

The third phase of the pension reform coincided with the SAP minority government's tenure in office. The implementation group, now chaired by a Social Democrat, also had to resolve a number of technically difficult and politically divisive questions. As a consequence, the introduction of the new system had to be postponed several times. The bulk of the legislation was only passed in June 1998 (to become effective in 1999), whereas the final legislation (concerning the automatic balance mechanism) was ultimately adopted only in May 2001. Apart from the immense technical problems associated with the creation of a new premium pension authority (*premiepensionsmyndigheten*), it was mainly political conflicts within the government which led to a massive delay in the reform process.

First, large parts of the SAP's rank and file (including many LO members) criticised the contents of the reform. As a matter of fact, the strongest opposition to reform came from within the Social Democratic party itself. Many party members refused to acknowledge the necessity for changing the old system (Palmer 2000). They were, in particular, fiercely opposed to the planned shift to parity employer-employee financing and the introduction of the premium pension scheme. At a party congress in September 1997, the majority of SAP members even called for a rejection of the five-party agreement. While the SAP leaders largely resisted these pressures, they demanded a partial re-negotiation of the cross-party agreement. While the bourgeois parties fiercely criticised this demand, they achieved a new compromise with the SAP after hard negotiations in early 1998. Wage earners would obtain a tax relief measure rather than a wage increase as compensation for the introduction of individual pension contributions.[16] Moreover, the SAP enforced a provision, according to which a public fund was to be established as part of the new premium reserve system for those who did not choose any of the private funds. In return, the bourgeois parties asserted an increase in the premium reserve contribution from 2 to 2.5% (Haag 2000; Lundberg 2001).

Second, the reform process was detained by conflicts between the Ministry of Finance and the Ministry of Social Affairs. While the former was eager to keep the burden on the public budget resulting from the extension of tax-financed pension benefits as low as possible, it was the primary interest of the latter to create a financially robust pension system capable of providing for adequate benefits. As a consequence, a protracted tug of war developed between these departments around the volume of financial means that were to be channelled from the AP funds (expected to maintain a buffer function even under the new pension system) to the state budget (Haag 2000).

Explanatory factors for the political success of the Swedish pension reform

The portrayal of the political decision-making process that led to a far-reaching restructuring of the Swedish pension system raises two interrelated questions. First, why have various political parties with clearly different ideological orientations in social policy been able and willing to arrive at a formal consensus on pension reform? Second, given the pronounced diversity of social policy ideas among the parties concerned, why did this consensus lead to a significant deviation from the status quo in pension policy rather than to an agreement based on the lowest common denominator (as we might have expected from Tsebelis' veto player approach)? Quite clearly, a range of different factors can help account for this policy outcome. No one factor can be said to have been enough to resolve the reform issues. However, at least in hindsight, *most* of these factors appear to have been necessary conditions for the final agreement.

The existence of a mature earnings-related public pension system was a crucial precondition for the emergence of a broad cross-party consensus concerning the make-up of the new pension system. Given the serious "double payment problem" associated with a changeover from a public pay-as-you-go financed pension system to a private fully funded system, an abolition of the public earnings-related pension pillar (to be replaced by private old age provisions) was eliminated de facto from the policy menu. In the 1950s, the bourgeois parties and the Social Democrats were still fighting fierce ideological battles over the question of whether the state should introduce an earnings-related pension system to provide for income security during old age or confine itself to providing a universal system of basic security. In the meantime, a large share of the population had accumulated sizeable benefit entitlements within the ATP system. As a consequence, all of the bourgeois parties in Sweden arrived at the conclusion that even a gradual abolition of this scheme in favour of private old age provisions would be economically and politically unfeasible. Hence, they abandoned the idea that more than 15% of contribution revenues should be used to enhance the premium reserve system. In this case, the overall contribution burden would have become much higher than was considered acceptable. In short, the fact that the ATP scheme had been in place for several decades created "factual constraints" which bourgeois politicians could not ignore and which therefore reduced ideological conflicts between the various parties (Lindbom 2001).

On the other hand, even the SAP – one of the most powerful proponents of earnings-related social insurance in Swedish politics – had become increasingly aware of the distributive and economic weaknesses of the existing pension system. In the face of severe fiscal and demographic pressures (strongly amplified by the sharp economic recession in the early-1990s), even Social Democratic policymakers in principle acknowledged the need for pension reform which included cost containment measures. Thus, both the bourgeois and the Social Democratic camps have become increasingly aware that pragmatic considerations have pushed ideological debates on basic principles into the background, which ultimately facilitated the common search for solutions.

Furthermore, the persistence of minority governments meant that multiparty co-operation would be necessary for successful policy changes. Therefore, the bourgeois minority government, eager to advocate a reform of the pension system, essentially had to rely on the SAP's co-operation. On the one hand, on several occasions the populist right-wing New Democracy proved itself to be an unreliable ally, with whom a stable political platform for pension reform could not be relied upon. On the other hand, the SAP's support was needed to ensure the durability of reform even after a (likely) change in government. Conversely, even the SAP government would not have been able to enact pension reform unilaterally. Moreover, it would have been virtually impossible for the Social Democrats to implement major changes in pension policy (such as the shift to a defined-contribution system) with the co-operation of leftist parties, i.e., the Greens or the communist Left Party. Hence, the SAP also needed at least one ally from the bourgeois camp to gain a parliamentary majority for pension reform.

Both the SAP and the bourgeois parties also shared a common interest in keeping the pension issue out of the electoral arena, which again favoured a policy-oriented bargaining process. The Social Democrats had their incentives for electoral gains softened by their expected return to power with the elections in 1994. As the former leader of the SAP, Ingvar Carlsson, pointed out, participation in the five-party agreement was not an electoral sacrifice for the Social Democrats because the economic crisis and the austerity measures imposed by the bourgeois government had paved the way for an SAP election victory (Lundberg 2001). The Conservatives, however, had little incentive to break up the five-party agreement with the SAP for electoral reasons, as their market-liberal profile prevented them from presenting themselves as defenders of the existing pension system in the eyes of the electorate (Kitschelt 2001).

The timing and the procedure of the bargaining process have also facilitated consensus-building across the five key parties and favoured the accomplishment of a comprehensive package deal. As noted above, shortly after the 1991 elections, the bourgeois government installed a parliamentary pension working group in which the social partners and other special interest groups were not represented. As Lundberg (2001) points out, it would have been much more difficult for an SAP government to have kept the social partners out. Moreover, at a later stage, the Left Party and New Democracy ended up also being excluded from the working group. As a consequence, the number of participants in the working group was manageable and several (potential) reform opponents were afforded no opportunities to block or delay the negotiations, while the remaining five parties were interested in coming to an agreement. In addition, the negotiations all took place in closed sessions in order to avoid major public debates about the issues discussed in the working group. These conditions combined to create an institutional setting, which allowed for package deals that facilitated mutually acceptable and welfare-increasing solutions even if a number of the individual elements (such as the premium reserve system) would not have been acceptable to individual parties (Scharpf 1997b). The short reaction period after the final report was issued also limited the abilities of interest groups, most notably the trade unions, to fundamentally criticise and alter the content of the reform package. The bargaining results were discussed and anchored within the respective party leaderships and party organisations only after a consensus had been established within the working group (Lundberg 2001). As a consequence, traditionalists within the SAP party organisation could only insert minor belated changes into the reform package. The five-party agreement ultimately made it easier for the reformist forces within the SAP to achieve more far-reaching changes than they would have been able to obtain from within their own party.

Although the Social Democrats party's dissatisfaction with the pension reform package was great, the SAP ultimately did not defect from the five-party agreement. To a great extent, this may be attributed to the tacit agreement of the LO. For one, the LO's leadership had a basic interest in the sustainability of the pension system and feared a potential breakdown of the ATP system as a consequence of Sweden's dramatic fiscal crisis in the early-to mid-1990s. It therefore eventually accepted the reform package by and large. Moreover, the LO was internally split among the various individual unions. Because of their own earnings career, a large number of LO members stood to profit from the shift to lifetime earnings and a higher guaranteed pension. In other words, resistance to the reform was lowered by the fact that it created losers *and* winners and that the sheer complexity and multitude of changes prevented groups from fully comprehending who stood to profit or lose under the new system.

Finally, two specific factors facilitated the establishment of the premium reserve system. First, the bourgeois parties made it clear that this reform element was not negotiable. As Lindbom (2001) points out, the bourgeois parties arguably expected that the expansion of private fully funded pensions would foster a public climate in which higher priority would be given to fighting high inflation. Second, the partial switch towards a fully funded system based on individual accounts was facilitated by the fact that considerable capital reserves accumulated by the public AP funds could be used to finance the transition costs (Myles and Pierson 2001).

5   Italy: Corporatist Concertation in the Shadow of EMU

Key features of the Italian pension system in the late-1980s

The Italian pension system provides for old age, disability, and survivors' benefits. It is divided into a number of mostly public occupational schemes. Private schemes are usually only of rudimentary significance. There are four types of public schemes:

1 a general scheme for dependent workers;
2 schemes for the self-employed;
3 schemes for civil servants;
4 schemes for special occupational groups, some of which complement the general scheme.

In addition, there is a means-tested social pension for people over age 65 with insufficient resources who are not eligible for benefits under any of the other schemes.

The benefit structure and the level of benefits vary greatly from scheme to scheme. Dependent workers insured under the general scheme receive a maximum pension of 80% of their earnings during the last five years up to a certain ceiling, after 40 years of contributions. The minimum contribution period is 15 years. The standard retirement age is 55 for women and 60 for men. However, people with a contribution record of at least 35 years are entitled to a "seniority pension" irrespective of their age.

The self-employed are not entitled to earnings-related pensions. Instead, their pensions are based on the actuarial revaluation of their contributions. No pension, however, can be lower than an established minimum. The age requirement is 65 for men and 60 for women, and the minimum contribution period is 15 years.

Civil servants enjoy earnings-related pensions, with a replacement rate of 80% after 40 years service; this rate may reach 100% for certain categories. Civil servants must retire at 65, but a pension may be claimed, regardless of age, after 20 years' service, and in some cases after only 15 years' service.

All pensions are linked to the minimum contractual industrial wage.

The general scheme operates on a pay-as-you-go basis and is financed through earnings-related contributions paid by employers (two-thirds) and employees (one-third). Together these amount to about 24% of earnings. The self-employed pay a flat-rate contribution, whereas civil servants pay an earnings-related contribution of around 7%. Financing conditions are more varied for the special schemes. The state covers any deficit with special contributions that are particularly heavy in the case of schemes for the self-employed.

The main administrative agency of the Italian pension insurance system (*Istituto Nazionale della Previdenza Sociale, INPS*) is governed by a board consisting of eighteen representatives of the workers' trade unions, nine employers' representatives, nine representatives of the self-employed and three state officials (Ferrera 1987).

Italy's pension reform record in the 1990s

In Italy, the long-term cost-containment effects of the recent pension reforms are roughly comparable to those of the Swedish reforms. Like Sweden, Italy has initiated a shift from a defined-benefit system towards a defined-contribution one. However, the transition period in which the new rules are phased-in is much longer.[1] Italy has also harmonised the different pension provisions between the public and the private sector. Moreover, significant steps were taken to promote fully funded types of old age provisions, albeit thus far with only limited progress.

Pension politics throughout the 1980s

Given the marked resistance to the reform of the Italian pension system throughout the 1980s, the scope of reforms adopted in the 1990s is remarkable. In contrast to the other countries studied, public pension benefits in Italy were still increased until the early 1990s. Between 1980 and 1992, public pension expenditures climbed from 9% to almost 15% of GDP (Germany -0.6%, Austria +0.9%, Sweden +1.8%, France +2%; OECD 2000a), contributing to a rapidly growing deficit between contributions and outlays. Measures aimed at containing pension costs such as the introduction of tighter eligibility criteria for minimum pensions in 1983 were exceptions to the rule (Klammer and Rolf 1998). While virtually every Italian government tried to contain the explosion of pension outlays and to strengthen private fully funded pensions, all these efforts were stalled by an "iron triangle" consisting of members of the Parliamentary Commission on Pension reform, various interest groups, and managers of the INPS, the main state pension body managing about two-thirds of the pensions (administered by a board composed of representatives of trade unions, employers, self-employed and the Labour Ministry).

Until the early 1990s, many of the reforms also enhanced the generosity of the system and thereby led to even higher pension costs. For instance, in 1988, the benefit ceiling for high incomes was abolished (hitherto only a contribution ceiling had been in place). In 1990, benefits for self-employed people were substantially improved. Hence, the dynamics of growing pension expenditures remained unbroken throughout the 1980s and early-1990s (Klammer 1997). To a large extent, this worrisome development was caused by the coexistence of a highly particularistic-clientelistic party system and an extremely fragmented social insurance system, which offered manifold possibilities to distribute differentiated benefits to specific party constituencies. This also gave rise to pronounced distributive disparities across sectors and occupational categories, in particular between private and public sector employees (Ferrera and Gualmini 2000a; Franco 2000).

In the 1990s, this unfortunate dynamic was largely brought to a halt. After 1992, virtually all of Italy's governments were determined to scale back Italy's hypertrophic pension system. However, not all of these reform initiatives met with success. Quite the contrary, while some reform efforts were successful, others failed almost completely. Below I will sketch the politics of pensions leading to these different outcomes. Four major reform attempts can be identified in the 1990s:

1 the Amato reform ("*riforma Amato*") in 1992;
2 a failed reform attempt by the Berlusconi government in 1994;
3 the comprehensive pension reform of the Dini government ("*riforma Dini*") in 1995; and
4 a follow-up to the Dini reform in 1997 adopted by the Prodi government.

The Amato reform (1992)

In 1992, the first successful effort was made to curb the rising costs of public pensions on a broad scale. Faced with a serious fiscal crisis and Italy's involuntary exit from the European Monetary system in September 1992, the Amato government sought to adopt a tight budgetary policy in order to restore the confidence of international financial markets. To that end, the Amato government[2] launched an "emergency plan" which also included a number of austerity measures in the realm of pension policy:

- a gradual increase in the retirement age to 65 years for men and to 60 years for women;
- a gradual increase in the number of "best years" on which the reference salary is based and – for younger workers only – a shift to lifetime earnings;
- a change of indexations of current pensions from wages to prices;
- a step-by-step tightening of eligibility criteria for seniority pensions in the public sector by raising the number of minimum contribution years (prior to the reform between 15 and 25 years) to 35 (as had already been the case for private employees);
- the suspension of new seniority pensions for workers in the private sector for one year.

The long-term impact of these measures on pension spending is significant. In the absence of this reform, treasury forecasts suggested that pension outlays would have increased from a level of 14.2% in 1998 to more than 23% of GDP by around 2040. With the Amato reform, the expected peak in pension outlays was projected to remain below 19% of GDP (OECD 2000b). By the same token, income replacement rates would be much lower for future pensioners, when the Amato government changes became fully implemented. For instance, a private sector employee with a contribution record of 35 years, who would formerly have received about two-thirds of his final salary, would only have received 47% under the Amato reform rules (Antichi and Pizutti 2000).

Although the reform was a significant first step to contain pension costs in the long run, it was clearly not enough. First, many changes were phased in very slowly, thereby limiting the reform's short-term impact on the public budget. Second, it did not touch the most salient (and probably most problematic) features of the old system. For instance, the accrual factor (i.e., the percentage of relevant earnings that enters into the pension formula per contribution year) was kept at 2% per annum. More importantly, the original plan to raise the number of minimum contribution years for entitlement to a seniority pension from 35 to 36 was withdrawn after informal consultations with the unions. This led to the counter-productive situation that elderly workers began trying to retire as early as possible. This was because for this group a postponement of retirement would have resulted in lower rather than higher pension payments (Antichi and Pizutti 2000; Baccaro 2000).

Despite these shortcomings, the Amato reform constitutes a remarkable and decisive divergence from the previous policy of unchecked benefit expansion. This was, among other things, facilitated by changes in the political reform process. Against the background of a severe economic and political crisis,[3] Parliament had empowered the Amato government to adopt legislative decrees (*legge delega*). This instrument allowed the executive to change legislation without the approval of Parliament. The only way for the Parliament to block these changes would have been to overthrow the government.

At the same time, the Amato government sought to back up the reforms by informally consulting with trade unions in order to obtain at least their tacit consent. Although the unions had launched general strikes in the fall 1992 against the policy proposals of the Amato government, they simultaneously signalled their co-operativeness during their peak.[4] The government entered into informal consultations with the trade unions and made concessions in certain areas, most notably with respect to the eligibility criteria for seniority pensions. Hence, the trade unions did not oppose the final reform package, although they did not formally approve the proposal either. The effectiveness of Amato's strategy is illustrated by his following statement:

I was aware [that] it was increasingly difficult to build consensus through party channels and for that matter even through Parliament itself; I resorted to the social partners as an alternative channel which, at that time, was more directly in touch with public opinion. In a number of cases, this allowed me to follow a totally new procedure in pushing through my policy measures: I discussed them with the unions; on the basis of their total or only partial consent I drafted a text which I then presented to Parliament, and – building on the consensus I had reached out of Parliament – asked for a vote of confidence. (Fargion 2000)

The failed Berlusconi plan (1994)

As noted above, the Amato reform only partly addressed the structural deficiencies of Italy's fiscally unsustainable and highly inequitable pension system. Moreover, despite the reform, the public deficit fell only modestly in the early-1990s and still amounted to more than 9% of GDP in 1994 (OECD 2001). As a consequence, the issue of pension reform still figured prominently on the political agenda. Hence, in 1994, the conservative Berlusconi government made a further attempt at pension reform.

The government appointed an expert commission in the summer of 1994 to put forward proposals for a reform of the pension system, which was then included in the Finance act (*Finanziaria*) for the period 1995–1997. The Commission also included union and employers' organisation representatives. However, the commission members were unable to arrive at a consensus and hence did not present a final report. Despite its disagreements with the trade unions, the government presented its own reform proposal for the finance bill (Antichi and Pizutti 2000).

The reform proposal comprised a number of harsh austerity measures (EIRR 1994; Pitruzello 1997; Baccaro 2000):

- a faster rise of the retirement age than had been called for by the Amato reform (to be fully implemented by 2000);
- cuts in seniority pensions through an increase in the number of minimum contribution years from 35 to 40 and a reduction of 3% for each year preceding the legal age limit;
- a reduction of the accrual factor from 2% to 1.75%;
- a switch to a less generous indexation method (projected rather than actual inflation), including a freeze of indexation in 1995;
- the abolition of all pension privileges for public employees.

Viewed in its entirety, the proposed measures would have drastically reduced the generosity of the existing pension system. The Berlusconi government was also keen to phase in these changes very quickly in order to achieve tangible budgetary relief in the short run, thereby contributing to the fulfilment of the Maastricht criteria. At the same time, Berlusconi made no serious attempts to include the trade unions and the leftist opposition in the reform process.

Italian trade unions and their parliamentary allies had repeatedly acknowledged the basic need for pension reform. However, they fiercely opposed Berlusconi's radical and hegemonic reform approach. In particular, they criticised the size and the rapid phasing-in of the pension cuts, as well as their exclusion from the policymaking process. Instead, they demanded direct negotiations with the Prime Minister.

The three major trade union confederations mobilised forcefully against the Berlusconi plan. Throughout the process, the unions organised a number of strikes against the pension reform package, including a four-hour general strike on October 14. Moreover, unions launched massive street demonstrations in many major cities, mobilising some three million participants. For instance, about 1.5 million people took part in a demonstration in Rome (at that time, Italy's largest post-war demonstration).

Faced with the constant threat of an even longer general strike, Berlusconi entered into negotiations with the trade unions and offered smaller cuts than initially proposed as well as additional taxes on businesses as a way of reducing the public deficit. However, serious disagreements persisted and the unions announced another general strike against the government's pension plans.

Against this background of an increasingly militant labour movement, the parliamentary coalition supporting the Berlusconi administration started to crumble. From the outset the parliamentary weak and internally fragmented government had great difficulties in presenting a unified front vis-à-vis the trade unions. For instance, Labour Minister Mastella, from the centrist Christian party, the CCD, argued for a different approach both with respect to the contents and the methods of reform. In contrast to Finance Minister Dini, Mastella favoured modest and gradual cutbacks over an abrupt policy shock and emphasised the need for social equality and cohesion. He also pleaded for co-operation with the unions and the parliamentary left (Pitruzello 1997).

The eventual failure of the reform package was caused by the defection of Berlusconi's coalition partner *Lega Nord*. Faced with massive public protests, *Lega Nord* broke ranks with the coalition partners and opposed the swift increase in the retirement age and the reduction of the accrual rate. Berlusconi sought to reunite the government coalition by a vote of confidence, whereas *Lega Nord* had promised the trade unions that they would force a postponement to allow them to be included in the negotiations. Moreover, even Dini and the employers' confederation, Confindustria, fearing the disastrous economic consequences of continued strikes, now came out in favour of direct negotiations with the trade unions. Finally, the government approved the postponement of pension reform, and the unions withdrew their plans for another general strike (Pitruzello 1997). In an agreement between the government and the three main trade union confederations, it was stipulated that only very small pension cuts would be included in the 1995 budget. Moreover, the agreement set out broad guidelines for a comprehensive pension reform to be negotiated between the government and the social partners in the next year (EIRR 1996a). Thus, after several months of severe political confrontations, the Berlusconi plan failed, which again led to the government's resignation only a few days later.

The Dini reform (1995)

After the fall of the Berlusconi government, a caretaker government led by the former Finance minister Lamberto Dini took over. After three months of negotiations with the three trade union confederations, the new government hammered out a pension reform proposal, which was sent to Parliament for approval. The reform package comprised a number of substantial structural changes (EIRR 1996a; Antichi and Pizutti 2000):

– a separation of the public pension system from the rest of the social security system, including a more strictly division between "insurance" and "assistance" benefits (the former to be financed by social contributions, the latter out of the general state budget);
– a progressive harmonisation of the multitude of separate pension schemes leading to a unified system for all employed people;
– a gradual changeover from a defined-benefit to a (notional) defined-contribution design;
– a gradual abolition of the different retirement ages for men and women and the introduction of a flexible retirement age between 57 and 65 on a strict actuarial basis;
– a gradual phasing out of seniority pensions. Workers with more than 17 years of contributions (at the end of 1995) would be able to draw a seniority pension at age 57 and 35 years of contributions or, alternatively, with 40 years of contributions (after date: 35 years of contributions with no agelimit);
– a homogenous contribution rate of 32% of employees' gross salary for all categories of private and public sector workers;
– extension of compulsory insurance for certain occupational categories;
– establishment of a legal framework (including tax incentives) for supplementary pension funds, to be set up primarily on the basis of collective agreements.[5]

Like the Amato reform, the Dini reform would effectively curb pension spending in the long-term. It has been estimated that the reform would keep the pension expenditure ratio below 16% of GDP even during the demographic peak. Thus, compared to the projections made on the basis of the Amato legislation, the Dini reform would dampen the increase in pension costs by an additional 3% of GDP (OECD 2000b).

To summarise, both reforms entailed drastic reductions in replacement levels for future pensioners. It has been estimated that actual pensions for this group would vary from between 40 to 50% of one's last salary (as compared to a then-current level of 80%; Cioccia et al. 2001).[6] For current pensioners and elderly workers, however, the measures were clearly less harsh than those sought by the Berlusconi government. Extraordinarily long transition periods ensured that the rules of the new system would mostly not apply to older and even middle-aged workers (at least 18 years of contributions by the end of 1995) and only partly apply to younger workers (less than 18 years of contributions). Only those hired in or after 1996 would be entirely covered by the new system (OECD 2000b).

The establishment of very generous "grandfather clauses" can be largely attributed to the fact that Italian trade unions agitated for the maintenance of benefit entitlements that had been built-up prior to the reform. Another reform package measure included in response to strong trade union pressures was the introduction of a "strenuous work" (*lavoro usuranti*) clause, which meant that workers engaged in arduous work would be allowed to retire five years earlier than the normal retirement age. The social partners were to decide which workers would be covered by this provision in each sector and then proposed an exemption in their behalf to the Labour Minister, who would adopt a corresponding decree. In return for these concessions, the unions accepted a gradual phasing-out of seniority pensions (EIRR 1996a).

The Dini reform was highly controversial among workers. Most notably, the tighter eligibility criteria for seniority pensions triggered strong criticism. However, the three trade union confederations proved capable of generating a sufficient degree of consensus among their rank and file. The preliminary accord between government and trade unions was subjected to a referendum by workers and pensioners (both union and non-union). About four and a half million people participated in a referendum with 64% voting in favour of the reform proposal (Baccaro 2001). It should be noted, however, that the level of agreement was much higher among pensioners (91%) than among active workers (58%).

The reform proposal was presented to Parliament following the referendum. The government made it clear that major changes to the proposed reform would be unacceptable. Nevertheless, the opposition sought to amend the proposal, leading to protracted negotiations with the government, which left the bill the subject of a vote of confidence. Given its skimpy majority, the government won its vote of confidence by striking a deal with Berlusconi's *Forza Italia*.[7] The latter succeeded in accomplishing a greater role for private insurance companies in offering supplementary pension funds, whereas the left-wing parties obtained certain guarantees for workers suffering hardships. In the end, the legislation was adopted without fundamental modifications to the original proposal. Only the Communists and the ex-fascist *Alleanza Nationale* voted unanimously against the bill (EIRR 1995a; EIRR 1996a).

At an early stage, the employer confederation *Confindustria* had withdrawn from the bargaining table and ended up not signing the agreement, because it believed the reforms had not gone far enough. In particular, it criticised the overly long period for the phasing-in of the changes and the non-reduction of social contributions (the bulk of which is financed by employers). Moreover, it was critical of the plan for using parts of the severance pay funds, which provided employers with cost-free working capital, to finance capitalised supplementary pensions (EIRR 1996a; Baccaro 2000; Cioccia, Turcio et al. 2001; Economist 2002).

The Prodi amendments (1997)

As noted above, the Dini reforms would only become full effective after a lengthy transition period. At the same time, Italy was experiencing extraordinarily strong short-term pressure to meet the fiscal convergence criteria laid down in the Maastricht Treaty, which only allowed for a maximum budget deficit of 3% of GDP from 1997 onwards. Given the fact, that Italy's budget deficit in 1996 still exceeded 7% of GDP (OECD 2001), drastic steps were necessary to reduce the budget, including new pension cuts, most notably seniority pensions. A re-opening clause established in the 1995 accord provided for a joint revision of the Dini reform in 1998, in the case of fiscal imbalances. Because of the extraordinary fiscal pressures imposed by the Maastricht Treaty, this re-examination was conducted a year earlier (Baccaro 2000).

In January 1997, the government set up a special commission (the Onofri Commission) to propose measures for a comprehensive reform of welfare programmes. With respect to pensions the Commission recommended a fortification of the Dini reform. The key proposals were (D'Ercole and Terribile 1998):

– a clearer separation between social assistance and old age pensions, with the former financed by general taxation and the latter by individual contributions;
– a complete harmonisation of different pension schemes;
– a more rapid changeover to the new defined-contribution system (also including workers with more than 18 years of contributions);

- tighter rules for seniority pensions (such as the immediate enactment of the eligibility requirements foreseen by the Dini reform for 2008);
- higher contribution rates for the self-employed;
- increase in the minimum retirement age.

On the basis of these proposals, the government entered into negotiations with the unions. As in 1995, Italian trade unions signalled their readiness to support in principle further adjustments if necessary. For instance, they proposed the introduction of a "solidarity contribution" to be paid by pensioners as a contribution toward the fulfilment of the Maastricht criteria (Baccaro 2000). In September 1997, the government arrived at an understanding with the unions on several welfare reforms to be included in the finance act for 1998. Moreover, they were about to arrive at an agreement on pension legislation changes after the government offered a number of concessions. For instance, the extension of the pro-rata-system to workers with a contribution record of more than 18 years, as proposed by the Onofri Report, was not included in the final reform package.

Despite these concessions, union support was not enough to guarantee the political feasibility of the reform package. The Communist Reconstruction Party *(Rifondazione Communista)*, hitherto a backer but not a member of the left-centre minority government, announced that it was blocking the finance law in Parliament. As the bourgeois opposition had already announced it was voting against any budget with higher value-added taxes, the government was forced to win the support of the Communists (*The Economist*, 4 October 1997). The *Rifondazione Communista (RC)* criticised the government for ignoring its proposals, concerning, among others, the reduction of the work week to 35 hours and the reform of the pension system. Basically, the RC was against any form of welfare and pension cuts. This triggered a serious crisis within the government and even led to the temporary resignation of the Prime Minister and the suspension of the negotiations with the social partners. The crisis was resolved after negotiations between the government and the RC, which finally withdrew its resistance to the finance law after the Government made a number of concessions including, for instance, the introduction of the 35-hour work week (a move that had been opposed by both employers and trade unions as an undue state intervention into the sphere of collective agreements between social partners). The RC also won a desired concession to leave blue-collar pensions unaffected. This group would have been the most adversely affected by the accelerated increase in retirement age. Apart from these concessions, the Communists' final approval of the government's savings package was motivated by strong pressure from their own supporters. In withdrawing their support from the Prodi government and triggering a veritable government crisis, the RC had not only endangered Italy's entry into EMU but also the political survival of Italy's first left-wing government since the second world war. Faced with this unfavourable scenario, its own supporters pressed the RC to re-approach the Prodi government (*The Economist*, 18 October 1997).

As soon as the government had won the Communists' approval of the 1998 finance act, it resumed its negotiations with the social partners. This resulted in an agreement between the government and the three major trade union confederations in November 1997, whereas the employers' confederation voiced criticism as it considered the measures insufficient. The content of this agreement was approved by Parliament with only limited changes (Eiroline 1997a; Trentini 1997).

The final legislation included the following measures (OECD 2000b):

– a quicker harmonisation of private and public sector pensions and the abolition of other special pension provisions;
– a gradual increase of contribution rates for the self-employed to 19%;
– a more rapid phasing out of seniority pensions for white-collar workers (leaving seniority pensions for blue-collar workers unaffected);
– suspension of automatic inflation-indexing for pensions above 3.5 million liras (about 17,000 euros) in 1998 and a lowered adjustment coefficient in the following three years;
– a three-month freeze of inflows of new entrants into retirement.

The Italian trade unions supported the reforms for a number of reasons. On the one hand, the reforms had achieved greater equity between public and private sector workers and reduced the privileges of certain other categories. On the other hand, unions welcomed the fact that blue-collar workers – who would have been most seriously penalised if the retirement age had been increased – remained unaffected by the new retirement-age restrictions. The trade unions also acknowledged their deliberate inclusion in the political reform process as such (Trentini 1997).

The government's concessions to both the trade unions and the RC weakened the savings volume originally envisioned by the government. Originally, the government had intended to cut pension spending in 1998 by 6,000-7,000 billion liras (about 3-3.5 billion euros). By the end of September, negotiations with the trade unions had led it to reduce the savings volume to 5,000 billion liras. In response to RC demands, the expected savings on pensions were further scaled down to around 4,000 billion liras. Moreover, the financial contribution of current pensioners was limited to the suspension of indexation on high pensions. However, albeit modest in scope, the reform became immediately effective and contributed to a reduction of the budget deficit from 1998 onwards by about 0.2% of GDP (D'Ercole and Terribile 1998).

After the Prodi amendments, no significant cost containment measures were introduced regarding pension policy. The current right-wing government – of Silvio Berlusconi – has announced, however, its intention to proceed with pension reforms. Most recently, the government presented the guidelines for further major pension reforms. These include a liberalisation of the retirement age allowing employees to continue working beyond the regular retirement age (60 for women, 65 for men), improved possibilities of combining seniority pensions with work income, a reduction of employer contributions by 3% to 5% for employees hired on open-end contracts and the dissolution of the severance payment system, the resources of which are to be used to promote the establishment of supplementary pension funds.

Trade unions were critical of the proposed measures as they see the fiscal balance of the public pension system being threatened. However, they acknowledged that the bill does not imply further constraints on seniority pensions. Given the outright failure of his unilateral attempt at pension reform in 1994, it appears that this time Berlusconi was being less radical in his reform approach and more reluctant to enact a unilateral pension reform package that again may be fiercely opposed by all three major trade union confederations. Strangely enough, Berlusconi even *increased* public pension spending recently by increasing minimum pensions from about 360 to 516 euros per month for about 2.2 million people, a measure that he had announced in his election platform (EIRR 2002; Pedersini 2002).

A number of further measures were implemented most recently in order to strengthen the role of supplementary pensions. In particular, tax incentives for contributions allocated from the end-of-service allowance to supplementary pension funds based on collective agreements were massively improved by a legislative decree adopted in February 2000 (Eiroline 2000a; Paparella 2001). Thus far, however, the expansion of fully funded old age provisions has only proceeded at a very slow pace. According to calculations of the Brambilla Commission conducted in October 2001, the real take-up ratios clearly fall short of original expectations. The Dini reforms were expected to lead to supplementary pension funds amounting to more than 1800 billion liras (about 0.9 billion euros), whereas the most recent figures only indicate a volume of some 360 billion liras (about 0.18 billion euros).[8]

In conclusion, the attempts by successive Italian governments in the 1990s to reform the economically unsustainable public pension system have been at least partly successful. Since 1992, Italy has been able to bring the dynamics of unchecked benefit expansion to an end. Moreover, Italian pension policymakers have successfully set in motion a process, which will lead to a more sustainable and equitable pension system, in which undue privileges for certain occupational groups (most notably public sector employees) will cease to exist. However, the bulk of these changes will only become fully effective in the distant future, leaving current pensions as well as pensions for middle-aged and older workers largely untouched. Hence, cuts in current pensions have done little to solve Italy's budgetary problems of the 1990s, let alone lead to a significant reduction of current levels of non-wage labour costs. By the same token, the content of recent changes in pension policy is hard to justify from the point of view of inter-generational equity, as the burden of adjustment will be first and foremost imposed on the younger generations, who will face a sharp deterioration of their future pensions. Finally, as noted above, the steps to promote supplementary pension funds have so far proven to be insufficient.

Explanatory factors for Italy's mixed reform record

Italy's mixed record in pension policy reform cannot be attributed to one single factor. Instead, we must focus on specific aspects of the overall reform record and try to identify the various factors that have either facilitated or hampered policy adjustments in particular instances. In the following section, I will briefly recapitulate and explain the most salient policy results that were enacted by recent pension reforms.

The most striking aspect is Italy's radical turnaround in pension policy after 1992, when a multitude of reforms were launched to contain spiralling pension costs and put a stop to uncontrolled benefit expansion. Obviously, the political conditions for a large-scale restructuring of the pension system have changed radically since 1992. This was facilitated by a number of partly interrelated factors:

First, the old clientelistic parties (which were the main culprits for Italy's overblown pension system) had been seriously weakened or even replaced by more reform-oriented parties. By the same token, quite a number of leading politicians in the 1990s such as Dini and Prodi (as well as numerous ministers in the Amato cabinet) enjoyed good reputations as relatively independent economic experts with no links to the old corrupt party establishments. Moreover, the Dini government was a caretaker government, whose incumbency was a priori limited and which therefore was not concerned about its own re-election. Thus, these governments were able to partly distance themselves from the electoral process. In combination with modified parliamentary rules providing the executive with greater control over the budgetary process, these factors reduced the opportunities of various interest groups to block legislative decisions (Gohr 2001a, b).

Second, throughout the 1990s, the dynamics of European integration (in particular the fiscal pressure imposed by the EMU criteria) and its beneficial impact on the political discourse at the national level has been an important driving force behind the reform of the Italian welfare state in general. Given two-digit budgetary deficits in the early 1990s, the Maastricht Treaty forced Italy to adopt an extraordinarily tight fiscal policy. While it is true that the immediate impact of the pension reforms adopted in the 1990s on the current public deficit was very modest, their long-term effect on the financial sustainability of public pension system will be considerable. Thus, in the long run, these reforms will also help to substantially reduce Italy's huge public debt, which according the Maastricht Treaty must be brought down to under 60% of GDP. Against that background, it should not come as a surprise that several EU member states accepted Italy's membership in the monetary union only under the condition that Italy reform its pension system (Cioccia et al. 2001). As Pitruzello (1997) has argued, the Maastricht Treaty represented a legally binding obligation for Italian governments and exerted powerful pressures within a relatively short period of time. While it is true that the pressures from international capital markets to reduce public deficits had already been strong in the 1980s, these pressures did not enforce compliance with concrete deficit criteria at a definite point in time. This difference matters, especially if politicians are presented with a very short time frame as was the case in Italy, and where the frequency of changes in government have been very high by international standards. As long as the binding criteria of the Maastricht Treaty did not force the short-lived Italian governments to adopt tight fiscal policies in a very short time frame, they could easily shift the task of balancing the deficit and securing the fiscal viability of public pensions onto subsequent governments. When the tight constraints imposed by the Maastricht Treaty meant that Italy could no longer postpone painful reforms, the political discourse regarding pension reform (and welfare reform, in general) changed fundamentally.

Moreover, the project of European integration enjoys extraordinarily strong support among the Italian public. Most notably, Europe is seen as a proper device for overcoming the lack of discipline and the clientelism of domestic party politicians (Featherstone 2001). Italy's membership in the European monetary union also promised substantial economic and fiscal benefits, as their high interest rates would be reduced to that of among lowest of European countries. This again would stimulate investment and considerably diminish expenditures on public debt service.[9] These prospects also fostered an increased willingness among political actors to reform Italy's highly unsustainable and inequitable pension system. This pressure from the EMU allowed successive Italian prime ministers to convey the message regarding the costs of non-adjustment, pointing to the necessity of sacrifices in the short-run (such as benefit cuts) in exchange for the promise of future benefits. This also helped reduce the electoral costs usually associated with the retrenchment of highly popular welfare programmes (Pitruzello 1997; Ferrera and Gualmini 2000a; Ferrera and Gualmini 2000b; Gohr 2001a/b).

What is more, the dramatic rise of fiscal pressures went hand in hand with the increases in influence of the Prime Minister's Office and the Ministry of Treasury with regard to pension policy proposals and a less dominant role of the Labour Ministry (Franco 2000).

Reform pressures were emphasised by the currency crises of 1992 and 1995, which led to Italy's temporary withdrawal from the European Monetary System. One needs to remember that one of the Maastricht criteria was a stability of exchange rates, which requires that a national currency remain within the stipulated bandwidth of the European Monetary System for at least two years. Italy would not have been allowed to enter the Monetary Union in the first stage, if the currency crisis of 1995 had been repeated one or two years later.

Italian trade unions have by and large played a supportive and constructive role in the process of pension reform. They were well aware of the distributional flaws and the financial unsustainability of the old pension regime. Equally important, they had had come to realise that retention of the status quo in pension policy would also jeopardise Italy's membership in the EMU. Against this background, Italian trade unions at least in principle acknowledged the necessity of pension reform.

Union support was crucial in order to sustain the political feasibility of pension reform in Italy. This is because a sufficiently stable consensus on pension reform is difficult to achieve in the party politics arena. The persistent fragmentation and instability of Italy's multi-party government coalitions plus the high degree of electoral competition strongly hamper consensus building within the government (let alone a consensus across the political camps). Even in those cases, where opposition parties offered their support to the government (as Berlusconi did in 1997),[10] alternating majorities would be the likely result. This again would endanger the internal cohesion of government coalitions.

Against this background, alliances between government and trade unions were the only way to forge a stable political base for pension reform. As Baccaro (2000) aptly remarks,

> in Italy, the presence of quarrelsome governmental coalitions based on a multiplicity of parties in constant competition with one another and relying on slim parliamentary majorities (or even, as in the case of the "technocratic" governments of the early- to mid-1990, devoid of clear and stable majorities) rendered interest-group inclusion in all major policy reforms, not just pension reform, almost a functional necessity.

The effective inclusion of trade unions in the reform process facilitated by their relatively comprehensive organisational structures. Italian trade unions are organised on the basis of confederations that represent simultaneously both white- and blue-collar workers in all economic sectors. To that extent, Italian trade unions possess the strategic capacity to sacrifice the interests of some members for the greater benefit of the collective. This explains why they have supported the large-scale harmonisation of the hitherto strongly fragmented pension system and accepted the abolition of pension privileges for public sector employees. Moreover, while the traditional ideological cleavages between the three major trade union confederations (reinforced by strong ties to their respective allies in the partisan arena) have led to a high degree of inter-union competition and thereby restricted their capacity of co-ordinated action, Italian trade unions have shown that they are in principle able to overcome internal divisions. This was regularly witnessed during the crisis situations of the 1990s. Most importantly, by putting aside their internal differences, Italian trade unions found it easier to persuade their rank and file about the necessity of unpopular reforms, as they did in the case of the Dini reform (Regini 1997; Culpepper 2000).

In this case, compliance of union members was also facilitated by the application of binding referenda among the workforce. The divergent pension policy interests within the trade union camp were effectively aggregated by a democratic majority vote at the grassroots level rather than by some hierarchical decision of trade union leaders, which had been an Italian union tradition. The key problem associated with the traditional hierarchic decision-making process lies in the fact that the potential losers may reject this decision on the grounds that it (allegedly) does not reflect the will of the majority of workers. In the past, this perceived lack of democratic legitimacy often gave rise to local strikes, which were decided upon by local unions rather than by national union leaders. This time, however, even the union members that were strongly opposed to the reform content acknowledged the procedural justice of the vote and therefore abstained from striking. This also explains why even those occupational groups which had voted in the majority against reforms (such as education employees) or which stood to lose disproportionately under the new regulations (i.e., public sector workers) accepted the outcome. Thus, as pointed out by Baccaro (2002), the empirical instance of the Dini reform is partly at odds with traditional neo-corporatist theory suggesting that union member compliance with loss-imposing reforms can only be achieved through a hierarchical and internally undemocratic organisational structure enabling interest group leaders to impose reforms on their members to which they would not normally subscribe to voluntarily (Schmitter and Lehmbruch 1979; Streeck 1994).

However, the question arises *how* the majority of voters could be encouraged to approve the Dini reforms. To begin with, the referenda were preceded by thousands of workplace assemblies in which Italian unions could use their strong presence at the local level to persuade workers about the necessity and fairness of the proposed pension reform. Moreover, due to its substantive policy content the Dini reforms were acceptable to a majority of workers. More specifically, the decision by majority vote effectuated a constellation in which a minority of workers who were intensely against the reforms was outvoted by a majority of workers, who had a positive, but less intense interest in the success of the reform plans. In that respect, a majority in favour of the reform could only be achieved if the pension entitlements of elderly workers and pensioners were largely exempted from the cutbacks (Baccaro 2001). This requirement resulted from the pronounced (and steeply growing) age-bias within the membership of Italian unions (about 50% of union members are pensioners). Thus, together with the elderly workers, pensioners form an extraordinarily strong majority among the unions' rank and file (Fargion 2000).[11]

Finally, Italian trade unions' co-operativeness vis-à-vis the technocratic Dini government was also motivated by the fear that the referendum's failure might prompt a subsequent, potentially more labour-hostile government to impose even harsher anti-union reforms (as Berlusconi attempted in 1994).

As noted earlier, Italy's pension reform record also displays a number of weaknesses.[12] The most critical of these (especially compared to the Swedish reform) is the very lengthy transition period, which severely limits any positive impact on public finances and non-wage labour costs in the short- and medium-term. Moreover, it imposes a one-sided burden on the younger generation. This, however, was the price Italian governments had to pay in order to obtain union approval. Given their pronounced age bias, Italian unions fiercely defended the interests of pensioners and elderly workers. Therefore, Italian unions mobilised on a massive scale against the Berlusconi plan, which primarily sought to achieve budgetary savings through immediate cuts in seniority pensions. While the expected budgetary savings resulting from the Dini reform were virtually equivalent to those envisioned by Berlusconi, the Dini reform expected more modest and gradual cuts in seniority pensions as well as higher pension revenues, in particular, by extending social security coverage to atypical workers, a measure that was enthusiastically welcomed by the unions (Baccaro 2002). Besides the co-operative style adopted by the Dini government, these are the aspects that facilitated an amicable agreement with the unions. The eventual failure of the Berlusconi plan can be attributed to the weakness and ideological fragmentation of the Berlusconi government, which proved unable to withstand the fierce opposition of a unified trade union front which organised large-scale and prolonged popular protests (including strikes and mass demonstrations) against the reform.

Another shortcoming that needs to be explained is the very slow expansion of supplementary pension funds. As Franco (2000) points out, excessively high contribution rates and large public deficits reduced the leeway for an expansion of the pre-funded pillar of retirement income provisions. Therefore, the system of severance payments was considered the only sizeable financing source suitable to the establishment of a strong fully funded pillar. However, even this changeover was seriously hampered by a number of factors (Eiroline 2000a; Franco 2000; Paparella 2001):

– While the Dini reform created the legal possibility of establishing supplementary pension funds, it provided only very limited tax incentives as the public budget was still in dire straits at the time. Only in 2000, when the public deficit had fallen to just 0.3% of GDP, was it possible to massively expand tax deductions in order to promote supplementary pension funds.
– Another factor that delayed expansion of supplementary pension funds was due to the divisions among the social partners. Employers were unwilling to accept the loss in financial liquidity associated with the allocation of money from the severance pay system, which allows for a sizeable share of self-financing at a relatively low cost for small and medium-sized companies in an otherwise relatively under-developed capital market (OECD 2000b). Moreover, social partners are divided on the issue of whether the changeover should be regulated by collective agreements (as suggested by the CISL, one of the major trade union confederations, and

by the employer confederation Confindustria) or by law (as demanded by CGIL, another major trade union confederation).

– The level of membership in supplementary pension funds is particularly low in the under-unionised sectors, most notably in the service sector, where most workers are not covered by collective agreements.

– More generally, employees' incentives to invest in pension funds were lowered by the fact that the public pay-as-you-go system continues to offer relatively high benefit levels for elderly and middle-aged workers and thereby reduces the pressure for additional pension savings.

6   Germany: From Consensus To Conflict

The key features of the German pension system in the late 1980s

German pension insurance (*Gesetzliche Rentenversicherung*) provides for old age, invalidity, and survivors' pensions. It comprises institutionally distinct schemes for blue- and white-collar workers with ultimately identical provisions. Civil servants draw pensions under the tax-financed civil service scheme (*Beamtenversorgung*), which provides benefits that equal 75% of final pay after 35 years' membership. Other public employees are compulsory members of a special supplementary scheme based on collective agreements (*Zusatzversorgung Öffentlicher Dienst*), designed to augment pensions under the workers' and employees' scheme, in order to provide pensions similar to those of tenured civil servants. Members of various professions are covered by self-governing compulsory insurance institutions (*Versorgungswerke*). All dependent workers and recipients of unemployment benefits are compulsorily covered for pension insurance. Self-employed people are usually not compulsorily covered, but may join the insurance system on a voluntary basis.

Old age pensions are earnings-related and designed to maintain the relative standard of living attained by the recipient during his/her working life. Entitlement to an old age pension presupposes a minimum insurance record of 5 years of contributions and attainment of the age limit of 65 years. Women and the long-term unemployed are entitled to a full pension from the age of 60. People with 35 years of contributions may opt for a pension from the age of 63, or 60 if handicapped. The amount of individual pensions basically reflects the contribution record of the insured person and the level of his/her earnings (*Lebenseinkommensprinzip*). A worker with a contribution record of forty years and life-time earnings corresponding to the average income of all insured people will receive an old age pension equalling 60% of recent average earnings. All pensions have been indexed since 1957. The annual adjustments generally reflect the development of average gross earnings.

Pension insurance schemes are financed by earnings-related contributions which amount to 19.2% of earnings (1986). Employees and employers each pay one half of this rate. Earnings above a certain ceiling are exempted from contributions. The federal government contributes about 20% of aggregate resources. The insurance schemes operate on a pay-as-you-go basis with a minimum reserve fund of one month's expenditures. Contribution rates must be increased if financial forecasts show that reserves are to fall below one month's expenditures.

The pension insurance schemes are run by self-governing bodies under state supervision. Insured people and employers each delegate one half of the members of the board of directors and the board of supervisors (Alber 1987).

Germany's pension reform record in the 1990s

An inspection of recent developments in German pension policies reveals a mixed record. Among the countries studied, Germany was the first to embark on a strategy of cost containment in pension policy. The German pension insurance has since 1977 been subjected to numerous curtailment efforts by both the Social-liberal coalition (in office until 1982) and the Christian Democratic-liberal coalition (Alber 1998). Until the late 1980s, these measures were largely aimed at the short-term stabilisation of contribution rates in the face of rising unemployment and low wage growth. As a result of these efforts, the pension expenditure ratio was even reduced slightly throughout the 1980s. Among the countries studied, only in Germany did pension spending decrease between 1980 and 1992 (by about 0.6% of GDP), although this development was also favoured by a falling old age dependency ratio. At the same time, pension outlays increased significantly in most other OECD countries (OECD 2001).

From 1989 onwards, a number of more incisive and long-term oriented reforms have been initiated in order to reduce the increase of pension costs that will result from demographic ageing. Due to these reforms, pension expenditures (and thus contribution levels) will increase much more slowly than was originally projected. Prior to the "big" 1992 reform contribution rates (amounting to 18.7% in 1990) were projected to reach a level of more than 36% in 2030. Currently, it is expected that contribution levels will not exceed 22% until 2030 (see table 6.1), albeit, this assumption may turn out to be somewhat too optimistic.

However, Germany's achievements with respect to the containment of public pension costs in the long-term do not appear to be particularly im-

Table 6.1 Projected contribution rates for statutory pension insurance*

Projection year	1990	2000	2010	2020	2030
1989 (without "1992 Reform")	18.7	22.0	24.5	28.1	36.4
1989 (with "1992 Reform")	18.7	20.3	21.4	22.8	26.9
1994	-	19.7	21.5	23.1	27.0
1996	-	20.4	21.6	23.2	26.2
1996 (with WFG measures)[1]	-	20.1	20.6	22.6	25.5
1996 (with "1999 Reform")[2]	-	19.7	19.1	20.0	22.42
2000	-	19.3	19.6	20.5	23.62
2000 (with "Riester Reform")	-	-	18.7	19.7	21.9

* Contribution rates required to balance the budget and to meet reserve requirements of the scheme. Note that this scheme does not include civil servants pensions. Until 1989, projections referred only to West Germany.

Sources: compilation by the author, based on Bönker and Wollmann (2001).
1. Wachstums- und Beschäftigungsförderungsgesetz
2. In 1999, the Pension Reform Act 1999 was suspended, which led to a temporary increase in the projected contribution rate.

pressive when compared to the other countries studied. Based on the standard scenario calculated by the Economic Policy Committee (2001), Germany is expected to face a stronger increase in pension expenditures over the next 50 years (4.9% of GDP between 2000 and the expected peak year) than Austria (4.2%), France (4%), Sweden (2.6%) and Italy (2.1%), albeit from a substantially lower starting point than Austria and Italy (see also table 2.2). In contrast to Sweden and Italy, Germany has not implemented a complete switch towards a defined-contribution system, albeit important steps in that direction have been undertaken. Quite remarkably, however, the most recent reform is geared toward establishing a multi-tiered pension system, in which private and occupational pensions will partly substitute the pension payments out of the public scheme. However, German pension policymakers failed in their attempt to make private old age provisions compulsory. Instead, the 2000 pension reform tried to promote private pension insurance efforts via direct subsidies and tax incentives. A major weakness of German pension policy – in particular in comparison with the successful efforts in Austria and Italy – is that only limited efforts were made to harmonise civil servants' pensions with the general scheme.

In this chapter I will analyse the recent German pension reforms in chronological order. I will start with the pension reform act 1992 (*Rentenreformgestz 1992*), which is said to be the first big pension reform, which aimed to drastically reduce the imminent increase in pension costs.

Pension politics in Germany has followed a rather erratic pattern in recent years. Until the early-1990s, all major pension reforms were – at least in the final vote in Parliament – commonly supported by the two large political parties, the CDU/CSU and SPD (Hinrichs 1998). By the 1980s, pension policy had become comparatively de-politicised in the sense that the issue of pension reform was largely kept out of the electoral arena. This – albeit fragile – consensus between the major political parties was also backed by the social partners. In terms of policy substance, this consensus revolved around the idea that the statutory pension insurance (*Gesetzliche Renten- versicherung, GRV*) had to at least approximately maintain the previous living standard during retirement. Moreover, the community of pension policymakers agreed that necessary reforms should be made within, rather than outside, the public system (Nullmeier/Rüb 1993; Hinrichs, 1998). The Pension reform act 1992, legislated in 1989 and implemented as of 1992, is a textbook example of this approach. The key features of this reform were:

– a switch from gross to net wage indexation;
– a phased increase of the retirement age to 65 years with actuarial reductions in the case of early retirement (to be implemented from 2001 onwards);
– the curtailment of non-contributory benefits (exception: improved credits for child rearing);
– an increase of the federal subsidy (*Bundeszuschuss*) to a constant share of 20% of total expenditures.

This reform would generate (and to a great extent already has generated) remarkable savings. It has been estimated that without this reform the pension contribution rate would have increased from a level of 18.7% in 1990 to more than 36% in 2030, instead of only 27% with the reforms (see table 6.1). Nevertheless, the reform did not change the net replacement rate for a fictitious standard pensioner[1] (70% of earnings). However, by changing indexation from gross to net earnings the reform effectively prevented a situation in which after-tax pensions were rising faster than the take-home pay of wage earners. At the time, policymakers acted on the assumption that the overall tax wedge would continue to increase even in the long run. In this case, retaining gross wage indexation would have led to an ever stronger divergence between net wages and net pensions to the benefit of the latter. Given that net wages had been virtually stagnating in real terms since the early 1980s (VDR 2001), pension policymakers (even within the trade unions) considered this scenario unacceptable. Thus, this element of the reform went largely uncontested from the outset (Nullmeier and Rüb 1993:231).

By contrast, the issue of increased retirement ages was highly controversial among the actors involved and even threatened to thwart the cross-party consensus. While the government parties (in particular the Liberals) sought to implement an increase in age limits at a relatively early stage, the Social Democratic opposition (along with the trade unions) demanded that this measure be postponed as long as unemployment remained high. Nevertheless, the SPD acknowledged that retirement ages needed to be raised in response to the long-term changes in the population's age structure. In the final compromise, the Social Democrats achieved a postponement of the increase in age limits by eight years above the original government plan (Nullmeier and Rüb 1993).

The negotiation process included several stages. In 1985, a working group composed of representatives of the employer organisation BDA, the German trade union confederation DGB, and the white-collar union DAG, as well as a commission chaired by the VDR[2] (the peak association of all the public pension funds), was created, which successfully paved the way for a consensus among the social partners about the main principles of a reform (albeit, the issue of increased retirement ages remained contested). In 1987, a working group comprised of coalition partners and representatives of the Labour Ministry was created to work out a government proposal on pension reform, which then became the negotiation basis for the Social Democratic opposition. These negotiations led to a commonly supported legislative proposal in March 1989, which was eventually adopted without major modifications (Nullmeier and Rüb 1993). While the agreement among the social partners in the preliminary stages of the negotiation process was clearly highly conducive to a corresponding agreement in the partisan arena (Niemeyer 1990), the final consensus was primarily based on a compromise between the Christian-Liberal government and the Social Democratic opposition.

What factors account for the development of such a broad cross-party pension consensus? Pension policymakers from all of the major political parties shared the conviction that an unaltered status quo in pension policy would be fiscally and economically unsustainable in the long run. Moreover, for reasons of inter-generational equity they considered an equal distribution of the rising demographic burden between contributors and pensioners as necessary.

At the same time, both the Social Democrats and large sections of the coalition parties shared the view that the basic structure of the existing pension system needed to be preserved. Even within the governing parties, demands for a radical change of the system such as a changeover from an earnings-related to a tax-financed basic pension could not win a legislative majority. Thus, the government and the opposition (except the Greens, who pleaded for a universal minimum pension) advocated changes *within* the public system.

The government coalition had a powerful motive for seeking the consent of the Social Democrats because it had an interest in sharing the blame for unpopular pension cuts with the largest opposition party in order to minimise electoral retribution. Norbert Blüm, the Christian Democratic Labour Minister in charge of the reform, had another motive for bringing the SPD on board. Because he belonged to the employee-wing of the CDU, Blüm advocated a more modest reform than his party's liberal coalition partner and the strong market-liberal forces within his own party. As Nullmeier (1996) points out, the traditional split in pension and social policy issues between the labour wing (*Arbeitnehmerflügel*) and the business wing (*Wirtschaftsflügel*) of the Christian Democrats favoured a constellation in which both sides sought to incorporate the interests of a third party into a pension compromise in order to strengthen their own standing within the party. The business wing attached great importance to the market-liberal demands of the coalition partner FDP. By contrast, the Christian Democratic Party's labour wing advocated a pension consensus with the SPD in order to compensate for its own intra-party weaknesses. Consequently, the concessions necessary to obtain the consent of the SPD produced an agreement closer to Blüm's own ideals than would have been the case had the reform been negotiated only within the government coalition.

The Social Democratic opposition was very confident of winning the next election at that time, and thus had only a limited incentive for launching an election campaign against a pension reform which it actually favoured in general. By agreeing to a compromise with the government, the party was able to move the reform outcome closer to its own ideal point. At the same time, the Social Democrats were expecting that the delicate issue of pension reform would be out of the way prior to them taking office.[3]

Finally, trade union leaders informally encouraged the Social Democratic negotiator, Rudolf Dressler, to sign the pension contract with the government. Trade unions had reasons to fear that an SPD withdrawal from the bargaining table would result in even harsher cutbacks and a more rapid increase in retirement ages and thus lead to a less favourable outcome from a union's point of view. Given the at least tacit support from the trade unions, Dressler eventually settled for a pension pact with the government.

In a nutshell, this consensus became possible because the policy positions of the signatory parties were similar enough that they could come up with a substantive pension reform agreement, while conflicting government and opposition incentives were not substantial enough to thwart a policy-oriented bargaining process.

The fading away of the pension consensus in the 1990s

The 1992 reform was designed to supersede the established practice of relatively arbitrary short-term adjustments. To that end, the reform aimed at stabilising the system at least until 2010, rendering further legislative interventions largely superfluous (Nullmeier and Rüb 1993). However, the terms under which this reform had been adopted changed fundamentally with German reunification, which – directly and indirectly – put the public pension system under increasing fiscal strain.

For one, from 1992 onwards, the West German pension system was extended to the East German *Länder*, a measure that was still being supported by all major parties. As a consequence, the pension payments for East German pensioners increased dramatically. Moreover, due to the higher labour market participation of women in the former GDR, benefit claims for women in the new federal states were higher than in West Germany. Most importantly, the collapse of the East German economy led to a sharp decline in employment levels. Due to these developments, the shortfalls for East German pension insurance bodies grew rapidly. Between 1991 and 1997 the East German pension insurance funds accumulated a deficit of about 75 billion DM (about 38 billion euros) (Meinhardt 1997). In response, West German pension bodies had to channel considerable financial transfers to East Germany (Ney 2001b).

In addition, even in West Germany steep increases in unemployment (and a concomitant explosion of early retirement) as well as the growing significance of atypical employment (at the time not subject to mandatory social insurance contributions) amplified fiscal pressures on the pension system. Since no additional funds had been diverted into the statutory pension insurance, the contribution rate had to be adjusted on several occasions. Between 1993 and 1997, pension contribution rates increased from 17.5 to 20.3% (VDR 2001). Moreover, the combined social insurance contribution rate even increased by 7%, from a low of 35.1% in 1990 to 42.1% in 1997 and thus surpassed the politically sensitive threshold of 40%. Consequently, the reduction of non-wage labour costs below 40% became increasingly salient in the government programme (Nullmeier 1996; Hinrichs 1998). At the same time, the public budget, still displaying a surplus of 0.1% of GDP in 1989 had turned into a deficit of 3.4% in 1996 (OECD 2001). Given the 3.0% deficit criterion stipulated by the EMU, this constrained the possibilities of increasing the federal subsidy to the pension system in order to reduce contribution levels.

In response to those pressures, the government sought, among other things, to discontinue the increasingly costly use of early retirement options. At the same time, the leader of the powerful metal-workers trade union *IG Metall* submitted a proposal for a tri-partite "Alliance for Jobs" (*Bündnis für Arbeit*) as a way of addressing the problem of mass unemployment in a joint effort by the government and the social partners. Initially, the Kohl government seemed to be quite open to this idea. In February 1996, the tripartite negotiations yielded an agreement about the introduction of an "elderly part-time work" scheme (*Altersteilzeit*). This reform aimed at containing the increasing misuse of legal early retirement options while at the same time it also sought to reduce youth unemployment. The new scheme encouraged part-time employment for employees over age 55 and refunded a certain share of employers' social insurance contributions to firms that hired an unemployed worker or former apprentice. In order to contain pension costs, the age limit for this type of pension (Rente wegen Arbeitslosigkeit) was to be gradually raised from age 60 to 63 with a reduction of 3.6% for each year of early retirement. However, as a concession to union demands, the higher age limit would not apply to unemployed people over 55 at the time of the legislation (Nullmeier 1996; Hinrichs 1998).

Interestingly, the Social Democratic opposition was entirely excluded from this tripartite agreement. Likewise, the SPD parliamentary representatives were also shut out of similar talks concerning tax, pension, and labour market issues. This triggered serious tensions between the trade unions and leading SPD politicians, which accused the trade unions of currying favour with the Kohl government. In response, the leader of the German chemical workers trade union IG Chemie, Hubertus Schmoldt, argued, that the trade unions were not concerned with election dates when they were dealing with the issue of unemployment (cited in Geissler 1998:79). This suggests that even a left opposition has a hard time denouncing social policy reforms as labour-hostile when these are being developed with trade union collaboration.

However, within the bourgeois coalition government, strong disagreements persisted about the question of whether collaboration with the trade unions was an appropriate strategy for bringing about substantial social policy reforms. While the Christian Democratic labour wing continued to advocate a co-operative approach, the market-liberal forces within the coalition strongly urged unilateral action as a way achieving more rapid and far-reaching adjustments. The latter position gained the upper hand when the employers threatened to quit the "Alliance for Jobs", which they had increasingly perceived as a rather useless institution, and also after the coalition parties won three *Länder* elections in March 1996, where the liberal FDP could especially strengthen its position. Shortly after the elections, the government took a clearly less conciliatory attitude vis-à-vis the trade unions and adopted a reform package unpalatable to the trade unions.

The Growth and Employment Promotion Act (*Wachstums- und Beschäftigungsförderungsgesetz*) was intended to cut sick pay from 100% to 80% and to lower employment protection rules, two measures that were absolutely unacceptable to the trade unions (Nullmeier 1996; Geissler 1998). With respect to pension policy this reform entailed further cuts in non-contributory benefits and an accelerated phasing-out of all early retirement options without permanent benefit reductions. In particular, the plan to increase women's regular pension age from 60 to 65 between 1997 and 2001, rather than between 2000 and 2012 as stipulated in the 1992 reform, triggered fierce criticism from the SPD and the trade unions, also because this measure was not accompanied by improved credits for child rearing (as had been demanded in a 1992 decision by the constitutional court). In the Pension Reform Act 1992, the increase of the retirement age for women had been made contingent on the development of the labour market situation. The reasoning then was that a higher retirement age was not desirable during high unemployment. Given that by 1996, unemployment had increased (rather than decreased), the SPD and the unions saw this step as a clear breach of the 1989 cross-party agreement. In response to their massive protests, the government postponed this measure for three years (Nullmeier 1996).

The cutbacks proposed in the Growth and Employment Facilitation Act not only led to the breakdown of the "Alliance for Jobs", but also provoked a massive counter-mobilisation by the trade unions. In June 1996, the German trade union confederation DGB launched the hitherto largest demonstration (approximately 350,000 participants) against the Kohl government's welfare cuts. Moreover, this reform put an end to the pension consensus in the partisan arena. In May 1996, the SPD's social policy spokesman, Rudolf Dreßler, officially revoked the present pension consensus with the government parties and refused to participate in the government's pension reform commission, which was drawing up further reform

Table 6.2   Change in vote shares between the federal elections of 1994 and 1998

Age group	Total			Women only		
	SPD	CDU/CSU	FDP	SPD	CDU/CSU	FDP
18-24	1.0	-1.7	-0.4	0.3	-0.3	-0.9
25-34	2.3	-3.5	0.7	-0.7	-2.0	0.7
35-44	4.7	-6.8	-1.5	5.3	-8.3	-1.3
45-59	6.0	-9.0	-0.5	7.2	-10.4	0.0
60+	5.8	-6.2	-1.1	8.6	-8.8	-0.9
All	4.5	-6.2	-0.7	5.3	-7.4	-0.5
Share	40.9	35.2	6.2	41.2	34.8	6.1

Source: Emmert et al. 2001

measures. At the time, the Social Democratic opposition considered pension cuts unnecessary and pleaded instead for a refinancing of non-contributory benefits (including the additional burden for the statutory pension insurance resulting from German reunification) out of the federal budget (Nullmeier 1996; Hinrichs 1998).

It is noteworthy that the government passed this law without consulting the Social Democrats, let alone seeking their consent (Ney 2001b). In hindsight, a case can be made that at the time, the government underestimated the political risks associated with its unilateral approach. In doing so, the government faced a broad alliance of reform opponents (including parliamentary opposition, trade unions and – to a certain extent – the churches), which could successfully exploit the widespread rejection of welfare cuts (in particular pension cuts) among the electorate. For instance, the government's decision to increase the regular retirement age for women faster than planned severely undermined the Christian Democrat's electoral standing among women aged 45 to 59. In the 1998 federal elections, the CDU/CSU suffered its strongest decline precisely within this group (see table 6.2). According to Heiner Geißler (1998:81), a leading Christian Democratic politician, the decision to enforce important social policy and labour market reforms through a hegemonic rather than co-operative approach inevitably destroyed the "Alliance for Jobs" and paved the way for the subsequent defeat of the Kohl government.

The Pension Reform Act 1999 (Rentenreformgesetz 1999)

Despite the fierce political controversy triggered by the Growth and Employment Promotion Act, the impact of this reform on the long-term development of pension contributions is very limited (see table 6.1). Moreover, the reform did not even prevent a further increase of contribution levels in the short run. In 1997 the pension contribution increased from 19.2 to 20.3% and threatened to rise to a further all-time high of 21% in 1998 (Hinrichs 1998). Against this backdrop, the Kohl government decided to take further and even more comprehensive measures in pension policy prior to the 1998 federal elections. In 1997 it adopted a major reform of the public pension insurance (Pension Reform Act 1999). The key elements of this reform were:

– a lower adjustment of pensions due to the introduction of a demographic factor into the pension formula. This would lead to a reduction of the standard pension level from 70% to 64% (for both current and future pensioners);
– tighter eligibility criteria for disability pensions;
– improved credits for child rearing (to be credited *in addition* to employment-related entitlements);
– a higher federal grant aimed at covering non-contributory benefits and financed by a 1% increase in the VAT;
– improved conditions for the development of occupational old age provisions through various labour law measures (Niemeyer 1998; Arbeiterkammer Bremen 2000).

According to official estimates, the 1999 reform would have dampened the long-term increase in contribution rates by about 3% (see table 6.1). Moreover, by raising the VAT rate from 15% to 16% and channeling the additional revenues into the public pension insurance the reform allowed for a short-term stabilisation of the contribution rate at the 1997 level (20.3%).

However, apart from the latter measure, the reform never became effective, because the red-green government suspended implementation shortly after it assumed office in 1998. In the following section, I will briefly portray the decision-making process that led to the adoption and subsequent suspension of the Pension Reform Act 1999.

As mentioned above, in May 1996, the Kohl government set up a commission, chaired by Labour Minister Blüm, to prepare a comprehensive pension reform plan. Initially the commission was supposed to include representatives of all the major parties and relevant interest groups. However, from the outset, the Social Democrats refused to co-operate and set up their own pension commission. The government commission was also supposed to represent a broad spectrum of pension experts including those who favoured a radical restructuring of the pension system. However, the majority of commission members (more or less determined by the Labour minister) advocated incremental reforms *within* the existing system. Hence, not very surprisingly, the final report (published in January 1997) recommended that the basic principles of the statutory pension insurance (e.g., equivalence principle, pay-as-you-go financing) should be maintained. The commission proposed the introduction of a demographic factor in the pension formula that would gradually reduce the net replacement ratio for a standard pensioner (for both current and future pensioners) from about 70% to 64% over the period to 2030 (BMAS 1997; Richter 2001).[4]

Within the coalition parties, the reactions to this report were mixed. Even members within the CDU contested the commission's proposals. Representatives of the business wing in particular urged a more rapid reduction of pension levels and demanded an increase in the regular retirement age, a measure that had been considered unnecessary by the expert commission. Kurt Biedenkopf, the government leader of Saxony and a member of the party's pension commission proposed a more radical reform, calling for a universal public basic pension to be complemented by private old age provisions. However, these positions did not obtain a majority within the CDU. Ultimately, the proposal presented by the expert commission was largely accepted by the party's own pension commission and by the CDU/CSU national executive committee (*Bundesvorstand*). However, the CDU commission modified the proposal insofar as it suggested an increase of the federal subsidy to the pension system to cover a higher share of non-contributory benefits. This modification was primarily enforced by Blüm and his allies from the party's employee-wing against the resistance of the Finance Minister. It needs to be emphasised that the interest aggregation within the CDU's pension commission was achieved by majority vote rather than by negotiation.[5] As a consequence, the official position of the CDU did not take into account the minority interest of the party's business wing and therefore largely reflected the positions of the Labour Minister (Richter 2001).

The liberal coalition partner, by contrast, was rather critical of the expert commission's recommendations from the outset. The Liberals demanded a stronger and quicker reduction of the pension levels as well as a higher retirement age. These measures were intended to keep the necessary contribution rate below 20%. Moreover, the FDP summarily rejected the plan to extend social insurance coverage to various groups of atypical employees (such as persons in low-paid jobs), a suggestion made by the commission and seized upon by the CDU. The FDP also fiercely opposed the idea of increasing the federal subsidy of pension insurance (Richter 2001).

In April 1997, the government parties formed a joint working group (*Koalitionsarbeitsgruppe*), which basically agreed on the model proposed by the CDU (including the increase of the federal subsidy financed by a 1% increase of the value-added tax). However, as a concession to the FDP, it withdrew the plan to extend social insurance coverage. In principle, the decision-making procedures within the coalition working group largely followed a pattern of "negative co-ordination" (Scharpf 1997b). Each party entered the negotiations with a fixed catalogue of single demands and sought to block every proposal that ran counter to its own interests. This tended to favour the actor whose policy position was closest to the status quo, i.e., the Christian Democrats' labour wing. By contrast, the FDP, which sought greater changes to the status quo, had a much weaker bargaining position, the more so because it was the smallest coalition partner (Richter 2001).

After the coalition parties had worked out a common reform concept, they tried to obtain the approval of the Social Democratic opposition. The SPD, however, was unwilling to co-operate with the government. The Social Democrats had set up their own pension commission, whose reform proposals primarily addressed the revenue side of the pension insurance issue. According to these proposals, no benefit cuts were needed to consolidate the pension system. Instead, certain groups of hitherto non-covered employees were to have mandatory insurance. Moreover, the report advocated the financing of all non-contributory benefits through general taxes, rather than through wage-based contributions (SPD 1997).

However, the SPD's "official" position in pension policy obscured significant disagreements within the party. Its status as an opposition party prevented the emergence of intra-party conflicts between "traditionalists", eager to reject demands for benefit cuts, and "modernisers", basically acknowledging the indispensability of curtailments. In the absence of government responsibility, these disagreements could be more or less kept under control. At the same time, both wings shared a common interest in defeating the Kohl government in the approaching federal elections. Given the electoral salience of the pension issue, the SPD decided to launch an election campaign against the government's pension cuts. Consequently, the SPD denounced the benefit curtailments as "indecent" and announced a reversal of the pension reform after it returned to power (Reuber 2000).

In May 1997, the Labour Minister offered to negotiate with the social partners. It was only at this point, that the social partners were given any direct access to the decision-making process. However, Blüm was largely bound by the decisions made by the coalition partners and therefore had only limited leeway to make concessions. At the same time, trade unions were unwilling to accommodate the government in the absence of substantial concessions. Furthermore, the chances for an amicable agreement between the government and the trade unions had been radically diminished through the most recent measures adopted in the Growth and Employment Promotion Act. These measures had seriously poisoned the mutual relations and thereby impeded a policy-oriented bargaining process, even if the unions might have accepted modest pension cuts in principle. Consequently, the trade unions did not achieve significant changes to the 1999 pension reform proposal.

A case can be made that the earlier conflicts with the Kohl government had altered the unions' interaction orientation vis-à-vis the government. The German unions saw themselves confronted with a – from their viewpoint – increasingly hostile stance by the government concerning labour and social policy issues. As a consequence, they decided to forego minor concessions in the bargaining arena and instead embarked on a confrontational strategy vis-à-vis the Kohl government. In doing so, they contributed to the electoral defeat of the bourgeois government and its displacement by a more labour-friendly alternative. As a part of this strategy, German trade unions supported the election campaign of the Social Democratic opposition with generous donations in the hope that the Social Democrats would undo the social policy and labour market reforms adopted by the Kohl government. In hindsight, unions' mobilisation strategy against the Kohl government turned out to be successful.

In its initial version, the pension bill worked out by the governing parties required the approval by the upper house (*Bundesrat*) to become effective. However, the Social Democrats formed a majority in the *Bundesrat* at the time, and they would have definitely blocked the overall reform package. To circumvent the institutional veto power of the *Bundesrat*, the government decided to split the reform package into two parts. The first part comprised the actual pension reform law, which did not require *Bundesrat* consent. The second part concerned the increase of the value added tax from 15% to 16%. This money was supposed to be used to channel additional resources into the pension system in order to avoid rising pension contribution rates. The second part could only be adopted with the approval of the SPD-led *Länder* in the upper house. The split of the reform package confronted the Social Democrats with a dilemma. On the one hand, the SPD had itself repeatedly called for a higher federal subsidy for pension insurance as a means of financing non-contributory benefits. On the other hand, the Social De-mocrats feared that the public would misunderstand the SPD's approval of this part of the reform in the sense that they might also hold the SPD respon-sible for the pension cuts. After protracted negotiations in the mediating committee (*Vermittlungsausschuß*) the SPD decided to approve this bill without major modifications. Without its approval in the *Bundesrat* the SPD would have brought about an increase in the pension contribution rate from 20.3% in 1997 to 21% in 1998, a development for which it did not like to be held responsible (Hinrichs 1998; Richter 2001).

The imminent increase in the contribution rate, which loomed after the summer of 1997, also caused renewed tensions between the coalition part-ners. Initially the entire reform proposal was supposed to go into effect in 1999. However, in response to the immediate threat of rising contributions, the CDU executive committee, along with the FDP, decided to implement the reform in 1998 instead. This again was fiercely contested by the CSU, which was determined to avoid a non-increase of pensions in an election year. Only after protracted controversies within the government could a compro-mise be reached. While the increase in the value-added tax (needed to sta-bilise the contribution rate) and the enhanced credits for child-rearing would become effective in April 1998, the reduction of the pension level would only begin in 1999 (Richter 2001).

By and large, however, the reform concept decided by the coalition work-ing group was legislated without substantial modifications. Even in the for-mal legislative process the bill was only amended slightly. The final reform, comprising relatively modest benefit cuts without any changes in the archi-tecture of the overall pension system, primarily reflects the pension policy positions of Labour minister Blüm. Backed by Chancellor Kohl, Blüm con-trolled the political decision-making process from the outset and was able to contain the influence of the market-liberal forces within his own party. In particular, Blüm effectively prevented his intra-party opponents from join-ing forces with the FDP.

The issue of pension cuts can hardly be overestimated as a key factor in the disastrous defeat of the Kohl government in the 1998 elections. An over-whelming majority of German voters considered pensions one of the most pressing political issues in the run-up to the 1998 elections. According to an opinion poll conducted by the opinion research institute FORSA (1998), 60.1% of respondents regarded this task as being personally "very impor-tant", 35.9% as "important". Thus, this issue was highly salient among German voters (Klein and Ohr 2001). At the same time, many voters had lost their trust in the Christian Democrats' capacity to preserve pensions. While in 1989, about one-third of voters believed the CDU/CSU was the most competent party with respect to the preservation of the pension system, less than 20% of voters were still of this opinion in 1997 and 1998. By contrast, the corresponding share for the Social Democrats still scored above 30% (Forschungsgruppe Wahlen). These factors combined to contribute to the worst electoral defeat of the Christian Democrats since 1949. Table 6.2 displays the changes in vote shares for the government parties and for the SPD by age and gender. A number of interesting findings emerge: First, the Christian Democratic vote losses reveal a pronounced age-specific pattern. To a significant extent, the Christian Democrats suffered these losses among people of retirement age (60 years or older), who lack the capacity to compensate for cuts in public pensions through increased private saving. Within this group, the CDU/CSU vote share fell by 6.2%. The losses were even more pronounced among those close to retirement, i.e., people aged 45-59 (9%). Like pensioners, this age group has only limited abilities to balance lower public pensions by means of more private old age provisions. In addition, their pension entitlements enjoy a lower degree of legal safeguards than is true for current pension payments. By the same token, the increase in the legal retirement age legislated in 1996 was of great concern for this age group, whereas it was irrelevant for current pensioners. Hence, it should not come as a surprise that elderly workers were most likely to change their voting behaviour in response to the pension cuts adopted by the Kohl government. By contrast, the Christian Democratic losses were relatively modest among younger voters, in particular within the age group below 25 years (1.7%), for which pension cuts are not critical to their voting decision.

A further indication of the electoral salience of the pension issue in the 1998 elections was the fact that the age-specific profile of the voter drain from the CDU/CSU is most pronounced among women. As pointed out above, the swift increase in the retirement age for women from 60 to 65, that had been legislated in 1996 and went into effect as of 2001, may explain the fact that the Christian Democrats suffered dramatic losses among women aged 45-60 (10.4%). What is more, women's pensions are often considerably lower than those of men. Hence, pension cuts are likely to be more tangible for women. This may explain the fact, that CDU/CSU losses were higher among female pensioners (8.8%) than among male retirees (5.1%).

Finally, the Liberals only suffered minor electoral declines when compared to the Christian Democrats and their losses do not reveal a clear age-specific pattern. This suggests that the core FDP voters are mostly high-income earners with a sizeable private retirement incomes and are thus only modestly affected by public pension cuts. Thus, from a vote-seeking perspective, market-liberal parties advocating pension curtailments are at less risk from an electoral perspective than Christian Democratic parties.

By contrast, the SPD achieved its largest gains among elderly voters. The Social Democrats not only succeeded in enhancing the electoral salience of the pension issue, but also in undermining the government's reputation as a trustworthy defender of the existing public pension system. Moreover, the SPD successfully presented itself as a credible alternative in that respect and attracted the lion's share of voters dissatisfied with the Kohl government's pension cuts. At the same time, it was able to fully mobilise its own core voters. These trends are reflected in the fact that voter turnout in 1998 (82.2%) was significantly higher than in the previous federal elections in 1994 (79%). Consequently, for the first time in its history the SPD attained a massive lead of 5.7% over the Christian Democrats (Emmert et al. 2001).

Three factors account for the sweeping success of the Social Democratic pension campaign. First, since the SPD was an opposition party it could not be held responsible for the pension cuts legislated in the 1990s and thus, its reputation as a defender of the public pension system remained largely intact in 1998. Second, the SPD received massive support from trade unions, which had also opposed the Kohl government benefit curtailments. It was clear that union support helped the SPD mobilise its key constituencies. Third, the 1999 pension reform was adopted at a relatively late stage in the legislative term, which made it extra difficult for the government to keep this issue out of the federal election campaign.

Pension politics under the red-green government

Shortly after their election victory in 1998, the Social Democrats lived up to their campaign promise and suspended the demographic factor as well the reform of invalidity pensions.[6] Moreover, the red-green coalition government enacted a number of measures to strengthen the revenue base of the statutory pension insurance. In particular, it extended coverage of social insurance in the area of atypical employment. In addition, the Schröder government further increased the federal subsidy to the pension scheme, which was largely financed by a new tax increase on energy consumption. These measures helped lower the pension contribution rate from 20.3% in April 1999 to 19.1% in January 2001 (Bönker and Wollmann 2001).

However, these reforms largely exhausted the political and legal leeway for an enhancement of the federal grant within the logic of the existing system, revolving around the principle of contributory social insurance (Bönker and Wollmann 2001). The federal grant now covers virtually all non-contributory benefits, including credits for child rearing and the costs of re-unification. Even the public pension insurance funds, which had hitherto repeatedly called for an extension of the federal grant, now share this view (Standfest 1999). These reforms were adopted without major conflicts within the government coalition, all the more so since these steps had already been proposed by the SPD prior to the election.

Beyond these measures, however, no consensus whatsoever existed within the Social Democratic Party over the future course in pension policy.[7] The hitherto suppressed differences of policy positions between "traditionalists" and "modernisers" were now about to break out into the open. Within the government, the "modernisers" began to gain the upper hand after 1998. Gerhard Schröder, himself an exponent of modernisation, opted for another moderniser, Walter Riester, the former vice-chairman of IG Metall, as his Minister of Social Affairs over the "traditionalist" Rudolf Dreßler, who had been the party's social policy spokesmen for many years. Moreover, in the spring of 1999 Oskar Lafontaine, a representative of the party's left-wing, suddenly and unexpectedly resigned as party chairman and Finance Minister. He was replaced by Hans Eichel as Finance Minister, an outspoken proponent of a tight fiscal policy. Thus, within the SPD leadership the centre of gravity clearly shifted toward more reform-oriented forces. Social and fiscal policy increasingly concentrated on the goal of stable contribution rates and of a balanced public budget.

However, this re-orientation, in combination with the persistent financial problems of the public pension system, confronted the SPD with a dilemma of its own making. Any significant cut in pensions would violate voter as well as union expectations for the less painful reform that the SPD had announced in its election campaign. Moreover, by not co-operating with the Kohl government in 1997, the SPD had clearly undermined its chances of attracting Christian Democratic support for a broad cross-party consensus (Anderson and Meyer 2003).

From the outset, the Schröder government was aware of the necessity of incisive cost containment reforms in the pension system, which would compensate for the demographic factor. Moreover, as a consequence of the shift towards a tight fiscal policy, statutory pension insurance again became a primary target for retrenchment to increase budgetary savings. In an effort to gain time for a more comprehensive pension reform, the Schröder government took a number of – immediately effective – emergency measures aimed at cutting rising pension costs (and thus lowering the burden on the public budget). One of the most important – albeit, largely ignored – savings measures involved the drastic reduction of the assessment base of pension contributions involving military/civilian service and receipt of unemployment assistance.[8] This measure immediately relieved the federal budget (due to lower state contributions to the pension insurance) but would also entail correspondingly reduced pension entitlements for the groups concerned.

What is more, in striking contrast to its promise of only a few months earlier, in June 1999, the Schröder government decided to suspend the indexation of net wages for two years and to switch to consumer price indexation instead.[9] Due to lower taxes and improved child benefits, net wages increased dramatically during this time. Had the indexation of the development of net wages been retained, this would have caused a sharp increase in pension outlays and thus a higher contribution rate. In order to prevent this, the government temporarily switched to price indexation. Interestingly, the short-term effects of this measure on the net replacement ratio were estimated to dramatically exceed those of the suspended demographic factor. According to Labour Ministry calculations, the pension level would fall from 70% to 67.6% within two years (*Handelsblatt*, 19-20 June 1999).[10]

This measure triggered widespread public criticism, even within the Social Democratic party itself. The unions, too, fiercely rejected this measure. The opposition parties accused the government of having breached its election promise and having fooled pensioners with some arbitrary pension cuts.[11] The Christian Democrats picked the arbitrary pension cuts as a major theme in the subsequent *Länder*-level elections. In a letter to all German pensioners, they denounced the cuts as *"the greatest election fraud in the history of the FRG"* (*Süddeutsche Zeitung*, 17 June 1999).

According to Wolfgang Schäuble, the party leader of the Christian Democrats at the time, this campaign met with a far larger public response the party could have hoped for (Schäuble 2001). Consequently, the SPD suffered a dramatic decline in voter trust as a defender of pensioners' "acquired" rights. According to an opinion survey conducted in September 1999, only 18% of voters still believed that the SPD was the most credible party in the current pension debate (FORSA 1999a). The government's unexpected pension cuts also contributed to the disastrous electoral defeat of the SPD in the following elections at the local and the *Länder* levels. In some of these elections the Social Democrats suffered double-digit declines in their vote shares. This is probably due to the fact that many traditional Social Democratic voters didn't vote or – in East Germany – switched to the post-communist PDS (Universität Kassel 2002). But, on the other hand, with the exception of Thuringia, the CDU was unable to capitalise and attract these disillusioned voters. In three elections, the CDU also suffered substantial vote losses in absolute terms (albeit, not as dramatically as the SPD). Arguably, the German Christian Democrats owe their *relative* success in these elections to the fact that they undermined the reputation of the SPD on salient issues such as pension policy. The Social Democrats, therefore, had a very difficult time mobilising traditional core voters.

The temporary suspension of net-wage indexation was accompanied by the guiding principles for major pension reform as presented by the Labour Ministry (see also table 6.3). Riester's proposals sought among other things:

– the introduction of a supplementary pension pillar on a mandatory and fully funded basis financed by workers contributions amounting to 2.5% of gross earnings;
– the introduction of a tax-financed and means-tested minimum protection *within* the statutory pension insurance;
– the creation of independent (rather than derived) pension claims for married women;
– a reform of disability pensions.

Moreover, about one year later, the government presented further proposals to contain pension expenditures. Apart from cuts in widows' pensions for those under age 40, the reform draft presented in May 2000 proposed a radical reduction in benefit levels for future pensioners. The idea behind this so-called offset factor (*Ausgleichsfaktor*) is to make the benefit level in the public pillar dependent upon the specific capacity of each age group to set up old age provisions on a private basis. Current pensioners lacking the capacity to offset pension curtailments through increased individual retirement provisions would be spared from pension level reductions. By contrast, younger age groups, capable of pursuing individual old age provisions over the long term, would have to accept a substantially lower pension from the public scheme. Age groups retiring in 2050 would therefore only receive a standard pension level of 54% rather than the current 70%. Perhaps, the government was also hoping that the reform would be politically more feasible if current pensioners were exempted from the cutbacks. Interestingly, these reform plans went far beyond the plans of the preceding bourgeois government, which only sought a reduction of the standard pension level to 64% and had largely confined itself to reforms *within* the existing pension system.

The Schröder government had to overcome many political obstacles and was forced to modify the original reform package over and over again in almost every respect. Table 6.3 gives an impression of the many changes made in response to various political objections. From the outset, virtually all of the reform proposals presented by the red-green government were fiercely criticised on several fronts:

The concept of a private mandatory pillar became the first victim of widespread public criticism. Apart from the employers, all of the other relevant actors opposed the idea of making private old age provisions obligatory. The Christian Democratic opposition criticised this plan by arguing that it was a one-sided burden on low-wage earners. Trade unions were also critical of the idea of partly replacing public pensions with private old age provisions and regarded this as turning away from the principle of parity financing between employers and employees, a principle that is deeply entrenched in the German social insurance system. In the eyes of the trade unions, a substantial shift towards private old age provisions would distribute the rising financing burden for old age provisions solely on to the shoulders of the wage earners instead of equally between employees and employers. Serious concerns were raised against this proposal, even within the governing parties, in particular by the green coalition partner, who objected to it, calling it a form of "paternalistic social policy" (*bevormundende Sozialpolitik*). Moreover, from a constitutional point of view it was unclear whether a private mandatory solution would fall under the legislative competency of the federal state (Dünn and Fasshauer 2001). Perhaps most importantly, *BILD*, the largest German tabloid, campaigned heavily against this plan. This campaign shifted the balance within the government so that it ended up withdrawing the proposal within a few days (Reuber 2000). Faced with disastrous opinion poll data and a number of important *Länder* elections, the government apparently feared negative electoral repercussions and thus opted for a voluntary solution supported by state subsidies.

Another contentious point was the harsh reduction of pension levels that would have been associated with the introduction of the offset factor. The main critique towards the offset factor focused on the fact that it would leave a great share of future pensioners with pensions at or at least close to the level of social assistance and thus undermine the legitimation basis of the system. This criticism was not only shared by the unions, but also by the Christian Democratic opposition; the pension funds association, the VDR; and a large contingent of the SPD, particularly the party's left wing. Only the employers and the market-liberal FDP regarded this concept favourably. Thus, the government was again forced to reconsider its proposals (see below).

Table 6.3 The German pension reform 2001: The major stages of the reform process

	BMAS[1] Cabinet Draft decision	Draft by the coalition working group ("Eckpunkte-papier")	Concept paper by the coalition working group	Concept paper by the coalition working group	Legislative draft	Changes in response to public hearings in the Bundestag	Further changes in the final legislative acts
Date	17 June 1999/ 23 June 1999	15 Jan 2000	30 May 2000	18 July 2000	14 Nov. 2000	11-13 Dec. 2000/ 19 Jan. 2001	26 Jan. 2001 11 May 2001
Indexation	Net wage indexation replaced by consumer price indexation in 2000 & 2001				Return to net wage indexation in 2001		
Pension formulae	-		Compensation factor I: Level of newly granted pensions gradually lowered from 70% to 54% (until 2050). Modified net wage indexation for current pensions.	Compensation factor II: Level of pensions granted from 2011 onwards will be gradually reduced to 64%[2] until 2030. Modified net wage indexation for current pensions.		Compensation factor replaced by more modest cuts affecting both current and newly granted pensions.	"Niveausicherungs-klausel" Pension level not allowed to fall below 67% of net wages.
Fully funded old age provisions	Private mandatory old age provisions (2.5% of gross wage)	Voluntary. State subsidies for low-wage earners (2.5% of gross wage).	Voluntary. State subsidies for low- and middle-wage earners (4% of gross wage).	Voluntary. State subsidies or tax relief for all wage earners (4% of gross wage). Special supplements for families with children. Entitlement to convert 4% of gross wage into an occupational pension.			Tax-free allowance for private/occupational pensions stipulated at 4% of contribution ceiling. Promotion of home ownership. Introduction of pension funds.

	BMAS'[1] Cabinet Draft decision	Draft by the coalition working group ("Eckpunktepapier")	Concept paper by the coalition working group	Concept paper by the coalition working group	Legislative draft	Changes in response to public hearings in the Bundestag	Further changes in the final legislative acts
Minimum protection	Tax-financed means-tested minimum protection within the GRV.[3]		Eased eligibility criteria for pensioners claiming social assistance.				
Old age provisions for women	"Optionsmodell"	Limited "Optionsmodell"		Cuts in widows' pensions with child-related supplements (later amended by the option to split entitlements between spouses)	Cuts in widow pensions softened. Pension splitting confined to people with at least 25 contribution years.		Cuts in widow pensions further softened.

1 Ministry of Labour and Social Order
2 Corresponding to 61% according to the old formulae
3 Statutory pension insurance
Source: Compilation by the author based on Dünn and Fasshauer (2001)

Finally, the government's plan to establish a system of minimum protection within the public pension system met with considerable political resistance, in particular from the bourgeois opposition parties, employers, and the VDR. The main criticism centred around the idea that the separation between contribution-related pension insurance and means-tested social assistance geared towards poverty prevention had to be maintained at all costs. The critics of this reform element also feared that the institutional blurring of the difference between social insurance and social assistance would give rise to an expanded black economy and further undermine the acceptance of the statutory pension insurance with its strong emphasis on the principle of equivalence between contributions and benefits (Ruland 1999; Bönker and Wollmann 2001; Dünn and Fasshauer 2001).

The widespread criticism and fierce protests triggered by the proposed reform package may have been in part the result of the fact that the Ministry of Labour developed the reform guidelines more or less single-handedly, without appropriate preparation and without really consulting the social partners and the public pension insurance bodies.[12] Faced with such a broad front of critics both inside and outside the government, Labour Minister Riester added a number of far-reaching substantive changes to the original reform concept. These changes were primarily aimed at meeting Christian Democratic demands. The government had at least three powerful reasons to seek their approval. First, given the potential electoral salience of the pension issue, the government sought to share the political costs associated with highly unpopular pension curtailments. Second, by forging an alliance with the opposition, Schröder tried to limit the influence of trade unionists and leftist reform opponents within his own party. By striking a pension deal with the Christian Democrats, the "modernisers" within the government would be able to achieve a more comprehensive reform than would be politically feasible if the interests of trade unionists and leftist forces within the party had to be taken into account. Third, parts of the reform required the approval by the *Bundesrat*, in which the SPD-led *Länder* lacked a clear majority.

The government made concessions to basically all of the Christian Democrats criticisms. The original plan of a private mandatory pension pillar and of a minimum protection plan within pension insurance (both elements had been strongly opposed by the CDU/CSU) were dropped at a relatively early stage. They did, however, retain the offset factor, which had been severely criticised, but they modified it so that the standard pension level would not fall below 64% even beyond 2030 (in September 2000 the government also announced the return to net wage indexation for the year

2001). In addition, the government made concessions in the area of widow pensions. Most importantly, the government – against the bitter resistance of the Finance Minister – even over-fulfilled Christian Democratic demands for a substantial extension of state subsidies and tax relief to private old age provisions, in particular for families with children (Reiermann and Sauga 2000).

Despite these numerous and comprehensive government concessions, the Christian Democrats continued to reject a common pension reform agreement with the red-green coalition. A strong case can be made for the notion that the Christian Democrats were not opposing the reform on policy content grounds. To a large extent, they shared the principles underlying the government's reform proposal. Like the government, they acknowledged the need for cuts in the pension levels and advocated a move to a multi-pillar system (Bönker and Wollmann 2001). It appeared that the Christian Democrats were internally split on the question of whether they should back the government or not. In the end, the opponents of a consensual solution gained the upper hand, which again led to a break-down of the extra-parliamentary compromise talks in October 2000. Perhaps, the successful Social Democratic pension campaign against the Kohl government in 1997 and 1998 had considerably diminished the government's prospects for attracting the support of the opposition for a cross-party consensus (Anderson and Meyer 2003). Now it was the Christian Democrats who sought to exploit the pension issue in the electoral arena. They also had a strong competitive interest in having the intra-governmental conflicts over pension reform continue, so as to again damage the government's electoral prospects. A swift agreement with the government would have most likely put an end to the quarrels within the government and thus – albeit, indirectly – diminished the electoral standing of the Christian Democrats.

Interestingly, the oppositional FDP appeared to be much more willing to arrive at a pension consensus with the government than the Christian Democrats, who left the extra-parliamentary consensus talks with the government parties, while the FDP continued to engage in cross-party negotiations, in which the key guidelines for a reform of the pension system were worked out. Leading Liberals publicly acknowledged the compromise orientation of the red-green coalition, whereas they blamed the Christian Democrats for thwarting a cross-party consensus (*Handelsblatt*, 13 July 2000 and 16 August 2000). Given that the FDP tends to take prominent market-liberal positions in social and economic policy, its pension policy positions were by no means congruent with those of the government. However, the FDP had only limited incentives to exploit the pension issue in the electoral arena. More specifically, in contrast to the Christian Democrats, the Liberals had no serious hopes of attracting a significant share of swing voters alienated by the pension cuts adopted by a leftist government. However, by offering its co-operation to the red-green government it sought to move the final reform outcome closer to its own ideal point and by this, strengthen its attractiveness vis-à-vis its own core voters, who were likely to accept pension cuts in exchange for lower taxes and contributions. Finally, the degree of positional conflict with the SPD was softened by the fact that the FDP had an interest in presenting itself as a potential coalition partner to the SPD after the election. Yet, an agreement with the Schröder government was doomed to fail as soon as the government was forced to make substantial concessions to the trade unions and thereby distanced itself once again from the FDP's positions.

Without the backing of the Christian Democrats, the government became dependent on the unconditional support of its own deputies in order to obtain a majority in parliament. However, the SPD faced massive difficulties in aligning trade unionists and its left-wing representatives. Initially, Riester was successful in averting the amendments put forward by these groups. In the party executive, nine members, largely union representatives and left-wingers, voted against his reform concept but were overruled by a majority of 19 votes. Even within the parliamentary group, the concept was approved by a majority of 70% (*Handelsblatt*, 5 July 2000). However, in the autumn of 2000, about 30 Social Democratic deputies publicly announced they were voting against the bill, unless the government substantially modified its reform concept. Without their votes, Riester's reform plan would lack a parliamentary majority.

As a consequence, the government had to make substantial concessions to the Social Democratic leftwingers and to the trade unions, which used their influence within the SPD parliamentary group as a bargaining chip vis-à-vis the government. Only after a number of their key demands were met, did the unions offer their consent. In response to these pressures the government once more changed its pension plans. First, the offset factor which was supposed to gradually reduce the standard pension level as of 2011 for newly granted pensions (while leaving current pensions untouched) was expunged. Instead, unions pushed through an alternative indexation factor (affecting current and future pensioners alike), which was to reduce the future pension level to a lesser extent than with the offset factor. The success of the unions in overthrowing the offset factor was facilitated by the fact that numerous other actors both inside and outside the government (such as the Greens, opposition parties, the VDR and BfA, the VdK,[13] employers' organisations, the churches, as well as the overwhelming majority of academic pension experts) also opposed the offset factor. They were all critical of the idea that the pension level should become dependent upon the point in time at which a person retires and thus entail benefit cuts only for those retiring after 2011. This method would impose an undue burden on the younger generation and hence violate inter-generational equity. At a public hearing held in December 2000, the offset factor was met with almost unanimous criticism (*Deutscher Bundestag* 2000).

Second, unions achieved the acknowledgement that collectively-agreed pension provisions would take precedence over private provisions (*Tarifvorbehalt*). This was to give the unions a say in the area of fully funded supplementary old age provisions.[14] The unions were able to achieve these modifications by forging a strategic alliance with the SPD's leftwing. This alliance gave the reform opponents a strong veto power as is illustrated by the following quotation from Andrea Nahles (2001), a prominent leftwing party representative:

> For strategic reasons, the SPD leftists needed the trade unions and their backing in society as leverage. Conversely, trade unions would not have been able to exert such a large influence without the blocking power of the left-wing within the party's parliamentary group" (translation by the author).

After the protracted conflicts between the government and the trade unions were settled, it was still unclear whether the pension bill would pass the *Bundesrat*, where the Social Democratic *Länder* lacked a clear majority. Therefore the government decided to split the reform package into two parts. One part, concerning the reform of statutory pension insurance, did not require the approval of the second chamber. Apart from a significant last-minute modification,[15] this part of the reform passed the legislative process largely unaltered.

The other part, which concerned the promotion of private provisions and the new regulations for a means-tested basic security for disabled and elderly people within the framework of social assistance, could only become a law if a majority in the *Bundesrat* voted in favour of the bill. A number of contested issues still had to be resolved in order to muster this majority. For instance, the financing of the pension reform was a highly controversial subject between the *Bund* and the *Länder*. Even the SPD-led *Länder* were concerned about huge expenditures associated with the administration of the private system and the introduction of the means-tested basic security and about high tax shortfalls resulting from the promotion of private pensions. Hence, they pressed for a stronger financial engagement of the *Bund*.

Moreover, the SPD and the Greens did not have a majority in the *Bundesrat*. The government could not count on the support of the *Länder* governed by the Christian Democrats (or by a conservative-liberal coalition), who would most likely block the reform and demand higher subsidies for low-income earners, the withdrawing of the cuts in widows' pensions, and the inclusion of home ownership into the catalogue of products under old age provisions that were to profit from state subsidies. Against this background, the government depended on the additional support of at least two of the *Länder* where the SPD shared power with either the CDU (Brandenburg, Berlin, Bremen), the FDP (Rhineland-Palatinate) or the post-communist PDS (Mecklenburg-Western Pomerania). In the first round, the *Bundesrat* rejected the pension bill and commissioned the reconciliation committee (*Vermittlungsausschuß*) to hammer out a compromise.

After protracted negotiations, the Schröder government finally won the approval of the *Bundesrat* in May 2001. This success was largely based on a deal between the federal government and the two *Bundesländer* Berlin and Brandenburg, both of which faced extraordinarily strong budgetary pressures. This deal provided that the new agency for the administration of the state subsidies to private old age provisions would be placed in Berlin and Brandenburg, which would create about 1,000 new jobs for a region suffering from very high unemployment. As a further concession to the Christian Democrats, the government also agreed to moderate the curtailments of widows' pensions, although this reform element did not actually require the approval by the *Bundesrat*. Furthermore, the social-liberal coalition in Rhineland-Palatinate approved the compromise, after the government had included home ownership in the catalogue of products of old age provisions to be subsidised. Finally, the government also offered increased financial compensation to the *Länder*.

The final pension legislation adopted in 2001 deviates strongly from the original reform concept in almost every respect:

First, the volume of curtailments was to be considerably lower than initially thought. Cuts in widows' pensions would be far less severe, and the standard pension level would not fall below 67% of net wages,[16] whereas the offset factor – in its initial version – would have meant a standard pension level of 54% by 2050. Nevertheless, the overall effects of this reform on future contribution rates will be at least as strong as those of the suspended "demographic factor" introduced by the Kohl government.[17] Moreover, two-thirds of these cutbacks will become effective before 2005 (Hain and

Tautz 2001), a finding which is at odds with the idea that pension reforms are likely to be designed in a way so that the bulk of savings will only accrue in the distant future and leave current pensioners – or, like in Italy, even the majority of current wage earners – largely untouched.

Second, the fully funded pension pillar was to be voluntary, not mandatory. Moreover, in contrast to the original concept, the public promotion of private old age provisions would not be confined to relatively modest subsidies for low-wage earners but include either subsidies or tax incentives for all wage earners at a very generous level. The current reform also offers strong incentives for the strengthening of occupational pensions on the basis of collective agreements, whereas the initial plan focused exclusively on private old age provisions.

Third, there was to be no minimum needs-based standard of benefit for the elderly within the statutory pension insurance. The final law only states that needy pensioners no longer have to rely on alimony from their children before they can claim social assistance.

Characteristic features of German pension politics and their relevance for reform outcomes

A number of facts are puzzling about the German reform process. Most importantly, it is noteworthy that the reform aspirations of the red-green Schröder government were clearly more comprehensive than those of the bourgeois Kohl government. Not only did the Schröder government seek more incisive pension cuts than its predecessor, it also forcefully pursued the partial privatisation of the German pension system, whereas the 1999 pension reform was only a reform *within* the existing public system. In that sense, the Social Democratic pension reform agenda had a much stronger neo-liberal imprint than the reform attempts of the previous Christian-Liberal coalition. As Hering (2002:46) correctly points out, the German case is symptomatic of the phenomenon that it is increasingly difficult to derive governments' pension policy preferences from their partisan complexion. This is especially true for governments led by Social Democratic and Christian Democratic parties, both of which must incorporate relatively heterogeneous social policy interests. Under these conditions, the *preferred* policy outcome seldom depends primarily on the general ideological orientation of the governing parties as such, but more specifically on the ideas and interests of the crucial pension policymakers within the government, most notably the Labour Minister, the Finance Minister, and the Chancellor. Under the Kohl government, pension policy was decisively shaped by a traditionalist Labour Minister, who favoured incremental and modest reforms within the public system, an approach that was by and large also supported by Chancellor Kohl himself. By contrast, the terms of pension policy under the red-green government were – at least in the beginning – largely formulated by Walter Riester, whose approach was a rather pragmatic one and whose primary objective was the stabilisation of contribution rates. Moreover, after the leftist Finance Minister Oskar Lafontaine resigned, Riester's retrenchment efforts were not only backed by Chancellor Schröder, but also by the new Finance Minister Hans Eichel, whose primary aspiration was to balance the public budget.

However, although the Social Democratic "reformer" Walter Riester had much more ambitious reform goals than his "traditionalist" Christian Democratic predecessor Norbert Blüm, the 2001 pension reform was only slightly more effective in stabilising contributions than Blüm's demographic factor. In the case of the 1999 pension reform, the market-liberal forces within the bourgeois Kohl government could not enforce a more radical reform against the resistance of Labour Minister Blüm, who had a strong influence on the formulation of the government's pension policy proposals and who could effectively veto overly ambitious retrenchment efforts. By contrast, Riester was forced to water down his far-reaching retrenchment plans in the face of massive resistance by leftwingers and trade unionists within his own party, who could exercise their parliamentary veto powers. In other words, Blüm was not only the crucial agenda setter in the reform process, but also – in contrast to Riester – an outspoken defender of the existing pension system and thus of the status quo, a position in which he had a powerful strategic advantage vis-à-vis his intra-governmental opponents.

While Riester largely missed his target to stabilise contribution rates in the long term, he was more successful in accomplishing the goal of establishing a private and fully funded pension pillar. The Schröder government's move towards a partial privatisation of the pension system was at least partly driven by an electoral dilemma of its own making. While facing the necessity of dampening the growth of pension expenditures, the Schröder government was also bound to its election promise of replacing the "asocial" demographic factor with a reform approach more palatable to wage earners and pensioners. Quite obviously, merely replacing the demographic factor with another indexation factor with a similar impact on benefit levels would hardly have done much to convey the image of a truly innovative and more equitable reform concept.

Against this background, the creation of a private pillar of old age provisions pointed the only way out of this dilemma. First of all, this approach would not only reduce the increase in social insurance contributions but (if successful) also help secure the living standard for future pensioners.

Second, by generously promoting private retirement savings the government could greatly enhance citizens' willingness to devote a larger share of their incomes to old age provisions, in particular because low-income earners with many children would profit disproportionately from state subsidies. In contrast to both benefit cutbacks and to mandating private old age provisions, the promotion of private and occupational pensions through generous allowances and tax incentives was an opportunity to claim some credit. Public promotion of private old age provisions can be framed as a benefit rather than an added burden for wage earners. This finding is clearly confirmed by recent German opinion polls. Only a small number of German citizens (between 14% to 27% depending on the design of the opinion survey) would favour a mandatory solution, whereas a clear majority (between 60% to 78%) is against it. However, 59% support the idea that contributions to private old age provisions should be tax-free, whereas only 28% disagree (FORSA 1996; FORSA 1999b; FORSA 2000a). This suggests that the political costs of a voluntary solution are considerably lower than those of a mandatory solution, irrespective of the simple fact that tax relief measures are not necessarily a "free lunch" but have to be recouped through higher taxes elsewhere.

Third, the promotion of private pension plans offered the opportunity to switch to a less generous indexation mechanism without a lowering of the formal replacement rate. As rising (voluntary) contributions to private old age provisions will henceforth be taken into account for the calculation of net wages and the yearly pensions adjustments (see footnote 100), the formal standard pension (expressed as a percentage of net wages) was to remain at a seemingly higher level than with the demographic factor (which did not alter the defintion of net wages). This, the government hoped, would appease pensioners.

Finally, the large-scale subsidisation of private and occupational pensions was motivated by the government's desperate effort to obtain the consent of the parliamentary opposition and, after this had failed, of the trade unions. As noted above, the Christian Democratic opposition had pressed for a massive expansion of financial incentives to private old age provisions. In an attempt to pave the way for a pension consensus with the CDU/CSU, Schröder decided to meet this demand. The decision to spend up to 10 billion euros for the subsidisation of supplementary old age provisions was maintained, although the Christian Democrats continued to refuse to cooperate. After the government realised that the Christian Democratic opposition would oppose the pension reform anyway, it intensified its efforts to at least bring the trade unions on board. To that end, it adjusted its reform concept in line with union demands by taking specific steps to strengthen occupational pensions within the framework of collective agreements between the social partners.

This brings us to a further puzzle concerning the German case. In recent years, trade unions have fundamentally altered their attitude concerning the role of collectively-agreed retirement provisions in the German pension edifice. Occupational pensions traditionally played only a marginal role for employees in the private sector and in most branches were provided as a voluntary fringe benefit by the employers and thus not regulated through collective agreements between the social partners. German trade unions used to consider old age provisions first and foremost as a function performed by statutory pension insurance. Occupational pensions were primarily regarded as a possible supplement rather than as a substitute for the state pillar. Meanwhile, however, German trade unions came to accept that occupational pensions based on collective agreements must be created in order to compensate for the cuts in the public pension tier:

First, German unions became increasingly aware of the fact that they would be unable to prevent a decline of benefit levels within the public pension tier in the long run, all the more so because they lack the powerful mobilising capacity of their French and Italian counterparts. Against this background, they considered the expansion of occupational pensions through collective agreements as a necessary step to compensate for the eroding income replacement function of the public pillar. As opposed to an expansion of private forms of old age provisions, collective solutions would achieve broader coverage among low-income earners and comprise solidarity-related elements of redistribution between occupational groups with different risk profiles. Moreover, only collective solutions create the opportunity that the symbolically important principle of parity financing between employers and employees can be retained.

Secondly, German trade unions recognised that the regulation of occupational pension within the framework of collective agreements would also lie in their organisational self-interest. As German enterprises have become increasingly reluctant to accept wage settlements established by collective agreements in recent years, German unions see their institutional role as bargaining partner at the industry level seriously threatened. Hence, trade unions saw the shift of occupational retirement provisions into the collective bargaining arena also as a strategy to reinvigorate the dwindling impact of collective bargaining agreements in the German system of industrial relations. For this reason, it was mainly the collective bargaining experts in trade union organisations which supported the new approach. By contrast, social policy experts within the German trade unions were more sceptical of an expansion of occupational pensions at the expense of statutory pension insurance. They particularly feared a financial erosion of the social insurance system since contributions to occupational pension schemes would be partly exempted from social contributions. However, even within the powerful metalworkers' union IG *Metall*, where the social policy department traditionally has a prominent position, the collective bargaining experts gained the upper hand, after the Schröder government had offered very attractive tax incentives for occupational pension plans. Moreover, the trade unions in the chemical branch (IG BCE) and in the public sector (ÖTV) had negotiated industry-wide supplementary pensions at an earlier stage and therefore strongly supported the government's plans to forcefully promote occupational pensions (Hering 2002).

The generous promotion of occupational pension plans prompted the unions to accept a significant reduction of the public pension level, a reduction which they had opposed in connection with the 1999 pension reform. We can interpret the growing interest of both governmental pension policymakers and trade unions in collectively negotiated pension arrangements as the result of a learning process in which both sides detected a potential – but so far largely overlooked – win-win solution to the pension problem in Germany.

While Germany has started to rapidly expand the private/occupational pillar of its pension system, the basic features of the main scheme, the statutory pension insurance, has been remarkably resilient. Unlike in Sweden and Italy, Germany did not introduce a completely new public pension system, but only adopted minor reforms *within* the public system. Any attempts to establish a means-tested minimum pension within this system were blocked. The same is true for efforts to radically scale down the standard pension level or replace the contributory system with a tax-financed basic pension. The pension formula is still strictly based on lifetime earnings. Even the attempt to introduce a differentiation of the benefit level between existing pensions (*Bestandsrentner*) and newly granted pensions (*Zugangsrentner*) through an offset factor, as applied in Italy and Sweden, failed. Moreover, the statutory pension insurance continues to predominantly cater to blue- and white-collar employees, with self-employed and civil servants still covered by separate schemes with entirely different benefit regulations. For instance, civil servants' pensions in Germany remain based on the last salary, whereas in Italy and Austria they will be gradually aligned to the country's general scheme.[18] In summary, the key features of Germany's public pension system remained extraordinarily stable. This remarkable institutional resilience is a result of the interplay of various factors:

First, the link between earnings and contributions was already very close in the German system. In contrast to the other countries studied, the principle of lifetime earnings had been established from the outset. As a consequence, Germany didn't need to change two central parameters of the pension formula, i.e., the reference salary and the period of assessed contributions. By the same token, however, these parameters could not be altered in order to achieve savings (Anderson and Meyer 2003). German pension policymakers had to rely on changes of the accrual factor in order to achieve substantial savings. This again will inevitably boil down to an across-the-board reduction of the benefit level for all pensioners. The political problem is that this sort of retrenchment is likely to be less acceptable than the more targeted and selective cutbacks resulting from changes such as an increase in the number of "best years". The latter approach was frequently applied in other Bismarckian countries and could be more easily legitimised on grounds that this would enhance the distributive equity within the system (Myles and Quadagno 1997).

Second, the number of partisan and institutional veto players in the German political system is relatively high. Typically, Germany is ruled by multiparty governments with relatively weak parliamentary majorities. To that extent that pension reforms entail legislative changes that affect the fiscal interests of the *Länder*, governments depend on the approval by the *Bundesrat*, which may again be dominated by the parliamentary opposition. Moreover, a powerful constitutional court watches over the compliance of constitutional rules, which also implies that changes in pension legislation must not violate the property rights associated with contributory pension entitlements. Similarly, a reform of civil servants pensions towards the principle of lifetime earnings would require a change of the constitution, which again would necessitate a two-thirds majority in both the *Bundestag* and the *Bundesrat*. Due to these multiple veto factors, the defenders of the existing pension system are in a strategically advantageous position.

A further stabilising factor is the deep ideological entrenchment of the equivalence principle in the "cognitive maps" of German pension policymakers. One of the strongest proponents of this principle is the pension funds' major association, the VDR, which not only incorporates the interests of the social partners but also continues to play a dominant role as one of the main think tanks in German pension policy. On occasion, the VDR could exert a powerful influence on the preference formation of pension pol-icymakers and also end up defending the traditional core principles of the statutory pension insurance.

Moreover, the political price that German governments have to pay for unpopular and unilaterally imposed measures in pension policy is perhaps higher than in most other countries. In Germany, two traditional welfare state defenders, the Social Democrats and the Christian Democrats, are the key competitors in the electoral arena (Kitschelt 2001). In addition, fre-quent elections at the *Länder* level with a potentially powerful impact on the majorities in the *Bundesrat*, amplifies the political risks of pension re-trenchment.

Finally, the strong alignment of party competition towards two powerful welfare state parties (*Sozialstaatsparteien*) makes it even more difficult for a leftist government to keep trade unions happy with their reform policies. Union members and executives basically know that an alternative bourgeois government does not necessarily pursue a more market-liberal social policy than a Social Democratic government. Hence, they may punish liberal re-forms launched by a left-wing government via political defections (Kitschelt 2003).

To some extent, concertational strategies may overcome the political bar-riers to a major reform of the pension system. As the 1992 Pension Reform Act has shown, both the partisan and the corporatist arenas constitute a po-tential basis for a broad consensus on pension reform. However, the Ger-man case also illustrates that the political conditions for negotiated adjust-ment in pension policy may change considerably over time. Thus, it appears that in Germany situational rather than structural factors explain the suc-cess or the failure of concertational strategies in pension policy. It remains to be seen whether Germany will be able to resume the tradition of a broad political consensus in pension policy.

7   Austria: Reform Blockage by the Trade Unions

The key features of the Austrian pension system in the late 1980s

The Austrian old age pension system closely resembles the German system although the equivalence principle is weakened by a number of strong redistributive elements. Like in Germany, there are two major pension schemes for blue- and white-collar workers, which are institutionally distinct but identical in their material provisions. The self-employed in the trade and commerce sectors as well as farmers are compulsorily covered in separate schemes.

Pension regulations for civil servants differ from those of private and public employees; the latter are covered by the general schemes for dependent workers. Civil servants draw their pensions under a separate and completely tax-financed scheme like they do in Germany. The calculation base is 80% of the last gross monthly salary, reached after 35 years of service.

All gainfully employed people (except civil servants) are compulsorily insured under the general schemes granting old age, survivor, and invalidity benefits. Entitlement to old age pensions requires at least 15 years of contributions. Entitlement to benefits is also conditional on the payment of 12 monthly contributions within the last 36 months. People satisfying the contribution requirements are entitled to draw regular old age pensions from the age of 65 (men) or 60 (women). Unemployment pensions may be paid to unemployed people from the age of 60 (men) or 55 (women), on condition that they have been in receipt of unemployment benefits for the preceding 52 weeks. Early retirement pensions are payable from the age of 60 (men) or 55 (women). The necessary insurance period is 35 years, and the insured must have paid 24 monthly contributions within the last 36 months. Pension payments are based on average gross earnings over the last five years. The full pension at standard retirement age corresponds to 79.5% of assessed earnings after 45 years of contribution. The accrual factor corresponds to 1.9% per year for the first 30 insurance years, and 1.5% for the following insurance years. If the old age pension is below 50% of the calculated base, the social insurance administration may decide to pay additional benefits of up to a maximum of 10% of the calculated base. If the old age pension (together with income from other sources) is below a legally fixed minimum, the difference is paid in the form of supplementary benefits (*Ausgleichszulage*).

Pension schemes operate on a pay-as-you-go basis and are financed by earnings-related contributions (insured people 10.25% of gross earnings, employers 12.45% of payroll up to a certain ceiling). The government covers any deficits as well as the costs of the income-tested allowance.

The pension schemes are run by pension insurance institutes through a central office and provincial offices. These offices have a board consisting of two delegates from the insured employees, two from employers, and one institute staff member. Case decisions are taken unanimously or, where no agreement can be reached, by the administration (Weigel and Amann 1987).

Austria's pension reform record in the 1990s

Austria has until recently made comparatively limited progress in pension reform. The series of incremental reforms implemented since 1985 had a significant impact on public pension spending and will also dampen the future increase of pension costs. Nevertheless, without further reform of public pensions (among the highest among OECD countries), outlays are likely to rise substantially in the medium and long-term (see table 2.2). Projections by the Economic Policy Committee (2001:22) indicate that public pension expenditures in Austria – despite their very high starting point – are likely to increase faster (about 4.2% of GDP from 2000 until the peak year) than the EU average (3.2%).[1] In contrast to Italy and Sweden, Austria has not transformed its statutory pension insurance into a (notional) defined-contribution scheme. It extended the "number of best years" somewhat, up to 18 years in the general scheme, but did not establish the principle of life-time earnings in the calculation of public pensions. What is more, many changes, such as the higher retirement age for women, will be phased in extremely gradually. Moreover, fully funded pension plans remain largely underdeveloped by international standards. Quite remarkably, however, Austria has managed to extensively harmonise the benefit levels between the general scheme and the scheme for civil servants by altering the calculation basis for the latter from the last salary to the 18 best salary years (Tálos and Wörister 1998; Lißner and Wöss 1999; Prinz and Marin 1999).

Pension policy until the early 1990s

Since the mid-1980s Austrian pension policymakers have adopted a number of reforms that sought to address the financial problems of the public pension system primarily (but not exclusively) through expenditure cuts, although these cuts were accompanied by a number of selective expansionary measures, such as improved credits for child rearing. As a consequence, the rapid increase of pension costs and contribution rates was largely brought to a halt after 1985. Moreover, between 1987 and 1994 the level of state subsidies to the public pension insurance could be stabilised at between 44 to 48 billion Austrian schillings (about 3.1 to 3.4 billion euros) (Tálos and Wörister 1998).

Nevertheless, the pension reforms adopted in the second half of the 1980s and in the early 1990s entailed only very incremental changes at the margins of the public pension system. As budgetary pressures remained comparatively modest until the early 1990s, these half-hearted measures were sufficient to stabilise the pension system in the short term. However, they did not solve the long-term challenges to the Austrian pension system, in particular with regard to demographic developments. Most importantly, only marginal steps were taken to increase the actual retirement age, which is still very low by international standards. Even the 1993 pension reform, explicitly designed to tackle the problems resulting from demographic ageing, was comprised of only a few significant adjustments, such as a change of indexation from gross to net wages, which soon proved to be insufficient.

By and large, these adjustments were adopted without serious conflicts. Both the government parties and the social partners generally agreed to the goal of fiscal consolidation. Dissension only revolved around the most appropriate strategy to accomplish this goal. While both government parties[2] (in particular the ÖVP) as well as the employer organisations advocated expenditure-related consolidation measures, Austria's trade union confederation ÖGB pleaded for an additional strengthening of the revenue side (Tálos and Kittel 1999). In line with the Austrian tradition of social partnership ("*Sozialpartnerschaft*"), these conflicts were solved through intense and compromise-oriented negotiations between the ruling parties and the social partners. As a rule, the social partners initiated and negotiated proposals for pension reform before they were submitted to Parliament by the Social Ministry. Institutionally, the model of social partnership is reflected in the privileged participation of the social partners' major associations in the formulation and implementation of social and economic policy.[3] This corporatist framework also includes the so-called chambers, statutory bodies with

Table 7.1   Share of trade union functionaries in the Austrian parliament

	SPÖ		ÖVP		FPÖ		Plenum	
	absolute	%	absolute	%	absolute	%	absolute	%
1987	33	41.3	13	16.9	-	-	46	25.1
1991	30	37.5	7	11.7	1	3.0	38	21.0
1998	19	26.8	1	1.9	2	4.8	22	12.2
2000	12	18.5	1	1.9	1	1.9	14	7.3

Source: Tálos and Kittel 2001:73

compulsory membership: The Federal Economic Chamber (WKÖ), repre-senting Austria's independent entrepreneurs, the Chamber of Labour (BAK), which represents the interests of employees, and the Chamber of Agriculture (LWK) representing the country's farmers. While the ÖGB and the BAK are traditionally linked to the Socialist party, the WKÖ and the LWK have tight links to the Austrian People's Party ÖVP (Linnerooth-Bayer 2001; Pernicka 2001a). In many cases there are multiple office-holders, i.e., one person performs key functions in both a political party and in an em-ployee or employer interest association. For instance, in the early 1990s, more than one-third of SPÖ deputies were still trade union functionaries (see table 7.1). Until recently, social partnerships had informal veto powers in the Austrian political system because no major decision in economic and social policy has been taken contrary to one of the social partners (Obinger 2001). In this constellation, trade unions were also able to exert a large in-fluence on the formulation of pension policy (Tálos and Kittel 1999; Linne-rooth-Bayer 2001; Tálos and Kittel 2001). As a consequence, only marginal adjustments were made to the Austrian pension system until the early 1990s. However, the very incremental nature of Austrian pension reforms until the early 1990s was also facilitated by the fact that the fiscal situation did not necessitate drastic savings measures at the time.

The failed "Sparpaket" of 1995

This situation changed rapidly in the first half of the 1990s. After 1992, the budget deficit increased from 2% to 5% of GDP within only two years (OECD 2001). This development coincided with Austria's aspirations to join the EMU, which necessitated a quick and substantial reduction of the public deficit. At the same time, employment in the business sector deteriorated rapidly. Against this background, an increase of pension contribution rates would have further aggravated the problematic situation on the labour market.

Hence, in the mid-1990s Austria was forced to adopt a very tight fiscal policy, which would also necessitate significant cuts in the pension system. Against this background, the government in 1994 single-handedly proposed a package of budgetary emergency steps without prior consultation of the social partners. This procedure clearly deviated from the traditional pattern of corporatist concertation, because the social partners were now being asked to negotiate a consensus on a reform that they had not initiated (Linnerooth-Bayer 2001). The original savings package proposal, largely worked out by the Finance Minister, sought a multitude of spending cuts in virtually all governmental departments and in most items of the social policy budget. With respect to pensions, the governmental programme included among others the introduction of actuarial reductions in the case of early retirement (Sebald 1998).

The consolidation package was met with fierce criticism, in particular by the trade unions. Both the ÖGB and the BAK argued that the package would impose a one-sided burden on wage earners and criticised the overwhelming emphasis on expenditure-related consolidation measures. Instead, they called for measures that would strengthen state revenues. Moreover, the trade unions fiercely criticised the fact that the savings package was only discussed at the party level without involvement of the social partners. The tensions between the SPÖ and the ÖGB reached a peak, when the leader of the Metal Workers Union and of the *Fraktion Sozialdemokratischer Gewerkschafter* quit the SPÖ bargaining committee under protest. At the same time, Socialist Federal Chancellor Vranitzky also made it clear that he was willing to implement the consolidation programme against trade union resistance if necessary (Sebald 1998).

The parliamentary opposition, furiously attacked the proposed savings measures as well. The Austrian Freedom Party FPÖ, a populist right-wing party, spearheaded this criticism. After 1986, this party had improved its electoral position dramatically at the expense of both the SPÖ and the ÖVP. In the 1994 elections, the FPÖ garnered an impressive 22.5% of votes. The electoral success of the Freedom party can at least partly be attributed to the unrestrained populism of its charismatic leader Jörg Haider, a populism that was exclusively motivated by the goal to maximise votes rather than creating a coherent programme. Hence, the FPÖ, while located at the right end of the political spectrum, also sought to exploit the issue of pension cuts in the electoral arena. For instance, Haider denounced the 1995 savings package as "unsocial" and "irresponsible" (Sebald 1998:13). By the same token, he fuelled widespread public dissatisfaction over the government's decision to increase pensions only slightly in 1995 (*Neue Züricher Zeitung*, 10 November 1994). Thus, the "grand coalition" government between the socialist SPÖ and the bourgeois ÖVP was confronted with a powerful and protest-oriented opposition party, a constellation which tended to amplify the electoral costs associated with unpopular welfare reforms.

After protracted conflicts, in particular between the SPÖ and the ÖGB, the government finally caved in and made numerous concessions to the trade unions. As Sebald (1998:101) points out, the SPÖ eventually proved unable to withstand persistent political pressures form the trade unions, especially after trade unionists in Parliament had threatened to vote against the bill. Given the numerical strength of the trade unionists in the Austrian parliament, in particular within the SPÖ parliamentary group (see table 7.1), the union threat potential was extraordinarily strong. In order to obtain the unions' consent, the government watered down the austerity package substantially. Among other things, it withdrew the planned reductions for early retirement pensions. While the initial savings plan sought to achieve the sought-after budgetary savings almost exclusively through expenditure cuts, the revised package, adopted in the spring of 1995, achieved almost 60% of the sought-after savings volume through revenue-sided measures. Moreover, the overall savings volume turned out to be considerably lower than originally planned by the government. Initially, about 250 billion schillings (about 18 billion euros) were supposed to be saved by 1998. A few months later, the government only expected to be able to save between 50 and 60 billions schillings (about 3.6 to 4.3 billion euros) (Sebald 1998).

The successful "Sparpaket" of 1996

The 1995 savings package proved to be largely ineffective with respect to the goal of fiscal consolidation. In 1995, the public deficit reached a peak of 5.2% of GDP (OECD 2001). Moreover, official forecasts by the government indicated that the budget deficit would reach about 8% of GDP in 1997 without further fiscal action (OECD 1996). Thus, only a few months after the adoption of the previous savings package in the spring of 1995 the government reinvigorated its efforts to improve the dire budgetary outlook.

This time, however, the government embarked on a more cooperative strategy vis-à-vis the social partners. At a very early stage, the social partners were asked to participate in the formulation of savings measures. In doing so, the government sought to avoid another clash with the trade unions, which had seriously disturbed the traditionally strong ties between the SPÖ and the ÖGB and eventually caused the failure of the previous *Sparpaket*. Now, the social partners themselves were asked to put forward proposals for a primarily expenditure-related reduction of the public deficit (Sebald 1998).

After protracted negotiations the social partners achieved a compromise and presented a joint report, which contained a catalogue of budgetary proposals. With respect to pensions, the ÖGB was initially able to avert a number of benefit cuts proposed by the WKÖ, such as an increase of the legal retirement age or actuarial deductions for beneficiaries of early retirement pensions. In return, the ÖGB abandoned its demands for the introduction of a solidarity tax and an increase of capital taxes. Instead the social partners agreed on a number of measures aimed at improving incentives for people to work longer. However, these proposals were very vaguely formulated and failed to achieve the government's savings targets.

This again provoked serious conflicts within the government. The ÖVP pressed for a more severe and strictly expenditure-related consolidation policy. In the area of pensions, the ÖVP called for a number of incisive benefit cuts, such as an increase in the early retirement age by two years in combination with an increase in the number of minimum contribution years from 35 to 37.5. In addition, actuarial deductions were to be introduced for all early retirement pensions. Given the dire situation on the labour market, the SPÖ fiercely rejected these proposals and instead advocated a reduction of the federal grant to the pension schemes for farmers and self-employed, which would have resulted in a drastic increase of pension contributions for those groups. Thus, each of the parties pressed for savings, which would each primarily affect the clientele of the other coalition partner. Despite minor concessions from both sides, the budgetary negotiations eventually failed – in particular, due to the conflicts over pension policy – and led to early elections in December 1995. A case can be made that intense political competition between the two parties had hampered a policy-oriented bargaining process. "Caught" in an unloved "grand coalition" government, both the SPÖ and the ÖVP were inevitably going to suffer severe vote losses to the populist Freedom Party FPÖ after 1986. As a consequence, both parties had an overwhelming interest in strengthening their electoral standing. Each party therefore sought to sharpen its policy profile at the expense of the other coalition partner by pursuing clientelistic interest politics rather than searching for solutions acceptable to both sides.

The consolidation of the public budget also became the major theme in the election campaign. The SPÖ primarily sought to present itself as the key defender of Austria's welfare system and mobilised against proposals to cut pensions, which was one of the most sensitive issues of the election. Apparently, this strategy proved to be very successful as the SPÖ was the clear winner in the elections and increased its vote share from 34.9% to 38.1%. In particular, the Socialists managed to mobilise non-voters and to retrieve a sizeable share of the voters it had previously lost to the Freedom Party (Sully 1996).

After the elections, the negotiations were reassumed. However, the ÖVP made clear that it would only form a new government with the SPÖ, if both parties agreed beforehand on a budget bill for the years 1996 and 1997. This agreement should specify the overall volume of budgetary consolidation and focus on measures that first and foremost address the expenditure-side of the budget. With respect to the former aspect, an agreement was achieved relatively easily. Moreover, the SPÖ hesitatingly approached the ÖVP and signalled its readiness to concentrate the budgetary measures on the expenditure side. In February 1996, both parties compromised on a four-year consolidation programme of about 100 billion Austrian schillings (about 7 billion euros) (for the Federal government), of which only one-third was to be achieved through increased revenues. This programme was agreed upon by the social partners and further elaborated in the draft budgets for 1996 and 1997 (OECD 1996; Sebald 1998).

In the area of pensions, negotiations proved to be particularly difficult. After a protracted bargaining process, the ÖVP and SPÖ achieved a certain rapprochement of their policy positions. The ÖVP accepted the retention of the early retirement age, while the SPÖ agreed to tighter eligibility criteria for early retirement. Moreover, against the fierce resistance of the ÖVP, the SPÖ advocated for a reduction of the federal grants offered to the pension schemes for farmers and the self-employed. In addition, the consolidation programme sought a number of other measures, most of which were explicitly aimed at increasing the actual retirement age. For instance, the digressive design of the accrual rate (i.e., the percentage of assessed earnings paid for each year of contribution), granting a higher value to the first 30 insurance years than to the subsequent insurance years, was moderated. Henceforth, the first 30 insurance years would be credited at 1.83% (instead of 1.9%), the subsequent insurance years at 1.675% (instead of 1.5%). This change was supposed to enhance the incentives for working longer. In addition, pension entitlements were reduced for people claiming more than one pension or those having additional incomes from employment. Moreover, the years on education would no longer be automatically compensated as insurance years.

Even after the presentation of the consolidation programme, different policy positions persisted with respect to the number of insurance years necessary for eligibility for early retirement. The ÖVP succeeded in increasing the number of minimum contribution years from 35 to 37.5. In return, it had to accept that this measure would only become fully effective beginning in 2001. This measure was incorporated in a draft by the Social Ministry, together with the proposals put forward in the consolidation programme. By and large, both social partners accepted the measures established in the ministerial draft. Although they were not directly involved in the negotiations, they were constantly informed and consulted by their respective allies in the partisan arena.

Severe criticism was only raised by organisations representing the interests of women. They claimed that the new pension insurance regulations would primarily affect women, who typically have less insurance years than men and who therefore stood to lose more disproportionately because of the sought-after increases in the number of minimum contribution years. However, their objections were not heeded. In summation, the pension policy proposals were adopted largely unaltered by the government parties in the Austrian Parliament (OECD 1996; Sebald 1998; Lißner and Wöss 1999).[4] Among the parliamentary opposition parties, it was again the right-wing FPÖ, which voiced the harshest criticism against the savings package.

The volume of curtailments in the area of pensions (as well as in the realm of social security as a whole) that was finally agreed to in the 1996 austerity package clearly went beyond the savings measures proposed by the joint report of the Austrian social partners a few months earlier. The volume of savings was also much larger than those in the 1995 austerity package. In the area of pensions, the overall consolidation results from the 1996 *Sparpaket* amounted to 0.6% of GDP by 2000 (see table 7.2). With respect to the scope and composition of the savings measures, the ÖVP was perceived the winner over the SPÖ. However, the ÖVP was incapable of launching a more comprehensive reform of the pension system including an increase in the age limit for early retirement.

The inclusion of the social partners in the reform process (at least at an informal level) helped to sustain the political acceptance and thereby the political feasibility of welfare retrenchment. This becomes particularly evident if we compare the two austerity packages launched in the mid-1990s with respect to the role trade unions played in the policy formulation process. In both cases, the trade unions had the same fundamental interest in Austria joining the European Monetary Union. Moreover, in 1996, they had agreed on a consolidation package that was tougher than the governmental savings proposals which they had vociferously opposed one-and-a-half years earlier. As Scharpf (2000:121a) has pointed out, trade union opposition to the first attempt of unilateral retrenchment was not primarily driven by disagreement over the substance of the government's policy proposals but by their institutional self-interest in maintaining their corporatist control over the economic and social policy choices of the government. Therefore, the government failed in its effort to impose an austerity package without concertation of the social partners. By contrast, in preparing the 1996 austerity package, the government asked the social partners to put forward their own proposals for a drastic consolidation of the public budget. The measures proposed in the social partners' report were subsequently specified and substantially extended at the government level. These amendments, however, were still made in permanent consultation with the social partners' associations. Throughout this process, the SPÖ leadership successfully mastered the delicate task of mediating between the interests of the ÖGB (and thereby large sections of its own party) on the one hand, and the more comprehensive policy positions of its conservative coalition partner on the other (Sebald 1998).

The watered-down pension reform of 1997

Only a few months after the commencement of the 1996 austerity package, the government announced a major reform of the pension system in order to secure the financial viability of the system in the medium- and long-term. Moreover, it sought a greater harmonisation of the different pension schemes. To that end, the government had commissioned the German pension expert Bert Rürup (1997) to put forward proposals for an overhaul of the Austrian pension system. The commissioning of an external and independent expert was probably motivated by the attempt to limit the influence of pension experts associated with the social partners already at the stage of problem definition. In doing so, the government hoped to obtain a realistic picture of the pension system's weaknesses, which again would create a more favourable political climate for more incisive reforms.[5]

The Rürup Report presented worrisome forecasts for the financial viability of Austria's pension system in the face of demographic ageing. If current benefits in the public pension insurance system (excluding civil servants) were to remain the same until 2030, the "mixed contribution rate"[6] would increase from 22.35% to 24.88% (in 2030), while the federal subsidy would increase from 2.59% to 6.06% of GDP. In response to the looming financial problems of the pension system, the Rürup Report presented a number of different reform options, which would significantly dampen the growth of public pension expenditures in the future. With the implementation of Rürup's proposals the "implicit contribution rate"[7] would only have increased from 30.21% in 1995 to about 35% in 2030 (rather than to 42.75% as forecasted in the status quo scenario). The cost containment effects could mainly be achieved through a strengthening of the actuarial fairness of the system and through the insertion of a demographic component in the calculation of the yearly pension adjustments. In addition, Rürup proposed starting with an increase in women's retirement age in as early as 2005[8] and including all employed people in the social insurance system (Rürup and Schröter 1997).

Initially, the government seemed willing to implement this reform concept without substantial modifications. In June 1997, it announced (without prior consultation of the social partners) a big pension reform, which needed to be adopted that same year (together with the 1998 budget) and which should largely follow the recommendations made in the Rürup Report (Tálos and Kittel 1999). Although the government did not embrace Rürup's proposal to increase women's retirement age in 2005, it proposed a number of other controversial measures, which were supposed to go into effect gradually in 2000 (EIRR 1997a):

- an increase in the reference salary from the best 15 to the best 20 years (until 2012);
- a reduction of the pension level for men (women) retiring before the age of 65 (60) at 2% per annum;
- a change in the reference salary for civil servants pensions from final salary to the last 15 years;
- a new adjustment formula (reducing the value of state pensions by 2% to 3%);
- an extension of pension insurance coverage.

Apart from the last item, the government's pension plan was fiercely opposed by the unions, in particular by the public sector union GÖD (*Gewerkschaft Öffentlicher Dienst*) which represents civil servant interests. Given their support of the voluminous *Sparpaket* adopted one year earlier, the unions were not inclined to accept the government's push for further substantial pension cuts in record time solely for the purpose of budgetary savings. As a consequence, a serious clash emerged between the government and the trade unions, which was also accompanied by union-led demonstrations against the government's plans. Despite concessions from the government, the negotiations with the social partners were extremely protracted and failed to produce any results. In the process, a number of leading politicians (mainly from the ÖVP) called for pension reforms without involving the social partners. However, they were unable to assert themselves within the government. Once again, the veto power of the trade unions vis-à-vis an internally estranged SPÖ/ÖVP government became evident. Given their large numbers within the SPÖ faction (see table 7.1), the trade unionists in the Parliament could credibly threaten to block the reform during a parliamentary vote. At a certain point, they even threatened to launch a no-confidence vote against the Socialist Chancellor if the government refused to withdraw its reform plans. In a last-minute deal, the social partners and the government agreed on a drastically watered-down version of the original reform plan. Thus, in the bargaining process Austrian trade unions were quite successful in defending the status quo in pension policy. In November 1997, the pension reform was passed (Tálos and Kittel 1999; Rürup 2000; Tálos and Kittel 2001).

In virtually every respect the government was forced to make comprehensive concessions. Initially, the government had planned to increase the number of "best years" from 15 to 20, beginning in 2000 with full implementation by 2012 (only for those taking early retirement). According to the final reform package, there was only to be an increase to 18 years, to be phased in from 2003 to 2019. Moreover, individual benefit reduction was not to exceed 7%. With respect to the actuarial benefit reduction for people retiring prior to the regular retirement age, a maximum ceiling of 10% was established, rather than 15% as was originally sought. Finally, the plan to modify the adjustment formula by introducing a demographic factor (taking into account rising life expectancy) was postponed (*Die Presse*, 21 January 2000). The cost containment effects of the 1997 reform were further undermined by the fact that the new rules actually included a number of benefit expansions. For instance, credits for child rearing were improved. Moreover, the accrual factor was harmonised at an even more generous level than before (2% instead of 1.75%). As a consequence, a full pension of 80% can henceforth be had at 40 rather than 45 years.

Despite this reform, however, pension expenditures for the general scheme were projected to rise from 10.4% of GDP in 2000 to 13.7% in 2030. In 2030, this would be only 0.5% (sic!) less than it would have been without the reform (see also table 7.2).[9] As Rürup points out, this reform realised less than 20% of the cost containment effects (in the general pension insurance) than would have been possible if one of the policy options presented in the Rürup Report (and initially accepted by the government) had been adopted (Rürup 2000).[10] Moreover, these calculations did not take into account the long-term financial effects resulting from the extension of the state pension scheme to the entire working population. While this measure strengthens the financial base of the pension system in the short-term (through a broadening of the revenue base), it also leads to new benefit entitlements and thereby to higher expenditures in the future. Therefore, it was possible that the 1997 reform would eventually make the Austrian pension insurance even more expensive in the long run (Marhold 1997:505).

It needs to be emphasised, however, that the 1997 pension reform achieved more comprehensive adjustments with respect to civil servant pensions. The calculation basis of civil servant pensions was to be altered from last salary to the salary of the 18 best years (as in the general pension insurance scheme). This measure would be gradually introduced between 2003 and 2020 (initially this change was to be phased-in more quickly). In the long term, this may lead to significant budgetary savings (Marhold 1997; EIRR 1998). It is expected that the 1997 reform will reduce expenditures on civil servant pensions by 0.2% of GDP in the year 2030 as compared to the baseline scenario (see table 7.2). As Rürup (2000) points out, this element of the 1997 pension reform can be seen as an exemplary contribution to the harmonisation of public pension schemes.

It soon turned out that the 1997 reform would contribute very little to the containment of rising pension expenditures. More specifically, it did not seriously address the problem of an overly low actual retirement age. Against this background, the issue of pension reform did not disappear from the political agenda. Only two years after the adoption of the 1997 pension reform, following the general elections in October 1999, the Socialist Chancellor, Viktor Klima, announced further pension reform plans. After protracted talks, the SPÖ and the ÖVP agreed on a coalition agreement in January 2000, which sought, among other things, an increase in the early retirement age by two years to be implemented within a relatively short time span. This plan triggered fierce protests by the unions and aggravated the existing tensions between the ÖGB and the SPÖ as well as within the SPÖ. These developments contributed to a massive crisis within the government. Under these conditions, Wolfgang Schüssel, the leader of the ÖVP, was unwilling to continue in the coalition with the SPÖ and finally entered into a coalition with the right-wing FPÖ in February 2000 (Eiroline 2000b).[11]

Pension policy under the right-wing government

In contrast to the "grand coalition" between SPÖ and ÖVP, the right-wing ÖVP/FPÖ government was more strongly oriented towards market-liberal ideas in social and economic policy. Pressed by the Maastricht Treaty, it was determined to balance the budget, in a very short time displaying a deficit of more than 2% of GDP in 1999 (OECD 2001). By the same token, this government showed a greater readiness to adopt tangible and short-term effective benefit cuts in pensions and other social programmes than its predecessor (Obinger 2001; Tálos 2001). This also holds true for the Freedom party, whose programmatic profile in social policy is basically characterised by demands for greater self-responsibility and less state influence. Against this background, its earlier attacks on the saving packages adopted by the previous government must be interpreted as an opportunistic move to attract potential protest voters.

Both parties announced a major reform of the pension system in their coalition agreement of February 2000. The government also appointed two commissions that were instructed to present proposals for a comprehensive reform of pension insurance and of civil servant pensions. In these commissions the social partners no longer represented the dominating force (traditionally chairing these commissions), but merely one actor among others. Independent pension experts played a particularly larger role in these commissions than previously (Linnerooth-Bayer 2001; Tálos and Kittel 2001). In April 2000, the coalition partners presented the crucial elements of their pension reform package (*Die Presse*, 3 April 2000):

- an increase in the early retirement age from 55 to 56.5 years for women and from 60 to 61.5 years for men, with a benefit reduction of 3% per year (hitherto 2%) for workers retiring prior to the normal retirement age (to be implemented from October 2000 until October 2002);
- an increase in the civil servant retirement age from 60 to 61.5 years (to be implemented from October 2000 until October 2002);
- a reform of widows' pensions: in October 2000, widows were to receive between 0% and 60% of the deceased spouse's pension (hitherto 40-60%). This measure only applies to newly granted widows' pensions.

These proposals were met by vigorous opposition from the unions and the parliamentary opposition. They specifically denounced the quick increase of the early retirement age as a "breach of confidence" of the existing regulations. By the same token, they announced that they were going to present this issue to the constitutional court.

Shortly after the presentation the government entered into negotiations with the social partners. However, these negotiations were virtually doomed to failure. Both sides accused one another of not negotiating sincerely. The government seemed unwilling to make any significant concessions to the trade unions. In particular, it refused to negotiate the speed and the financial volume of the sought-after pension cuts and declared that it would put through the pension reform even against trade union resistance if necessary. In response, the trade unions sought to mobilise their members and the general public and launched various protest actions against the government's reform plans (including a protest strike by transport workers) (Tálos and Kittel 2001). However, lacking the powerful mobilising capacity of their French or Italian counterparts, the union protests went largely unheeded by the general public.

At the same time, the unions tried again to use their party channels in order to prevent a parliamentary majority for the government's retrenchment plans. This time, however, their parliamentary power resources were much weaker. Under the new government constellation, the ÖGB could no longer rely on a sizeable number of trade union functionaries within the government factions. Instead, the ÖGB pressed the employee organisation of the ÖVP (Österreichischer Arbeiter- und Angestelltenbund, ÖAAB) to side with the trade unions on the issue of pension reform. To a certain extent, the representatives of the ÖAAB shared the objections of the trade unions against the proposed reform package. Most importantly, the ÖAAB had raised serious concerns with respect to the constitutionality of the government's pension plans. In particular, it claimed that an increase in the early retirement age without significant interim regulations would constitute a "breach of confidence" and might therefore be rejected by the constitutional court (*Die Presse*, 17 June 2000). In response to these concerns, the government added a number of temporary exception provisions for certain groups into the final law. For instance, men with 45 contribution years and women with 40 contribution years were exempted from the increase of the early retirement age for a five-year transitional period. However, the government did not change the overall time schedule of the reform, and most of the regulations became law in as early as October 2000.

In the run-up to the final vote in Parliament the trade unions called upon the 24 ÖAAB deputies to vote against the pension reform, in which case the government would not have had a parliamentary majority.[12] However, all of the ÖAAB deputies except one voted in favour of the bill, after the government had made a number of minor concessions (*Die Presse*, 8 July 2000). Apparently the MP's affiliated with the ÖAAB attached a greater value to their loyalty vis-à-vis the government than to their policy interests concerning a more modest reform approach. Moreover, the ÖAAB had a competitive interest in dissociating itself from the socialist trade unionists. The latter were portrayed as "fundamentalist" opponents of reform, who could only be found on the streets, while the ÖAAB presented itself as the true representative of workers' interests, which would use serious bargaining to achieve real improvements (*Die Presse*, 6 June 2000).

A case can be made for the notion that the ÖVP/FPÖ government had no serious interest in bringing the unions and opposition parties on board. The populist FPÖ appeared to be particularly determined to replace the traditional procedures of concertation entrenched in the system of social partnership (from which the FPÖ used to be completely excluded) with a more hierarchical approach (Obinger 2001). Through its repeated calls for a dismantling of corporatist structures and its attacks on the Austrian system of "favouritism" (*Günstlingswirtschaft*), associated with organisational privileges held by trade unions and their functionaries, the FPÖ had dramatically expanded its electoral support base since 1986. By the same token, the FPÖ continued to press strongly for a weakening of trade unions' institutional power bases. For instance, the competencies for labour law and labour market policy were handed from the Ministry of Social Affairs to the newly created Ministry for Economy and Labour in order to restrict the traditional ÖGB channels of influence. It is remarkable that FPÖ Chairman Jörg Haider even tried to make the adoption of the pension reform contingent on a 40% reduction of the compulsory levy to the Chamber of Labour (a public corporation, de facto managed by the trade unions). In doing so, the FPÖ sought to curb the unions' institutional influence. However, the ÖVP rejected this package deal (Tálos 2001).

The SPÖ opposition not only voted against the reform in parliament, but also started constitutional proceedings against parts of the reform, in particular the reform of widow pensions and the increase in the early retirement age. However, its main criticism was primarily directed at the extremely short transition rules, which were denounced as a breach of confidence. In principle, however, the SPÖ did not deny the necessity of further pension reform. Only a few months earlier it had signed a coalition agreement with the ÖVP according to which the early retirement age was to be increased by two years, making it more difficult for the SPÖ to exploit the pension issue in the electoral arena.

It is noteworthy that the overall volume of pension cuts realised by the 2000 reform is roughly equivalent to the expenditure cuts decided in the 1997 pension reform plan, both with respect to the general scheme and with

Table 7.2   Cost containment effects of recent Austrian pension reforms

	1996 Savings package	1997 Pension reform	2000 Pension reform
Saving effects in the the general scheme	0.6% of GDP until 2000	0.5% of GDP until 2030	0.5% of GDP until 2003
Saving effects in civil servants pensions scheme		0.2% of GDP until 2030	0.2% of GDP until 2003

Source: Buczolich et al. (2002)

respect to pensions for civil servants. However, while the measures adopted by the 1997 reform were to only be fully operational in 2030 and after, the measures of the 2000 pension reform were to fully implemented as early as 2003 and thus achieve the sought-after savings effect in a much shorter time span (see table 7.2).

The övp/fpö coalition also took cautious steps to strengthen fully funded forms of old age provisions. Most importantly, it reformed Austria's statutory severance pay system[13] and – like Italy – introduced an option of using the severance payments to fund occupational pensions as a supplement to the public pillar. The reforms entail the following changes:

- All private sector employees are entitled to severance pay from the first day of employment (hitherto only after three years of service with their current employer).
- Entitlement will apply regardless of the reason for the termination of the employment relationship (hitherto only in the case of dismissal by the employer).
- Employers are obliged to pay 1.5377% of employee wages to a central fund, from the time they are first employed until they leave/retire. Maximum level of severance pay is reached after 37 years. Previously, individual employers had to make provisions in their accounts for at least half of the severance pay entitlements that might fall due. These entitlements amounted to two months of final salary after three years service, three months pay after five years service, four months after 10 years, six months after 15 years, nine months after 20 years and a maximum of 12 months after 25 years of service.
- In principle, an employee leaving his/her company can either choose to take the severance payment at once or to save the entitlement for a future pension.

– As before, contributions to severance pay remain liable only to a flat-rate income tax of 6% and are exempted from social security contributions. However, no income tax will be levied if the severance pay is invested into a pension fund, thereby providing a tax incentive for private old age provisions.

Interestingly, in the severance pay reforms, the ÖVP/FPÖ coalition deviated from its previous policy of curtailing the influence of social partnership (particularly of the trade unions). The reason is that the coalition parties were unable to agree whether the entitlement to severance pay should be granted from the first day of employment – as preferred by the FPÖ (a position also shared by the Social Democratic opposition) – or – as demanded by the ÖVP – only after one year of service for the same employer. Against this background, the government decided to delegate the drafting of a new severance scheme to the social partners, which achieved a relatively quick compromise. After the government accepted the social partners' proposals without major modifications, the reform was unanimously adopted by Parliament in June 2002.

The main advantage of the modified scheme is the expanded scope of entitlement to severance pay compared to the earlier legislation, since virtually all employees (including those on unpaid leave) would be eligible for severance pay contributions. This element had been a key trade union demand. It is estimated that about 800,000 new employees would now be covered by severance pay. However, the individual amount of the severance payments provided under the new legislation is significantly lower than under the former law. This was the main concession to employers, which had a strong interest that the extension of severance pay coverage to all employees in the private sector not boil down to a higher financial burden on employers (Gächter 1998; Pernicka 2001b; Traxler 2001; Adam 2002; Arbeiterkammer Österreich 2002).

The reform of severance payments is only a limited step towards fully funded old age provisions, especially if compared with the other countries studied. Both in Germany and Italy, wage earners are able to divert a considerably higher share of their income tax-free into private or occupational pension plans than in Austria. Moreover, the still very generous benefits provided by the public system and the very half-hearted measures to curb public pension spending in the future, diminish the individual incentives for increased private retirement savings. On the one hand, the high level of contributions needed to finance public pensions restricts the capacity of individual households to pursue private old age provisions. On the other hand, the political attempt to ensure a high income replacement level within the public pension system even in the long-term may raise public expectations that enhanced private old age provisions are not needed to maintain one's individual living standard after retirement.

Pension politics in Austria – the conditional impact of the trade unions on reform outcomes

Table 7.3 summarises in a highly stylised fashion the fundamental transformation of the political decision-making process in Austrian pension policy since the late 1980s. In a nutshell, this transformation is characterised by a gradual decline in trade union influence. We can distinguish three distinct phases in Austrian pension politics, displaying varying degrees of union influence.

As pointed out above, since the mid-1980s Austrian pension policymakers have been concerned with the goal of cost containment. However, until the early 1990s, cost containment reforms were still largely developed within the traditional framework of social partnership. Pension reforms were typically initiated and negotiated by the social partners, or at least worked out in close concertation between the government and the social partners. To that extent, the trade unions could exert a powerful influence on the process, the content and the timing of pension reforms. The trade unions participated in the formulation of policy proposals at a very early stage. This was based on a relatively strong political consensus that no major decision in social and economic policy should be made without, or more strongly, *against* the social partners. At the same time, the pressures for budgetary consolidation were still comparatively modest. These factors combined to favour an extremely incremental reform process. For instance, a constitutional law adopted in 1993 sought a harmonisation of regular retirement

Table 7.3   Union influence on political decision making in Austrian pension policy

Period	Government constellation	Pressures for budgetary consolidation	Do unions have... proposal formation power?	political veto power?	Degree of adjustment / speed of implementation
1987-1993	SPÖ/ÖVP	Medium	Partly	Yes	Incremental / very slow
1994-2000	SPÖ/ÖVP	Very strong	No	Yes	Incremental / rather slow
2000-	ÖVP/FPÖ	Strong	No	No	Modest / very rapid

ages for men and women (by raising women's retirement age from 60 to 65), which would, however, only be implemented from 2018 to 2034.[14]

In the mid-1990s, this constellation began to change. Faced with extraordinarily dramatic budgetary pressures (reinvigorated by the 3% deficit criterion laid down in the Maastricht Treaty) the SPÖ/ÖVP coalition sought to get a tighter grip on the reform process. In particular, the government tried to determine the content and the timing of reforms (Tálos and Kittel 1999). Most importantly, it unilaterally established tight guidelines with respect to the overall volume of expenditure cuts to be made in the pension system. In two cases (1994 and 1997), it proposed major changes to the pension system without prior consultation of the social partners. By the same token, in striking contrast to the consensual tradition of social partnership, it even considered the adoption of reforms against trade unions' resistance. Clearly, the unions had lost influence in the formulation of policy proposals through corporatist bargaining. Instead, they increasingly tried to exert influence by lobbying and sought to block disadvantageous legislative changes via their parliamentary representatives. Due to their high level of representation within the SPÖ parliamentary group, they were still able to use their veto powers. Thus, the internally divided SPÖ/ÖVP government proved incapable of passing pension reforms against trade union resistance. This means that throughout the 1990s, Austrian pension policy evolved at a slow, incremental pace. A textbook example of this incremental approach was the 1997 pension reform, which for instance sought only a tiny increase in the number of "best years" (from 15 to 18). Moreover, this increase would only become go into full effect in 2019.[15]

Only in cases where the trade unions themselves acknowledged the necessity of quick and comprehensive savings measures was the government able to accelerate the pace of reform. However, this appears to be an exception to the rule. Only in the mid-1990s, when the deficit criteria imposed by the European Monetary Union required adoption of a very tight austerity policy, did the trade unions approve tangible and immediate short-term pension cuts as a temporary consolidation measure (e.g., a pension freeze of one year). Another area where trade unions showed a remarkable willingness to reform is in the partial harmonisation of civil servants' pensions with the (less generous) benefit rules applying to the general scheme.

Both instances shed light on the strategic capacity of Austrian trade unions, reflected in their highly centralised organisational structure. This capacity became evident in various dimensions. The first instance reveals its inter-temporal dimension. Given the potential future gains (associated with Austria's EMU membership) Austrian trade unions proved they were able to forego present satisfaction and accept temporary losses for their rank and file including pension cuts. The second instance reveals its inter-personal dimension. Since their power was highly concentrated near the top rather than at the branch level, Austrian trade unions have the capacity of sacrificing the interests of some occupational groups (e.g., of civil servants) for the greater benefit of the collective, which is more interested in an efficient and equitable pension system. Nevertheless, union willingness to co-operate with the government in a pension reform entailing losses for (parts of) their rank and file also rests upon a cognitive dimension. Only if unions *believe* that sacrifices are necessary to obtain larger overall gains (or to avoid larger losses) are they be prepared to sacrifice. Thus, even large unions will probably oppose pension retrenchment, as long as they don't recognise any associated long-term benefits.

Under the centre-right ÖVP/FPÖ government, union influence on social and economic policy has eroded further. As noted above, this government made little effort to bring either the Social Democratic opposition or the trade unions on board, especially after announcing the quick implementation of a major pension reform. It also appeared unwilling to make significant concessions to the trade unions or the SPÖ. Instead, the government remained adamant that final pension reforms must yield sought-after substantial savings for the public budget in a very short time span. Under this condition, it was unlikely that the unions (and the parliamentary opposition) would cave in, because their co-operation would not have changed the final reform outcome significantly. In other words, neither the unions nor the SPÖ would have realised significant policy gains by co-operating with the government. At the same time, they would have been forced to share the political costs associated with the adoption of a highly unpopular reform package. Institutionally, the unilateral approach adopted by the bourgeois government was facilitated by the fact that it had a solid parliamentary majority and that the trade unions – under this government constellation – were no longer able to drive a wedge between, and into, the governing parties. As a consequence, the pension reform 2000 entailed more incisive benefit cuts than its predecessors. For instance, it completely abolished all newly granted widows' pensions for retirees, whose own pension entitlements exceed a certain income limit. Moreover, while its long-term effects are still comparatively modest (as its primary intention was short-term budgetary savings), this pension reform has much shorter transition clauses than the previous reforms. For instance, the legislated early retirement age increase was implemented only a few months later, going into full effect in October 2002.

In the case of the most recent pension reforms, a number of favourable and fairly extraordinary conditions created a "window of opportunity" for the government to pursue its unilateral policy of pension retrenchment without large political risks. Since the reform was adopted at the beginning of the legislative term, the danger of electoral retribution was limited. Moreover, Austrian trade unions have only a limited capacity of counter-mobilisation in terms of mass demonstrations and strike actions. Perhaps most importantly, the government enacted the reform at a time when the sanctions of other EU member countries against the Austrian government clearly dominated the public debate and pushed other controversial issues into the background. This may explain why the government's policy interest in balancing the public budget clearly prevailed over concerns of electoral losses possibly associated with unpopular pension cutbacks. Apparently the government considered the electoral risks of the pension reform as comparatively limited and thus had no powerful motive to make significant concessions to the unions, which would compromise the government's budgetary goals.

Addendum: Most recent developments

While the research period of this study basically ends in 2002, another major pension reform was adopted in 2003. The financial effects of this reform are not included in the figures presented in chapter two. Nevertheless, they appear to be rather substantial and display a clear deviation form the traditionally prevailing pattern of marginal and incremental adjustments in pension policy. And so I have decided to complement this chapter with a brief analysis of the most recent pension reforms in Austria.

In December 2002, a special commission nominated by the ÖVP/FPÖ government presented a number of rather comprehensive proposals aimed at restoring the financial sustainability of the Austrian pension system in the long-term. The coalition, which had returned to office after the general election in November 2002, adopted most of these proposals and announced a number of rather harsh benefit curtailments such as (Eiroline 2003a):

– an abolition of early retirement pensions until 2009;
– an increase in the reduction of early retirement pensions from 3.75% to 4.2% per year of early retirement;
– a reduction of the accrual factor from 2% to 1.78% per year (as a consequence, a full pension of 80% of pensionable earnings would only be reached after 45 rather than 40 years);

– a calculation of pension benefits based on 40 rather than 15 or 18 working
years.

Taken together, these measures would have implied drastic and immediate
welfare cuts, which for some groups may have actually meant benefit reductions of more than 30%. As expected, the Social Democratic opposition and
the trade unions reacted with fierce criticisms. Quite unusually in the Austrian political context, trade unions even organised country-wide "defense
strikes" against the government's plans. According to recent surveys these
strikes were supported by 62% of the population. May and June 2003 saw
Austria's largest strikes since 1945 with over one million employees participating.

At the same time, the government's pension plans came under strong attack within its own ranks (see *Der Standard*, 14 May 2003). Representatives of the Freedom Party (which had suffered a tremendous defeat in the
previous national election and thus found itself in the role of small coalition
partner to the now dominant ÖVP), particularly the former and yet still
highly influential party leader Jörg Haider, called for milder benefit cuts and
a fixed time schedule for the harmonisation of the various public pension
systems. In addition, the FPÖ argued for a referendum on the planned cuts.
Quite remarkably, Haider even threatened to forge an ad-hoc alliance with
the Social Democratic opposition in order to block the government's pension plans and to that effect, entered into talks with SPÖ chairman Alfred
Gusenbauer.

Within the ÖVP, the government's pension proposals also went far from
uncontested. Especially the trade unionists within the party sought to soften
the sought-after pension cuts. Moreover, they called for a broad reform consensus including the social partners. Fritz Neugebauer, leader of the Federation of Christian Trade Unionists (Bundesfraktion der Christlichen Gewerkschaft, CFG) and of the Union of Public Services (Gewerkschaft
Öffentlicher Dienst, GÖD) repeatedly threatened to vote against the reform
in Parliament if the government refused to change the content of the reforms, i.e., by limiting the cuts for individual pensioners to a maximum of
10% compared with the then-current scheme.

Interestingly, even the employer-oriented Chamber of the Economy
(Wirtschaftskammer Österreichs, WKÖ), having traditionally strong links
with the ÖVP, criticised the government's unilateral approach. Instead, it
sought to find an alternative solution to the government's proposals and offered to present its own reform plans by early autumn jointly drafted with
the trade unions. The WKÖ thus sought to avoid a harsh confrontation with

the trade unions possibly resulting in a higher level of industrial conflict and also sought to maintain its influence within the traditional social partnership. However, Chancellor Schüssel refused the initiative of the social partners and declared that any delays would be unacceptable.

It is remarkable that even Federal President Klestil, member of the governing party ÖVP, argued for a postponement of the government's pension plans until the social partners could work out their own reform proposal. Moreover, he showed understanding for the strikes organised by the ÖGB, arguing that the government proposal would generate unacceptable cases of hardship. As a consequence, Klestil invited the government, the parliamentary opposition, and the social partners to a series of tripartite roundtable talks, a proposition which none of the parties involved could decline. Given the widespread criticism against the reform proposals, even within the governing parties, Chancellor Schüssel had to make a number of concessions in the bargaining process. In particular, he offered to limit the benefit cuts for individual pensioners to a maximum of 10% and a longer phasing-out period for early retirement pensions. However, the trade unions considered these concessions as insufficient, broke off the negotiations, and organised further nationwide strikes, which covered almost all of the economic sectors but remained very limited in terms of time. The government withstood these protests and in June 2003 pushed a modified pension reform through Parliament (Eiroline 2003b). Through these modifications, the government sought political support from potential reform opponents within its own ranks in order to ensure a parliamentary majority in favour of the reform bill. Finally, the governing factions adopted the pension bill unanimously. The final legislation contains a number of significant changes to the original draft:

- The proposed abolition of early retirement pensions is to be fully implemented by 2017 rather than 2009.
- The reference period for the calculation of pensionable earnings is to be increased to 40 years. However, for each child this period is reduced by three years.
- The reduction of the accrual rate is phased-in more slowly.
- A 10% ceiling for benefit reductions resulting from the new legislation, shall apply to all insured people.
- Moreover, special provisions are to be established for people performing physically demanding work (*Schwerarbeiter*) allowing them to draw an early retirement pension without actuarial reductions.

It is important to note, that the new pension rules will also apply to employees in the public sector as well as politicians, a demand which was of particular concern to the Freedom Party.

Despite the above-mentioned modifications to the original reform draft, the long-term savings effects of the reform are likely to be considerable. This is especially true in comparison with the pension reform of 1997, which was largely ineffective in terms of cost containment. In contrast to 1997, this time the trade unions had only a limited impact on the final reform outcome. It appears that the current ÖVP/FPÖ government is less prone to listen to union demands than its predecessors. Quite remarkably, it is the first Austrian government that has openly rejected a joint initiative of the social partners in such an important matter of economic and social policy. This can be seen as a strong indication that the creeping erosion of the Austrian model of *Sozialpartnerschaft* has gained momentum during the Schüssel administration. Moreover, this government appears to be less dependent on the unions' institutional support. Unlike with the previous SPÖ/ÖVP government, the current government does not offer the unions strong political veto powers mainly because the presence of trade unionists within the governing factions is much smaller. In contrast to their French counterparts, Austrian trade unions also lack the ability to organise country-wide strikes that can paralyse the national economy over a long period of time. Moreover, the massive public protests against the pension reforms may not dramatically harm the government's re-election prospects because the next regular national election is not until 2006.

8   France: Adverse Prerequisites for a Pension Consensus

Key features of the French pension system in the late 1980s

The French pension system comprises a large number of pay-as-you-go financed and categorically fragmented schemes with privately funded schemes of only minimal importance. Private sector employees (65% of the insured population) are covered by the *régime général*. For public sector employees (20%) and the self-employed (12%), a number of separate schemes exist side by side and are organised by employer and profession. Retirement age, contribution rates, and calculation of benefits vary greatly from one scheme to another (Bonoli 2000). Private sector pensions are essentially based on a two-tiered structure with a number of compulsory occupational schemes complementing the general scheme. Public sector pensions, by contrast, are usually provided in one tier (for an overview see table 8.1).

The *régime général* is financed by employers' and employees' contributions (8.2% and 6.4%, respectively, up to a certain contribution ceiling). A total of 37.5 contribution years are necessary to receive a full pension corresponding to 50% of the salary base earned over the last 10 years. The retirement age for both genders is 60 years. Apart from contributory pensions, the general regime also provides means-tested benefits (*minimum vieillesse*) for elderly people with insufficient resources.

Table 8.1	The basic structure of the French pension system		
	Basic insurance	Complementary schemes	
Private sector employees	Régime général: 14 million contributors, 9.2 million retirees	ARRCO: 15 million contributors, 9 million retirees	AGIRC (for executives): 3 million contributors, 1.6 million retirees
Public sector employees Self-employed	Special schemes: 4.7 million contributors, 3.5 million retirees		

Source: Neumann (1999); Veil (2000a)

As already noted, French employees in the private sector are also compulsorily covered by complementary schemes topping up the benefits out of the general scheme. The ARRCO (*Association des régimes de retraites complémentaires*) scheme covers virtually all private sector employees, whereas AGIRC (*Association générale des institutions de retraite des cadres*) provides a supplementary benefit for executives only. For an average worker, the combined replacement rate from the general and the complementary scheme roughly corresponds to 70% of previous wages. However, while the complementary schemes operate on a pay-as-you-go basis, they are (in contrast to the general scheme) of the defined-contribution type. Hence, there is no fixed replacement rate and benefits are adjusted downward whenever contributions fall below the level needed to maintain the scheme's fiscal equilibrium. In contrast to the general scheme, ARRCO and AGIRC were established through collective agreements and are exclusively managed by the social partners (Gillion et al. 2000).

Typically, the separate schemes for public sector employees (*régimes spéciaux*) provide more generous benefits than those for private sector employees. For instance, civil servants benefits are calculated on the basis of the last salary (rather than the salary of the last 10 years as in the general scheme) and the regular retirement age may also be substantially lower than in the private sector (Bonoli 2000).

France's pension reform record in the 1990s

Among the five countries studied, France shows the greatest overall deficiencies in making its pension system more sustainable. While the 1993 reforms of private sector pensions will generate substantial savings in the medium-term, contribution rates will continue to rise considerably over time. Moreover, while the reforms significantly tightened the connection between contributions and benefits, it neither produced a full changeover to the principle of lifetime earnings in the calculation of benefits nor provided a higher regular retirement age. The meager reform record is further tarnished by the Juppé government's failure in 1995 to implement an analogous pension reform of public sector employees. It has been calculated that their pensions will account for over 50% of the total deficit in the general pension system, although they account for less than one quarter of the insured (Taverne 2000). Finally, the plan to establish a new pillar of private and fully funded pensions launched by the Juppé government in 1997 was stalled by the subsequent Socialist government, which instead only introduced a small reserve fund within the public system to cover future pension costs. Beyond

that, the Jospin government largely avoided the delicate issue of pension reform. As a consequence, without further reform, contribution rates are projected to rise from 13.76% up to 25.9% in 2030 (Taverne 2000).

   Until the early 1990s, general pension costs were increasing more rapidly
in France than in the other countries studied with the exception of Italy's
public pension expenditures. Between 1980 and 1993, public pension
spending in France rose almost continuously from 9.5% to 12% of GDP.
Only after 1993 were pension outlays more or less stabilised at this level
(OECD 2000a). Moreover, from the mid-1980s to the early-1990s the general scheme displayed chronic fiscal deficits, which had to be (temporarily)
recouped with government money. These financing problems were largely
driven by a sharp decline in labour force participation by elderly workers.
Labour force participation rates among men aged 55 to 64 years were approximately 70% in the late-1970s but fell steadily until the mid-1990s
when it reached an all-time low of 41.5% in 1995, a more pronounced decline than in most other OECD countries (OECD Labour Force Statistics,
various issues). At the same time, French pension policymakers have done
very little to curb rising pension costs. Instead, they have repeatedly increased contribution levels to limit the shortfalls. At the time, increasing
contribution rates seemed like a politically more feasible adjustment strategy than adopting of pension cuts (Bonoli 2000).

Pension policy until the early 1990s

The absence of significant cost containment reforms until the early 1990s
seems all the more astonishing, because seven official commissioned reports
on pensions between 1985 and 1993 mostly displayed worrisome projections about the financial viability of the public pension system in the long
run. These reports also arrived at basically similar policy recommendations.
For instance, a White Paper published by the government in 1991, projected
an increase of the average contribution rate from 18.9% (in 1990) to more
than 30% in 2030 even under favourable demographic and economic conditions, if the status quo remained unchanged. The White Paper echoed previous reports by proposing a number of measures to curb pension spending
such as establishing a tighter link between contributions and benefits and a
longer qualifying period for full pensions (*Livre Blanc sur les retraites*
1991). Against this background, all of the major parties except the Communists thought that benefit cuts were needed to restore the fiscal balance of the
public pension system and to secure its long-term viability in the face of demographic ageing. In response to the rising fiscal pressures, pensions had

been regularly adjusted to prices (rather than wages) since 1987, with *ad hoc* legislation passed by Parliament every year (Bonoli 2000). However, prior to 1993, different political factors impeded any efforts to adopt more comprehensive reforms, whose necessity went basically uncontested in the partisan arena.

As Bonoli (2000) points out, all of the various coalition governments have been equally afraid of the public's (but particularly union) reactions to pension cuts, including Jacques Chirac's bourgeois government between 1986 until 1988. The Chirac government organised a major convention on the future of French social security which led to the publication of an expert report in autumn 1987. This report highlighted the necessity of substantial cost containment measures in pensions. However, because Chirac intended to run for Prime Minister in the 1988 presidential elections, he shied away from the very unpopular issue of pension reform, especially because he had already suffered important setbacks in his previous efforts to implement neo-liberal reforms. For instance, he withdrew his plan of partial privatisation of the higher education system in the face of large-scale strikes and demonstrations initiated by students' organisations (Bonoli 2000).

The political conditions for a major reform of the pension system became even more unfavourable during the socialist government's tenure from 1988 to 1993. French trade unions[1] continued to reject any curtailments of public pensions. Moreover, the Socialist government was dependent on the external support of the Communist party, which was unwilling to support any government initiative at pension retrenchment. Thus, prior to 1993, the delicate issue of pension reform had been repeatedly postponed (Bonoli 2000).

The successful Balladur reform

The general elections in 1993 produced an overwhelming parliamentary majority for the bourgeois parties (79.7% of seats). The Socialist government was replaced by a centre-right coalition government under Edouard Balladur. Unlike his predecessor, Balladur faced few parliamentary obstacles to the adoption of a controversial pension reform. At the same time, the economic recession and the EMU convergence criteria amplified the need for budgetary consolidation and thus the necessity of cost containment measures in the public pension system. From 1990 to 1993, the general budget deficit increased from 2.1% to 6% of GDP (OECD 2001). In part, this was caused by huge shortfalls in the public pension system. Within the *régime général*, the financial deficit grew from 6.6 billion francs (about 1 million euros) in 1990 to 39.5 billion (about 6 billion euros) in 1993 despite a comparatively favourable demographic structure at that time (Bonoli 2000).

In April 1993, the Balladur government announced major pension system reforms. To a large extent, Balladur picked up reform proposals made in the White Paper published by the previous Socialist government in 1991. The main elements of the proposed reform package for the *régime général* were (Vail 1999):

- the extension of the qualifying period for a full pension from 37.5 to 40 years (to be phased in from 1994 until 2003);
- an increase in the number of "best years" from 10 to 25 as the reference period for the calculation of benefits (to be phased in from 1994 until 2008);
- the indexation of pensions according to prices rather than wages for a five-year period (to be based on a government decree rather than a parliamentary vote);
- the creation of an "Old Age Solidarity Fund" (*Fonds de soldarité vieillesse, FSV*) to cover non-contributory benefits, financed by an increase in the *contribution sociale généralisé (CSG)* from 1.1% to 2.4%, an earmarked tax on all incomes (including income on capital and property) and duties on all alcoholic and some non-alcoholic beverages.

From the outset, the government sought to arrive at a tacit understanding at least with parts of the French trade union movement. A fully consensual solution including the formal approval of the unions regarding pension cuts would have been rather unusual in the French context as French unions typically lack the organisational capacities to mobilise consent for unpopular reform measures among their rank and file (Bonoli 2000, Culpepper 2000). The best, Balladur could hope for, was to prevent unions from organising large-scale public protests against his reform plans. This, he believed, would bring himself into a more favourable position for the 1995 presidential election. Hence, he employed a bundle of strategies to prevent the unions from mobilising against the sought-after pension cuts (Vail 1999; Bonoli 2000; Levy 2000; Palier 2000; Bozec and Mays 2001):

First, Balladur adopted a deliberate and non-confrontational policy style vis-à-vis the trade unions. He attached great importance to consulting with the trade unions and invited them to a conference where his pension proposals were to be discussed. Moreover, informal negotiations took place between the Ministry of Social Affairs, the employers' association, and the trade unions throughout April and May 1993.

Second, the reform package included important concessions to the trade unions, aimed at securing their role in the management and control over pensions. By creating the Old Age Solidarity Fund, Balladur fulfilled a key demand of the trade unions. This measure relieved the financial pressures on the *régime général* by reducing the deficits within the system. It also shifted parts of the overall pension system costs from wage earners to the broader population. Most importantly, through the organisational and financial separation of contributory and non-contributory elements, the government basically acknowledged the managerial role played by trade unions in the field of earnings-related social insurance. Thus, the creation of the FSV can be seen as a quid pro quo for unions' tacit acceptance of pension cuts.[2] Furthermore, limitations of price indexation to five years[3] and the avoidance of a direct increase in the formal retirement age[4] rendered the overall reform package more palatable to the trade unions. Moreover, the Balladur proposal deviated from the suggestions made in the White Paper insofar as it sought a more modest extension of the qualifying period for a full pension (40 instead of 42 years). Thus, Balladur's reform agenda was not overly ambitious in comparison to the proposals made in previous government reports. Instead, the Balladur reform was designed to mitigate political resistance through the inclusion of various concessions to the trade unions.

Third, by confining the reform to the *régime général* Balladur avoided a potential clash with the labour movement in the public sector where union density rates as well as their mobilising power is much stronger than in the private sector.[5] In other words, Balladur sought to exploit an institutionalised divide between the public and the private sector resulting from the existence of a fragmented pension system (Vail 1999).

His distinct approach in policy style and policy content allowed Balladur to obtain the acquiescence of at least parts of the French labour movement. According to a Ministry of Social Affairs civil servant who participated in the negotiations with the social partners, the two confederations, the CFDT and FO (Force Ouvriere), were the key targets of his efforts:

> It was important for us to gain the approval of the CFDT because we knew that the FO and the CGT would be hostile anyway.(...) We needed at least the neutrality of the other confederations. It was also important to avoid the FO adopting a position that was too violent. In fact, they were against it, but did not react as they had against the Juppé plan in 1995. They did not mobilise their members this time by claiming that the new legislation was shameful (cited from Bonoli 2000:139).

Officially, the French trade unions rejected the proposed reform package. The communist CGT even threatened to call a general strike. Even after a promised series of consultations, the major trade union leaders continued to oppose the reform and criticised the fact that Balladur – despite his rhetorical emphasis on consultation and co-operation – had in fact imposed a reform against the trade union's wishes (Vail 1999).

However, the actual union position towards the Balladur reform was more varied or at least less hostile than was officially proclaimed. The proposal was the subject of a vote at the administration board level of the basic pension scheme, the *Caisse Nationale d'Assurance Vieillesse* (CNAV), an agency that includes both trade unions and employer representatives. The social partners were asked to vote separately on the two reform elements: pension benefit cutbacks and the creation of the FSV. Regarding curtailments, only the employers and the Catholic CFTC voted in favour. By contrast, the set-up of the solidarity fund was supported by CFDT, FO, CFTC (and thus by the majority of French unions) and employers. Although this vote did not entail any legal consequences, the government interpreted it as a clear indication of the unions' true position regarding the entire pension reform package. Most importantly, the vote signalled the tacit support of the CFDT, the relatively moderate but largest trade union federation. Consequently, the government decided to go ahead, and adopted the reform without major changes on 22 July 1993 (law) and on 27 August (decrees). The reform became effective in 1994 and will be gradually phased-in until 2008 (Bonoli 2000).

At the same time, even the most radical federation, the communist CGT (which fiercely rejected the entire reform package) failed to mobilise its members – let alone the public at large – against the reform. Despite their hostile proclamations, the CGT leadership did not produce a large-scale protest movement (*Le Monde*, 30 August 1993, p.1). To a great extent, this may be accounted for the fact that the Balladur reforms only affected workers in the basically non-unionised private sector.

The 1993 reforms will significantly improve the financial outlook of the *régime général*, although it will not prevent a substantial rise in contribution rates in the medium and long term. As shown in table 8.2, the medium-term effects of the reform on the projected contribution rates hinge largely on the development of employment and real wage growth. Moreover, they also depend on whether or not pensions continue to be indexed in line with prices. In the former case,[6] the increase in contribution rates between 1993 and 2010 will be lower (between 1% and 5.2%) than in the case of pensions adjusted according to wage developments (between 3.5% and 8%). With-

Table 8.2   Projected development of the equilibrium contribution rate[1] to the general regime before and after the 1993 reform

| | Before 1993 reform | | After 1993 reform | | | |
| | | | Wage indexation | | Price indexation | |
	Favourable scenario[2]	Unfavourable scenario[3]	Favourable scenario[2]	Unfavourable scenario[3]	Favourable scenario[2]	Unfavourable scenario[3]
1993	18%	18%	18%	18%	18%	18%
1995	18.5%	18.3%	18.4%	18.3%	18%	18%
2000	20.2%	21.1%	19.8%	20.6%	18.3%	19.5%
2005	21.6%	23.8%	20.6%	22.6%	18.3%	20.8%
2010	24.5%	28.3%	22.5%	26%	19%	23.2%

1. Contribution rate required to finance all current expenditures from a uniform contribution levied on labour income.
2. Employment growth = 1% per annum, real wage growth = 1.5% per annum
3. Employment growth = 0% per annum, real wage growth = 1% per annum

Source: Office for Official Publication of the European Communities (1996:64)

out the 1993 reforms, contribution rates would have grown between 6.5% and 10.3% until 2010. It has been estimated that in 2040 the contribution rate will be about 7% lower because of the 1993 reforms (Office for Official Publication of the European Communities 1996:65).

The failed reform of public sector pensions

As pointed out above, the Balladur reform only concerned the *régime général* which only covers employees in the private sector. There were no re-forms of public sector pensions. This may be due in part because of the specific entitlement rules for public sector employees and the specific working conditions of certain categories of public sector workers (such as miners and rail workers), which differ from those in the private sector. This was also the official reason why both reforms were dealt with separately. Perhaps more importantly, however, successive French governments hesitated to tackle the politically sensitive problem of public sector pensions. As pointed out above, French unions are much more powerful in the public than in the private sector, both with respect to the degree of unionisation and with respect to their mobilising capacity. Workers in the public sector had repeatedly organised prolonged strikes and other protest actions (Bonoli 2000).

However, increased outlays for public sector pensions strains the public budget, partly because employment-related contributions cover only a limited share of total costs, whereas the lion's share is financed out of the state budget. For instance, civil servants only pay a pension contribution rate of 6%, while the majority of civil servant pension outlays is financed by the government (Wischeropp 1999). At the same time, overall budgetary pressures remained strong. In 1995, the public deficit amounted to 5.6% of GDP (OECD 2001). Thus, an extraordinarily tight fiscal policy was required to meet the 3%-deficit criterion of the 1997 Maastricht Treaty. These pressures amplified the need to complement Balladur's reform of private sector pensions with a similar reform of public sector pensions.

Moreover, after the presidential elections, the political power constellation was more conducive to a major overhaul of public sector pensions than before. In May 1995, the Conservative Jaques Chirac was elected President, who again appointed Alan Juppé as Prime Minister. The election of Jaques Chirac eliminated the earlier division within the French executive (typically called *cohabitation)* between a Socialist President (Francois Mitterand) and a conservative Prime Minister (Edouard Balladur) that had existed since 1993.[7] Moreover, in contrast to his predecessor, Juppé faced only limited electoral constraints to the adoption of liberal welfare reforms because the next election was some three years away. Juppé also inherited an extraordinarily comfortable parliamentary majority of 79.7% and presided over an ideologically cohesive two-party government (Bonoli 2000).

Moreover, in contrast to his Italian counterpart, the French Prime Minister has significant power over the appointment of ministers, which tend to implement his policies. In addition, he disposes of a highly centralised policymaking apparatus and faces no institutional veto powers, as is the case for German governments, which are often dependent on the support of the *Bundesrat*. Hence, Juppé faced no institutional constraints in defining and implementing the content and the method of pension reform (Pitruzello 1997).

However, he faced the problem that the adoption of welfare cuts would necessarily run counter to the promises made by Jaques Chirac during the presidential election campaign. Among other things, Chirac had declared he was going to cut taxes and leave social benefits untouched. Initially, the government honoured several of its electoral promises. For instance, the statutory minimum wage and minimum pensions were raised generously in June 1995. However, in an effort to reduce the public-sector deficit (another promise made during the campaign), the government quickly changed course and announced a major reform of the social security system that was suffering from a huge structural deficit (Vail 1999; Bonoli 2000).

The preparation of the reform blueprint lasted until November 1995. The precise contents of the reforms were kept secret until the day the proposal was presented to Parliament. The so-called Juppé Plan was conceived and prepared by only four appointed social advisors and high-level civil servants, the Prime Minister, and the President. Quite remarkably, the government at large was excluded as was the Minister of Social Affairs within whose purview the reform actually fell. While the CGT and the FO were never even contacted during the formulation process, and even the leader of the moderate and relatively reform-oriented CFDT was only informed of the details a few days in advance. However, even then the sought-after reform of public sector pensions remained a secret. Apparently, pension reform was regarded as the most controversial issue. It was even controversial within the government, especially whether the reform of public sector pensions should or should not be included in the overall reform package. The government had good reasons to fear trade union reactions. On 10 October 1995, a large-scale strike took place against government plans to freeze public sector wages in 1996, and – for the first time since 1978 – the leaders of the seven union federations marched together. Initially, the Minister responsible for public sector employment, Jean Puech, fearing the political repercussions of such a move, had managed to convince Juppé to drop plans for public sector pension reform. As a consequence, trade unions were unofficially informed that this controversial item was not going to be included in the final reform package. In fact, Juppé changed his mind on the night before the publication of the plan. In response to the pressure of his predecessor and fellow party member, Edouard Balladur, who demanded a tighter fiscal policy, Juppé ultimately decided to incorporate the pension issue into his reform plan anyway (Pitruzello 1997; Bouget 1998; Vail 1999; Bonoli 2000).

On 15 November 1995, Juppé presented his plan in Parliament. It included the following elements (Bonoli 2000):

- the introduction of a universal health insurance scheme;
- the reform of public sector pension schemes (*régimes spéciaux*), which was intended to (at least partly) harmonise pensions in the public sector with those in the private sector. This would include the extension of the qualifying period for a full pension from 37.5 to 40 years, the introduction of a minimum retirement age of 60 (some civil servants are allowed to retire as early as age 50) and the calculation of benefits on the basis of the best 25 years (in the public sector, pensions are often calculated on the basis of last salary);
- the freezing of family benefits in 1996 and their taxation after 1997;

- the partial shift of health insurance financing from employment-related to general contributions levied on all incomes;
- the increase of health insurance contributions for unemployed and retired people by 1.2% in 1996 and in 1997 (at that time at 1.4%, or 5.4% below the standard contribution rate for those working);
- the introduction of a new tax, levied at a rate of 0.5% on all revenues, earmarked for the repayment of the debt accumulated by the social security system;
- the introduction of a constitutional amendment which allows Parliament to vote on the social security budget.

At the same time, Juppé sought to restructure the loss-making national railway company SNCF, a move which was likely to trigger protests among railway workers.

While the Juppé plan was welcomed by French employers and by international economic organisations such as the IMF, it was rejected by the trade unions and the Socialist opposition. It is interesting to note, however, that the Socialists were initially divided. While they condemned the plan through their official spokesmen, individual party representatives actually took a positive stance vis-à-vis the reform plan.[8] It was only after some time that the Socialist leader, Lionel Jospin, was able to unite the party against the Juppé plan. However, the main criticism was directed against the government's hegemonic approach, rather than the plan's content. In fact, many elements of the reform package (including the realignment of public sector pensions) had also been favoured by previous Socialist governments only a few years earlier (Bonoli 2000). This fact clearly restricted the Socialists' ability to exploit the pension issue politically, all the more so because the next election was only three years away. In addition, Juppé requested legislative authorisation to adopt the reforms by government decrees, thereby combining the issue with a vote of confidence. Given a parliamentary majority of almost 80%, this procedure was politically safe and prevented parliamentary debates as well as potential obstructionism on the part of the Socialist opposition (Pitruzello 1997). Thus, the rejection of the reforms by the parliamentary opposition did not pose a crucial political threat to the government.

This cannot be said with respect to the trade unions and their powerful mobilising capacity in the public sector. All of the trade unions denounced Juppé's unwillingness to enter into negotiations about the content of his reform package. Even Nicole Notat, leader of the moderate CFDT, noted that she had "*never seen a government according so little importance to consul-*

tation" (Vail 1999:323). However, while the CGT and FO condemned the whole programme, the moderate CFDT rejected only the reform of public sector pensions but, otherwise, largely supported the other aspects of the Juppé plan. A case can be made that the unanimous rejection of the planned changes to public sector pensions by the trade unions was a result of the dominant role of public employees within the trade union organisations.[9] As a consequence, none of the major trade union federations can afford to act against the interests of public sector employees.

With respect to those parts of the Juppé plan that were unrelated to public sector pensions, the basic union positions varied significantly. This is especially true for the constitutional amendment allowing Parliament to fix annual spending limits and the introduction of a universal health care system combined with a gradual shift in financing structures from employment-related contributions to general contributions. These measures were opposed by the FO and CGT, which feared the increased governmental control over social insurance and a concomitant reduction of their own influence on the social security system. In fact, these measures threatened to undermine the organisational power base – especially that of the FO – which used to have a dominant position in the parity-based management of the national health insurance fund (EIRR 1996b). The following citation by FO leader Marc Blondel illustrates the importance of this aspect (cited from Bonoli 2000:145):

> [the Juppé Plan] is the biggest theft in the history of the French Republic. It is the end of the Sécurité sociale. By deciding that Parliament is going to direct social protection, it robs us of 2,200 billion French francs made up of contributions paid by employers and employees. We were told that we needed to act in order to save social security, but they are taking it away from us (*Le Monde* 17 November 1995, p.12).

By contrast, the CFDT leadership took a less critical or even positive stance towards these reform elements. For instance, the CFDT welcomed the replacement of employment-related contributions by a universal social contribution (CSG) in the financing of health insurance, a process which was completed by the left-wing Jospin government in 1998. In sharp contrast to the hostile reaction by the FO, it lauded this move as "a measure of equity and fairness, finally in line with the aims of the architects of social security. Everyone will contribute according to his or her income and will receive according to his or her needs" (Eiroline 1997b). Similarly, the CFDT approved the government's efforts to gain a tighter grip on the massive financing problems of the social security system (Eiroline 1997c).

The gradual reorientation of the CFDT leadership towards more moderate and reformist policy positions is accompanied by their endeavour to become the privileged partner of the government and of employers in the management of social insurance funds. In principle, this strategy proved to be successful. In the re-appointment of the heads of the social insurance funds after 1995, the CFDT allied itself with the employers' representatives and thereby managed to largely replace the FO, which lost all of its important positions, especially the head of the National Health Care Insurance Fund (EIRR 1996b; Palier 2000).

Against this background, the CFDT leadership initially took a less hostile position against the entire Juppé plan, which again caused serious tensions with the other trade union confederations, in particular with the FO, whose leader Marc Blondel accused his CFDT colleague of "speaking like a minister" (EIRR 1995b). A case can be made that the leaders of the CFDT – given their general support of the Juppé plan – might also have begrudgingly accepted the sought-after cuts in public sector pensions. It is telling that the CFDT initially refused to take part in a general strike called for 28 November by the CGT and the FO. Nevertheless, the rank and file of all the unions (including members of the CFDT) supported organised resistance against the Juppé plan. In fact, large sections of the CFDT base did not understand how a leftist trade union could support a conservative government's plans. As a consequence, the CFDT leadership proved unable to resist the demands for action raised by its more militant members and hence closed ranks with the other trade unions, which henceforth formed a unified front vis-à-vis the government (Bouget 1998; Vail 1999).

In response to the Juppé plan and the Prime Minister's refusal to accommodate their demands, the French trade unions (with the CGT and FO taking a leading role) launched a number of strikes at the end of November. Within a few weeks a gigantic, albeit incoherent, protest movement emerged against the Juppé government, fuelled by various social groups. This movement reached its climax in the second week of December when hundred thousands of protesters took to the streets in numerous French cities.[10] Initially, it was mainly railway workers who went on strike. These strikes, which effectively paralysed large sections of the French economy, lasted some three weeks. A few days later, other public sector workers (in the gas and electricity, postal and telecommunications sectors, air traffic, regional transport, hospitals, schools, ports, and the Bank of France) went on strike as well.[11] Thus, French unions were extraordinarily successful in mobilising public sector employees against the Juppé plan. Against this background, they radicalised their positions and called upon Juppé to withdraw his plans before negotiations could begin (EIRR 1996a; Pitruzello 1997; Bonoli 2000).

Initially, Juppé refused any dialogue with the unions and maintained his confrontational style. In a speech to Parliament on 5 December he confirmed his resolve to enact the reforms as a necessary means to maintaining international competitiveness and to meeting European commitments. However, in the face of continued paralysis, Juppé finally offered to include the trade unions in the reform process. With respect to pensions, he commissioned his labour minister Jaques Barrot to organise a roundtable with the union leaders to discuss the implementation of the reforms. The unions rejected this invitation and continued to demand a complete withdrawal of the reform plans. At the same time, they called for another general strike. Based on the (correct) perception that the sought-after reform of public sector pensions was the most controversial issue of his reform package, Juppé on 10 December rescinded this reform element while largely standing behind the other elements of the plan, including measures aimed at increasing government's control over social security. The decision to withdraw the planned cuts in pensions for public sector workers ended much of the strike action and took the wind out of the sails of the protest movement. In a nutshell, Juppé completely failed with his plan to impose pension cuts for public sector workers, whereas Balladur two years earlier had been quite successful in implementing similar curtailments in the private sector (Pitruzello 1997; Vail 1999; Bonoli 2000).

The reform of the complementary regimes

In the mid-1990s the complementary regimes for wage earners in the private sector, i.e., ARRCO and ARGIRC (for executives only), were reformed as well. This was done through collective bargaining agreements between the social partners without state interference.[12] In the 1993 and 1994 agreements, trade unions and employers' associations stipulated an increase in contribution rates. Within the ARRCO schemes, for instance, the minimum contribution rate (many employers and employees pay higher contributions on a voluntary basis) was gradually increased from 4% to 6% until 1999. In 1996, another contract was signed between the social partners, which sought the transformation of the 46 individual ARRCO schemes into a single scheme. Moreover, in order to ensure the financial equilibrium of these schemes until 2005, the agreement stipulated a further increase in contribution rates, lowered pension entitlements per contribution point, and lower nominal increases in pension levels. Under the assumption that the nominal

Table 8.3   Projections of gross replacement rates for three typical cases[1] (in % of previous wages)

	1996	2020	2040
	Blue collar, private sector[2]		
General regime	45.7	41.1	40.9
ARRCO	22.4	15.4	10.3
Total	68.1	56.5	51.2
	Executive worker, private sector[3]		
General regime	22.9	20.6	20.6
ARRCO	11.7	8.2	5.4
AGIRC	24.4	16.7	11.9
Total	59.0	45.5	37.9
	Civil servant		
Total	57.8	57.8	57.8

1. Including the impact of the 1993 reform for the general regime and of planned indexation rules for the complementary schemes ARRCO and AGIRC
2. Individual reaching the social security ceiling after 20 years of contributions
3. Individual at the 90 percentile of wage earners affiliated with the general regime

Source: Charpin (1999)

value of pension points will continue to be adjusted in line with prices and that real wages will double until 2040, this reform was to result in a drastic reduction of future replacement levels. For instance, the combined gross replacement rate (general regime plus ARRCO pension) for an average blue-collar worker in the private sector is projected to fall from a level of around 68% in 1996 to almost 50% in 2040. While only about 5% of this reduction results from the changes in the general regime, more than 10% can be attributed to the reform of the ARCCO scheme. The reduction will turn out to be even stronger for pensions from the AGIRC scheme providing supplementary benefits for executive workers. By contrast, due to the failure of the Juppé plan, replacement rates for civil servants will remain unchanged in the absence of reform (see table 8.3).

The successful implementation of cost containment reforms within the complementary regimes can be attributed to at least two factors. First, as set out in chapter one the complementary regimes are based on a defined-contribution design. As a consequence, the retention of the status quo automatically boils down to a decrease in benefit levels if demographic changes lead to a rapidly growing share of pensioners. Under these conditions, trade unions will only be able to defend current benefit levels if they have the power to change (instead of only defend) the status quo. This again requires the approval of the employers, which will resist a drastic increase in contribution rates. Moreover, as the complementary schemes are by their very nature exclusively financed out of wage-based contributions, trade unions cannot hope that the government will take over any of the financial responsibilities, as it has frequently done with respect to the general system in the past. Second, the complementary regimes cover only workers in the private sector. In this area, however, trade unions' power base is much weaker than in the public sector due to very low levels of organisation. Thus, with respect to the complementary regimes, the bargaining power of trade unions is comparatively limited. This may explain why French trade unions have not hesitated to sign agreements that impose tangible losses for about 14 million private sector employees, while they fiercely opposed cutbacks of public sector pensions (EIRR 1993; EIRR 1996c; Bozec and Mays 2001).

The Thomas Law of 1997 – a failed attempt to establish private pension funds

The Juppé government also took steps to create a third tier of pension provisions – based on private pension funds – in addition to the pay-as-you-go financed basic and complementary pension schemes. To this end, the French Parliament adopted a bill on retirement savings funds (known as the "Thomas Law" or *Loi Thomas*) earmarked for some 14.4 million employees in the private sector as well as agricultural workers. The establishment of these pension funds should make up for both the reduction in public pension benefits associated with the general regime reforms and in the complementary schemes. It also sought to strengthen the French equity market and counterbalance the growing power of foreign institutional investors.[13]

All private sector employees can voluntarily join the retirement savings funds (*plans d'épargne retraite*). The funds can be established on the basis of a collective agreement at the company or sectoral level. However, if no agreement is reached after six months of negotiations, subscription to the plan may also be unilaterally decided by the employer. Moreover, employees without access to a savings plan through an employer are allowed to join a scheme of their own choice. These funds were intended to provide for a life annuity during retirement, which would be subject to income taxes and which could be transferred to one's partner or children. Both employees and employers can freely decide the level of contributions. These contributions are tax-free, up to limit of 5% of the gross salary. (EIRR 1997c; Reynaud 1997). Moreover, employers payments would be free from social security contributions up to a certain limit (EIRR 1997; Reynaud 1997).

The Thomas Law was supported by the French bank and insurance industries and – at least in principle – by the employers' association. Interestinngly, it was the Minister of Economic Affairs who was in charge of applying this very law, rather than the Minister of Employment and Social Affairs, who was opposed to this bill. The left-wing parliamentary opposition and the trade unions saw it as an indication of the dominance of financial interests over social concerns. By the same token, they feared a "de-solidarisation" of old age provisions with only a small group of well-off employees profiting from the new private pillar. The fact that employer payments to these pension funds were deductible from social security contributions was also perceived as a potential threat to the financial viability of the pay-as-you-go financed pension schemes. The trade unions, in particular, feared that the establishment of private pension funds (which would be run by private insurance companies rather than collectively by the social partners) may over time lead to a gradual crowding out of pensions from the complementary regimes, the management of which provides for an indispensable job and income source for union functionaries. Another objection to this legislation concerned its incompability with the advantage rule (*Günstigkeitsprinzip*) as stipulated in employment law. The reason is that a company agreement or an employer's unilateral decision can prevail even if a more favourable agreement is concluded at the branch level. Given these concerns, the Socialist party committed itself to repealing the Thomas Law with a change of government. Thus, after the leftist election victories only a few months later, the new government decided against implementation of this piece of legislation (Reynaud 1997; Blanchet and Legros 2000).

Pension policy under the Jospin government

Although the huge right-wing majority in the *Assemblée Nationale* still had a year of its mandate left, in April 1997, President Chirac exercised his constitutional prerogative to dissolve Parliament and called for early elections. This decision was based on the assumption that the electoral outlook for the bourgeois parties would only worsen in 1997 as the EMU would require further unpopular austerity measures. Nevertheless, the bourgeois government parties failed to maintain their parliamentary majority. Their combined vote share fell from 39.5 to 31.5%, while both the left-wing and the extreme-right opposition substantially increased their vote shares. The electoral defeat of the Juppé government is at least partly due to Juppé's unpopular austerity policies combined with his confrontational and hegemonic policy style towards the trade unions. What is more, his austerity policy was a direct contradiction of Chirac's election promises during the 1995 presidential campaign. The election meant a left-wing parliamentary majority forming a shaky Socialist-Green-Communist coalition headed by Lionel Jospin. With their largest share of parliamentary seats since 1981 (6.6%) and two ministers in the cabinet, the Communists were able to secure a strong influence within the new government (Szarka 1997).

Jospin differed fundamentally from his predecessors with regard to policy style. In contrast to the technocratic and hegemonic approach adopted by Juppé, Jospin attached great importance to negotiation and concertation with the various social partners. In contrast to Balladur's post facto concertation, Jospin sought to incorporate the social partners in the early stages of policy formulation. To this end, he applied a technique that had been used frequently by French governments in the past. He commissioned experts to draft reports to test the reactions of the social partners before moving ahead with (or abstaining from) controversial reforms (Levy 2000).

With respect to pension reform, Jospin's first trial came with the publication of the Charpin Report by France's National Economic Planning Agency in co-operation with the social partners' pension experts in March 1999 (Charpin 1999). Although the government presented a diagnosis of the pension problem that was in general agreement with the views of the social partners, the report's proposals turned out to be highly controversial. Based on a rather gloomy scenario of the financial development of public pension schemes in the medium and long term, the report proposed a gradual lengthening of the qualifying period for a full pension to 42.5 years (previously 37.5 years in the public and 40 years in the private sector) over the next 20 years. In addition, it recommended beefing up the newly-created reserve fund within the public pension system (see below).

While employers' associations approved the extension of the contribution period (and called for even more comprehensive adjustments), unions reactions were mixed and ranged from cautious approval to open hostility. The CFDT in principle shared the overall philosophy of the Charpin Report and called for a progressive harmonisation of private and public sector pension schemes. However, powerful federations within the CFDT such as the rail workers' federation opposed this line and threatened to take industrial actions against any attempts to curb their pension entitlements (which were more generous than those of the general scheme). CGT and FO also condemned the report's proposals. They particularly rejected the extension of the qualifying period in the context of persistently high unemployment, in fact they were calling for a return to a contribution period of 37.5 years in the private sector (Sauviat 1999; Bozec and Mays 2001).

In an effort to find a more promising foundation for negotiations with the trade unions, the Jospin government distanced itself from the Charpin Report and commissioned the Council of Economic Analysis, an institution composed mainly of left-wing academics, to draft another report on the pension problem. In so doing, Jospin sought to present a more palatable reform concept to the trade unions. The so-called Taddéi Report, published in September 1999, presented solutions to the pension problem that differed from the Charpin Study. While rejecting the extension of the qualifying period (as proposed by Charpin), the Taddéi Report advocated a more progressive transition from activity to retirement.

Only a few months later, the so-called Teulade Report was published by the French Economic and Social Council (a consulting assembly provided for in the Constitution of the French Republic and representing a broad array of social interest groups), on its own authority and not the government's. Remarkably, the Teulade Report's conclusions were diametrically opposed to the Charpin Report's. For instance, it rejected the augmentation of the contribution period, especially in the context of high unemployment and disapproved of harmonising the special regimes with the less favourable rules of the general scheme. Noting that harmonisation should not lead to a deterioration of benefit rules in the special regimes but instead to an improvement of those in the general system. Moreover, the Teulade Report argued in favour of a return to wage indexation for private-sector pensions. Like the Taddéi Report, the Teulade Report also advocated the limitation of early retirement options and improved incentives for companies to keep older employees (based on training and flexible systems of progressive retirement departures). To relieve the pension system's finance problems, the report advocated fortifying the public reserve fund, increasing state-financing of non-contributory benefits and including revenues other than wages. Above all, it underscores the need to foster economic and employment growth. Based on the assumption of an economic growth rate of 3.5% per year until 2040(!), the report states that the long-term viability of the pension system can be ensured without benefit cuts.

The Teulade Report was heavily criticised by the employers' association and the right-wing political parties, which denounced its unrealistic assumptions. The CFDT was also critical of the report, asserting that economic growth and lower unemployment alone would not be enough to address the pension system's finance problems. It also criticised the absence of proposals that dealt with greater harmonisation of pension schemes. Most of the other trade unions, however, supported the general orientation of the report and its emphasis on employment policy (rather than on pension cuts) as a means of consolidating the pension system. This strong divergence of policy positions among the key actors in French pension politics made it virtually impossible to arrive at a broad political consensus on pension reform (Blanchet and Legros 2000; Sauviat 2000; Bozec and Mays 2001).

The fierce resistance of large sections of the French trade union movement against any form of pension retrenchment forced the government coalition (within which a number of leftist representatives partly shared unions' concerns) to postpone decisions on this controversial issue until at least after the 2002 general elections. Clearly, the big 1995 social protest movement against the Juppé plan and the subsequent withdrawal of proposal to cut pensions in the public sector had a deterrent effect on Jospin. Moreover, the post-1997 economic recovery associated with yearly growth rates well above 3%, falling unemployment, and an improvement of public finances created a situation in which pension cuts were not needed to reduce the budgetary deficit and stabilise contribution rates in the short term. This again made it easier for Jospin to pursue a non-decisive policy on the reform of the public pension system (Sauviat 1999; Bozec and Mays 2001). Jospin's only significant cost containment measure in the area of pensions was the temporary continuation of price indexation (rather than wage indexation). As the 2002 elections approached, however, the Jospin government deviated from this course in order to improve its election prospects and so in 2001 and 2002, pensions were raised by 2.2%, an increase significantly above the inflation rate.

Jospin's wait-and-see attitude was also evident in the promotion of private pension funds. As mentioned above, the Jospin government repealed the Thomas "law" on private pension funds, which had been adopted by the preceding bourgeois government. The abrogation was primarily prompted by the fierce opposition of trade unions, which criticised the fact that these pension funds would force out rather than complement the existing pay-as-you-go based pension schemes and give no role to the social partners. Hence, Jospin decided to first concentrate on fortifying the public pension system. In November 1998, the government set up a reserve fund within the pay-as-you-go system (*fonds de reserve*) to smooth over the effects of the imminent demographic shock. It has been financed by, among others, a "solidarity contribution" levied on companies, the surpluses from the general scheme, part of a 2% tax levy on capital revenues, dividends from part-state-owned companies, the proceeds of future privatisations, and profits from the sale of UMTS licenses. The reserve fund is invested in financial markets and largely managed by the government. Clearly, the relatively favourable budgetary conditions during Jospin's term in office facilitated the creation of the reserve fund. With an original endowment of 2 billion francs the fund is intended to achieve a volume of 1000 billion francs (152 billion Euro) in 2020 (in constant prices). However, in order to stabilise the pension system in the long run, the sought-after volume would have to be much higher (Sauviat 1998; Blanchet and Legros 2000; Bozec and Mays 2001; Math 2001).

The French trade unions – in contrast to the employers – in principle, supported the idea of a capital stock *within* the public pension pillar as a means of sustaining the financial viability of the pay-as-you-go system in the context of demographic changes. They were also in favour of the collective nature of this measure. In contrast to private pension funds, a public fund would not lead to a "desolidarisation" of old age provisions. The unions mainly criticised the management and organisation of the fund, which was characterised by the dominant role played by the government with only limited influence by the social partners (Math 2001).

While the Jospin government did not rule out the creation of private pension funds, it aimed to develop pension funds more in line with the preferences of the political left and the trade unions. Apart from the FO, French trade unions accepted the principle of pension funds. But unlike Juppé's plans, the trade unions wanted compulsory funds, that are managed collectively by the social partners and do not compete for funding with the pay-as-you-go systems. Jospin also promised not to authorise the establishment of private pension funds before reforms to sustain the long-term viability of the public pension system were adopted. Hence, France still lags behind the other countries studied with respect to the development of third-pillar pensions (Sauviat 1998; Levy 2000).

Explanatory factors for the slow pace of pension reform in France

By and large, French pension policymakers have made only limited progress in making the pension system more sustainable. In order to account for France's meagre reform record in pension policy we need only briefly recall the fact that the pension reform process after 1985 is divided into four distinct phases:

1 A period of non-decision until 1992, covering tenures of both bourgeois and Socialist governments.

2 The bourgeois Balladur government (March 1993-May 1995) adopted a substantial reform of private sector pensions. While yielding considerable savings in the medium and long run, the reform is less ambitious than the "big" pension reforms adopted in Sweden and Italy, both of which led to a radical shift from defined-benefit to defined-contribution systems. Moreover, the Balladur reform alone will not be enough to stabilise private sector pension costs in the face of demographic ageing.

3 The bourgeois Juppé government (May 1995-June 1997) failed in its attempt to impose a major reform of public sector pensions.

4 Finally, the Socialist-Green-Communist coalition government under Lionel Jospin (June 1997-May 2002) represents – by and large – a period of non-decision in pension reform.

Thus, for most of the time since the mid-1980s (before 1993 and again after 1997), French governments have basically pursued a policy of non-decision, refraining from launching major initiatives to reform the pension system, although in principle they acknowledged the need for reform. Only in three cases did French governments take the initiative to move forward with controversial pension reform plans. Two of these three attempts essentially failed, either because the government withdrew its reform plan in the face of massive social unrest (Juppé's plan to cut public sector pensions) or because the subsequent government reversed the reform (the creation of private pension funds through the Thomas Law). The only successful attempt at pension reform by the French government (the Balladur reform in 1993) was not enough to ensure the long-term viability of the pension system and left a number of critical issues (public sector pensions, the development of fully funded pension plans) unsolved. Hence, I will first summarise those factors which explain the remarkable resilience of the French pension system. Thereafter, I will briefly recapitulate the (exceptional) conditions which facilitated the success of Balladur's reform attempt in 1993.

The phenomenon that most French governments made no serious attempts to reform the pension system suggests that these governments considered the political costs of reform higher than the costs of non-reform. This is primarily due to the fact that a broad political consensus on pension reform is extremely difficult to achieve in French politics and that the potential losers of reform may be able to mobilise effectively against the curtailment of their pension claims. The specific features of the French party system tend to impede the emergence of an alliance for pension reform across the political camps. The party system is characterised by very strong competition between the left-wing and bourgeois blocs. This again results from

France's majority-style electoral system, in which even small electoral gains for one camp may transform into a huge majority of parliamentary seats. Moreover, the French polity until recently featured a double electoral cycle (with general elections every five and presidential elections every seven years), which additionally intensified the high degree of bipolar party competition (Bonoli 2000). These factors amplify the electoral cost of pension reform and render a broad pension consensus between government and opposition parties extremely difficult even if their pension policy positions do not deviate very much from one another. Moreover, under these conditions the left-wing governments between 1988 and 1993 and between 1997 and 2002 had to rely on the parliamentary support of the Communists, who tended to oppose significant cutbacks of public pensions as a matter of principle.

The most important impediment to effective pension reform, however, concerns the organisational structures and the mobilising capacities of French trade unions. A number of institutional factors hamper the strategic capacity of French trade unions to strike package deals with the government in the area of pension policy:

First, the unions are highly competitive among one another. Consequently, a trade union confederation co-operating with the government in welfare retrenchment can be easily denounced by other unions as a "sell out" of workers interests and may therefore jeopardise the support of its own members (Levy 2000).

Second, French trade union confederations have little control over their sub-organisations and their rank and file in general, which is often able and willing to organise spontaneous strikes at the grassroots level without the approval of their national leadership (Deutsch-Französisches Institut 2001). Given the categorical fragmentation of the French pension system, this favours the particularistic interests of individual occupational groups (i.e., public sector workers) at the expense of more comprehensive interests at the leadership level (such as the interest of the CFDT leadership in a greater harmonisation between private and public sector pensions). Hence, French unions largely lack the strategic capacity to organise consent for reforms which impose losses on some members at the benefit of the greater collective (Culpepper 2000).

Third, the unions are likely to fight any reforms which may threaten their institutional position in the social insurance administrative bodies (including the complementary regimes). The main reason is that French unions are insufficiently funded due to very low levels of organisation, especially in the private sector. Thus, their involvement in the management of social insurance bodies provides them with an indispensable job and income source for their functionaries (Bonoli and Palier 2000; Palier 2000; Ebbinghaus 2001). Hence, virtually all French trade unions were strongly opposed to the type of private pension funds established by the Thomas Law. According to this legislation, the management of private pension funds would primarily fall into the hands of private insurance companies rather with the social partners. Moreover, as contributions to these funds were deductible from contributions to the public pension system, the trade unions feared a financial erosion of public social insurance and a concomitant weakening of their organisational power resources (Veil 2000a; Veil 2000b).

Against this background it is not surprising that the representatives of traditionalist, strictly status quo oriented policy positions tend to prevail within the French trade union movement, whereas the more reformist forces have a difficult time making themselves heard. French trade unions, however, *do* show a considerable readiness and capacity to mobilise their members. This is especially true for the public sector, where the level of unionisation is considerably higher than in the basically non-unionised private sector. Certain occupational groups in the public sector such as railway workers are able to carry out strike actions that effectively paralyze strategic sectors of the national economy which can last for several weeks. As their successful protests against Juppé's attempt to cut public sector pensions have shown, French unions can even assert themselves against an institutionally strong and ideologically cohesive government (Pitruzello 1997). Against this background, it does not come as a surprise that French governments more often than not have sought to avoid direct clashes with the trade unions over the controversial issue of pension reform.

Of all the French governments since 1985 only the Balladur government could bring about a major reform of the French pension system. According to Vail (1999), the success of Balladur is based on the judicious choice of policy substance plus on the policymaking style on the part of the government. Both factors ensured the tacit acquiescence of the trade unions or at least the non-appearance of a major protest movement against the proposed reforms. Concerning policy substance, Balladur confined the reform to employees in the private sector and thereby avoided a conflict with the more militant unions in the public sector. In addition, Balladur included a number of important concessions to the trade unions in his reform package, such as a shift in the financing of non-contributory benefits from social contributions towards taxes. As Bonoli (2000) points out, this measure was a key demand of some trade unions. It relieved the financial pressure on social insurance schemes by reducing the deficits within the system. Moreover, through the separation of contributory and non-contributory elements, the government acknowledged the trade unions' managerial role in social insurance. By contrast, the Juppé reform in 1995 combined benefit cutbacks with an attack on trade unions' managerial role within the system by empowering the Parliament to vote every year on the social security budget. Finally, Balladur had a deliberately non-confrontational policy style and attached great importance to intense consultations with the trade unions, whereas Juppé developed his reform plan under complete secrecy and (at least initially) rejected negotiations with the trade unions, thereby reducing the scope for an amicable agreement.

Addendum: Most recent developments

As in Austria, a major pension reform was adopted more recently (July 2003). Unfortunately, the effects of this reform on the future development of public pension outlays have not yet taken into account in the spending projections reported in chapter two. Nevertheless, as in the Austrian case, there is strong reason to believe that this reform will dampen the expected increase of pension expenditures quite substantially. Thus, it appears appropriate to conclude this chapter with a brief assessment of the most recent developments in French pension politics.

The general elections in June 2002 saw the replacement of Lionel Jospin's left-wing government with a conservative government headed by Jean-Pierre Raffarin, which also gained a sizeable majority of Parliament seats. Shortly after assuming office, the new government began preparing a major reform of the public pension system. In May 2003, it issued a draft bill on pension reform concerning the general pension scheme, the civil servants' schemes, and the schemes for the self-employed. However, in contrast to the Juppé plan, the draft did not seek changes for the special schemes (i.e., for train and metro drivers). The draft proposed the following measures (Jolivet 2003a):

- By 2008, public sector employees would – as their counterparts in the private sector – have to pay 40 instead of 37.5 years of contributions in order to be entitled to a full state pension. Depending on the development of life expectancy, the contribution period could be extended to 42 years by 2020 (both in the public and private sector).
- All pensions would be adjusted in line with cost of living changes (as is the case for the general scheme since 1993).

– Civil servants' pensions would be based on the last three years salary (rather than over the last six months).
– Survivor's pensions would be simplified and means-tested.

While this draft also includes a number of compensatory elements (such as the inclusion of bonuses for public-sector workers in the calculation of their pensions or the lowering of the "reduction coefficient" for each year of early retirement from 10% to 6%) the overall effect of this package would be a substantial reduction of pension benefits in particular for employees in the public sector. Hence, the government's reform plan was sharply criticised by French trade unions. On 13 May 2003, the five major union confederations organised wide-scale strikes and demonstrations with 57.5% of central government employees taking part in the strike actions and with another one to two million people joining the demonstrations against the reform proposals (Jolivet 2003b). Furthermore, another one-third of the population approved of the protests (*The Economist*, 17 May 2003).

In contrast to the Juppé government, which had hammered out its reform plan in complete secrecy, Prime Minister Raffarin sought to involve the social partners at a relatively early stage. In February 2003, he had outlined the main points of his planned pension reform to the social partners. Moreover, his Minister of Social Affairs, François Fillon, had signalled the government's readiness to negotiate the reform plan with the trade unions (Jolivet 2003c). In particular, he had suggested that there was room to negotiate on several issues such as a rise in minimum pensions for low-salary employees or the maintenance of the option for retirement before 60 in the case of those with long working lives (*The Economist*, 17 May 2003). In hindsight, the government's willingness to enter into serious negotiations with the unions turned out to be much more effective than Juppé's unilateral approach. On 14 May, one day after the unions' large-scale protests, the government met the social partners and offered a number of significant concessions. Through these concessions the government was able to drive a wedge within the French trade union movement, which was internally divided in its pension policy positions. While the radical FO was demanding an even *shorter* contribution period in the private sector, the moderate CFDT only sought to obtain some selective improvements to the government's reform draft. This explains, why CGT and FO dropped out of the negotiations at a rather early stage, whereas the other confederations remained until the end of the meetings. Two of them, the CFDT and the (minor) CFE-CGC ultimately accepted the revised government's proposals, which contained 19 amendments. While seriously altering the government bill, the amendments did not challenge the key issue of the reform, i.e., the lengthening of the contribution period required to get a full state pension. The most important amendments concern (Jolivet 2003b):

– increase in the level of minimum pensions for those with a full earning career to 85% of the minimum wage (rather than 75% as originally proposed by the government);
– the option to retire before the age of 60 for those employed since the age of 16;
– lower actuarial reductions in the case of early retirement (5% instead of 10% per year);
– a 0.2% increase in social contributions to improve the financial balance of the pension system.

In addition, the final legislation also included some compensatory measures for civil servants:

– a new supplementary scheme would be created for civil servants which includes bonus payments received throughout the working career (up to a limit of 20% of the salary);
– the calculation period would continue to be based on the last six months of employment (rather than the last three years as proposed by the government);
– the possibility to repurchase years of studies;
– the validation of part-time employment as full-time.

The compromise agreement marked the clear end of a united union front against the government's pension plans. The unions that did not sign the pension deal announced further industrial actions against the reforms.[14] The government, however, stood firm against the trade unions. After one-and-a-half months the strikes crumbled. The government, through its deal with the CFDT, was not only able to ensure that basic public services would run (all the more since the special schemes for railway and electricity and gas utility workers had from the outset been excluded from the reform measures) but also to undermine moral support for the strikes by the general public. Quite remarkably, tens of thousands of people demonstrated in Paris *against* the striking union members, urging the government not to give in (*The Economist*, 28 June 2003). Moreover, given its comfortable parliamentary majority, the Raffarin government had few problems in passing its pension bill.

It was not surprising that the CFDT's agreement with the government caused harsh conflicts within the French trade union movement. Not only the other trade union federations but also some of its own members fiercely criticised the CFDT for its "hurried" decision to strike an agreement with the government (Jolivet 2003b). The CFDT leadership, by contrast, claimed that its negotiations with the government had resulted in concrete and important achievements for union members. In return, the CFDT criticised the FO and CGT for their unwillingness to enter into serious negotiations with the government, arguing that this strategy weakened the CFDT's position in the bargaining process (see CFDT 2003a). It must also be noted that the CFDT's agreement with the bourgeois government was also attacked by the Socialist opposition. Certain Socialist Party representatives even encouraged the CFDT's rank and file to abandon their union (see CFDT 2003b).

The recent pension reforms adopted by the Raffarin government were the first successful attempts to curb pension benefits in the French public sector. As this reform has demonstrated, the mobilising capacity of French unions in the public sector is not necessarily an insurmountable obstacle when it comes to painful curtailments for public employees. Moreover, their mobilising capacity is not unlimited. Raffarin's skilful bargaining strategy allowed him to split the French trade unions and thus weaken their protest movement against his pension plans. This shows that the ideological fragmentation of the French trade unions may under certain conditions constitute a strategic advantage for reform-oriented governments in that it also offers them opportunities to split the labour movement on certain issues and to isolate (or at least critically weaken) those forces within the trade union camp that unconditionally stick to the status quo.

9   Conclusion

Pension reform is difficult but it happens

Welfare retrenchment is a difficult undertaking. As Pierson (1997) points
out, the welfare state appears to be the most resilient aspect of the post-war
political economy, with pensions probably being the most resilient part of it.
This is particularly true for pension systems of the Bismarckian type covering large sections of the population and granting earnings-related benefits
typically perceived as "acquired rights" on the part of the beneficiaries.
Nevertheless, most governments in the countries studied have sought to reform their retirement income systems in recent years. In principle, this holds
true for both left and right governments, although the experiences in Austria, Germany, and Sweden show that Social Democratic party leaders often
had greater difficulties in organising support for painful pension cuts within
their own party organisations than did their bourgeois counterparts. Governmental reform efforts in pension policy were mainly aimed at dampening
the growth of non-wage labour costs, unburdening the public budget, establishing a tighter link between contributions and benefits, harmonising benefit regulations between different pension schemes and stimulating the expansion of fully funded old age provisions. As far as the goal of cost containment is concerned, the countries studied have made substantial progress
since the late 1980s. Pension policymakers in the Bismarckian countries
have adopted a number of cost containment measures in recent years. As a
consequence, public pension expenditures will now grow much more slowly
over the following decades than they would have done otherwise.

Huge differences in national sequences of pension policymaking

However, comparing the national developments conducted in this study
also revealed substantial variations *around* the trend line and, perhaps even
more importantly, in the timing and speed of reforms. Among the countries
studied, Sweden stands out as the only country that managed to ensure the

long-term sustainability of its pension system in one big step rather than in a long succession of numerous more or less piecemeal adjustments.

In Italy, pension policy continued to be expansive rather than contractive until the early 1990s. Thereafter, however, this policymaking pattern changed radically. Within only three years, two major pension reforms were passed, as a consequence of which, public pension outlays are likely to remain below 16% of GDP over the next 50 years rather than reaching a peak of more than 23% around 2040. In 1994, however, this process had suffered a severe, albeit temporary, set-back when Prime Minister Berlusconi failed in his attempt to impose a radical reform of the pension system on the trade unions.

In Germany, governments began reducing the generosity of the pension system as early as 1977. Since then, pension policy is characterised by frequent adjustments, most of them rather incremental. In sum, these adjustments resulted in substantial benefit reductions. Thus far, however, none of them have proven sufficient enough to stabilise pension contributions in the long run. Moreover, pension cuts were occasionally even reversed, for instance with the suspension of the Pension Reform Act 1999 (legislated in 1997) by the red-green government in 1999.

In Austria, the first cautious attempts at pension retrenchment took place in the mid-1980s. However, until the late 1990s these reform initiatives resulted in little more than a gentle trimming of one of Europe's most lavish pension systems. However, beginning in 2000, the reform process gained momentum with tangible benefit cuts implemented in a relatively short period of time.

In France, the first significant (albeit still insufficient) pension cost containment reforms were only adopted in 1993. In the following years, the reform process ground to a complete standstill. Since in 1995 a major attempt to cut public sector pensions had failed, no further initiatives to curb public pension spending were launched. It was only in 2003, when a French government took a new (and successful) initiative to contain public pension spending.

In my study, I have treated specific instances of pension reform (or non-reform) within each country as the crucial unit of analyses rather than countries as such. As we have seen, there is no invariable country-specific pattern of pension reform that would remain constant over time. Most of the countries studied have experienced both successful and failed reform initiatives as well as non-decision periods concerning pension reform. While some of the reforms were far-reaching, others were watered down beyond recognition. In summary, the conditions for successful adjustment in pension policy appear to vary considerably *across* but also *within* countries. This study has sought to explore the factors that account for this twofold variation.

Empirical findings reveal the insufficiency of functionalist approaches

The analysis of the political decision-making processes in the various countries revealed that pension politics goes beyond mere functional adaptation to external pressures. To be sure, the internationalisation of product and capital markets, the pressure for fiscal austerity, and especially the ageing populations constitute important driving forces for national policymakers to place pension reform on the political agenda. In some countries, most notably Italy, the politically binding criteria of the Maastricht Treaty clearly accelerated the pace of pension reform. However, even there the mere presence of strong external as well as internal pressures did not guarantee the successful implementation of pension reforms. The failed pension reform plans of the Berlusconi government in 1994 provide striking evidence of this. Supranational or functionalist models of social policy reform suggesting a seamless transformation of external pressures into corresponding policy decisions by national policymakers therefore tend to neglect the importance of domestic factors.

An actor-centred analysis of pension policy

In this analysis, the key focus centred on the *actors* involved in the politics of pension reform. Following the theoretical framework of actor-centred institutionalism (Scharpf 1997b), political actors are characterised by specific capabilities, perceptions, preferences, and interaction orientations, and operate in a specific institutional context. By drawing on these theoretical categories I sought to identify the causes of different outcomes in the area of pension policy. In what follows, I will briefly review how far the approach of actor-centred institutionalism can be applied to the analysis of the politics of pension reform in Bismarckian countries.

In order to adequately understand the actor constellation within the area of pension policy, we must recall the fact that pension reform is associated with considerable political costs. Broadly speaking, pension politics these days are as much about adjusting pension arrangements to changing demographic and economic conditions as they are about overcoming widespread political resistance to reforms that impose tangible losses on large parts of the electorate. As the ratio of pensioners to the number of employed continues to increase significantly in the future, pension reforms translating the secular trend of demographic ageing into legislative decisions ultimately boil down to a distribution of financial burdens. There is little doubt that pension benefits will become less generous while pension costs (including expenditures to occupational and private forms of old age provisions) will continue to rise. If current levels of financing are maintained, pension benefits are likely to fall. Conversely, if current pension levels are to be maintained, a much higher share of the gross domestic product needs to be channelled into the pension system. In other words, pension policymakers are inevitably faced with a "tragic choice" where all alternatives (reform as well as non-reform) are painful (Bovens et al. 2001). Under these conditions, pension reform is primarily an exercise in "blame avoidance" rather than in "credit claiming" and may trigger harsh political conflicts.

An actor-centred analysis of pension reform processes must not be confined to the role played by actors within the government camp. It must also take into account the parliamentary opposition and the trade unions as crucial players facilitating or impeding effective adjustment in pension policy. Each of these corporate actors has a distinct preference structure regarding pension policy:

The government, to begin with, is the first mover and has to decide whether it puts pension reform on the political agenda or not. In the policy dimension it has an interest to implement real changes (in particular, to effectively curb the growth of pension costs). At the same time, government politicians are aware of the great electoral risks associated with unpopular measures in pension policy and thus they have an interest in winning the approval or at least the acquiescence of those reform opponents who are capable of mobilising large sections of the electorate against the reform. The compliance of potential reform opponents will further increase the likelihood that legislative changes in pension policy (which often only reveal their full effects decades later) cannot be easily reversed by future governments.

The opposition parties have to decide whether they oppose or support a government's pension plans. They often have ambivalent preferences towards a pension consensus with the government. As policy seekers, opposition parties have an interest in influencing the contents of pension reform, which suggests co-operation with the government. If an opposition party has a realistic chance of regaining power in the near future, its preferences in pension policy often tends toward cost containment since economic and fiscal pressures force governments to consolidate public pension schemes primarily through savings on the expenditure side. However, as vote- and office-seekers, opposition parties have a competitive interest in improving their relative position vis-à-vis the government suggesting a more conflict-oriented strategy in issues of high electoral salience such as pension reform.

Trade unions, too, have contradictory preferences when it comes to pension policy both in the policy dimension and in terms of their organisational self-interest. In the policy dimension they have to balance their interest in stabilising the level of social contributions against their interest in maintaining the present level of pension benefits. However, for a number of reasons (discussed at length in chapter 3) unions are as a rule more critical of pension cuts than governments. But unions must also carefully ponder whether their policy interests in the retention of pension benefits (as well as their organisational self-interests) are best served through negotiations with or mobilisation against the government.

Empirical variation in the political support base of pension reforms

The bottom line is that governments will always be better off if they can avoid major conflicts over pension policy. This is not necessarily true for the parliamentary opposition and the trade unions for whom consensus with the government is not necessarily a value in itself. Their willingness to arrive at a pension consensus with the government cannot be taken for granted but always depends on specific contextual factors. Empirically, this assumption is confirmed by the observation that the numerous pension reform initiatives scrutinised in this study differ tremendously with respect to their political support base (see table 9.1). On the one hand, we see a number of instances where governments received neither the support of the opposition nor the backing of the trade unions in their pension reform efforts, often resulting in an escalation of the political conflict. At the other extreme, we also see reforms that were backed by both the opposition and the trade unions. Between these extremes are numerous pension reforms (and reform attempts, respectively) that can neither be characterised as fully consensual nor as purely unilateral. Quite a few pension reforms were hammered out between governments and trade unions while the parliamentary opposition remained opposed. In one case, the government struck a formal deal with parts of the union movement, while other unions continued to mobilise against the reform. In other cases, trade unions did not sign a formal agreement with the government but signalled their implicit agreement or at least abstained from large-scale protests. We detect similar shades in the strategic responses of parliamentary opposition parties. Most of the pension reforms analysed in this study did not enjoy the parliamentary support of the opposition parties. But the opposition did not always attempt to fully exploit the

Tab. 9.1   Political support of pension reforms and passage of legislation

Country/Year	Support by opposition parties?	Support by trade unions?	Reform adopted?
Sweden 1994	Support by SAP; Communists & New Democracy vote against.	Unions largely support the reform.	Yes
Italy 1992	No	Acquiescence	Yes
Italy 1994	No	Unions fiercely opposed, large-scale protests.	No
Italy 1995	Part of opposition votes against, other part abstains from voting.	Reform largely drafted & actively supported by all major trade unions.	Yes
Italy 1997	Bourgeois opposition votes against. After initial refusal, Communists vote in favour.	Yes	Yes
Germany 1989	Support by SPD; Greens vote against.	Unions largely support reform.	Yes
Germany 1997	No. SPD makes pension cuts a major electoral issue.	No	Reform later suspended by red-green government.
Germany 2001	No	After massive protests and far-reaching concessions by government, unions approve final reform package.	Yes
Austria 1993	No (but government is formed by a "grand coalition" of SPÖ/ÖVP).	Reform largely drafted & actively supported by the social partners.	Yes
Austria 1997	No (but government is formed by a "grand coalition" of SPÖ/ÖVP).	After massive protests and far-reaching concessions by government, unions approve final reform package.	Yes
Austria 2000	No	No	Yes
Austria 2003	No	No. Unions organise country-wide "defense strikes".	Yes
France 1993	No	No, but protests remain limited.	Yes
France 1995	No	No. Unions organise large-scale strikes.	No
France 1997 ("Loi Thomas")	No	No	Reform later suspended by Jospin government.
France 2003	No	CFDT strikes formal agreement with government. CGT and FO continue to mobilise against reform.	Yes

pension issue in the electoral arena. Moreover, a new government seldom fully reversed the pension policies of their predecessors as the German red-green government did in 1999 when it suspended the demographic factor introduced by the Kohl government. In the case of the Dini reform (Italy 1995), a number of deputies from the opposition Forza Italia abstained from voting in order to ensure a parliamentary majority for the reform.

It is important to note, that the deliberate inclusion of non-governmental actors in the reform process has a temporal dimension as well. In some cases, pension reforms were from the outset drafted in close co-operation between government and opposition or between a government and the trade unions. The Dini reform of 1995 and the Austrian pension reform of 1993 were in large part developed by the trade unions and the social partners, respectively. In many other cases, however, governments initiated reform plans unilaterally in the hope that trade unions (or opposition parties) would – on the basis of some limited concessions – ultimately accept the reform packages. In these cases, pension reforms basically became a source of harsh political conflicts, which were often only settled – if at all – via last-minute deals. In a nutshell, empirical analysis of pension reforms in the Bismarckian countries reveals huge differences in the degree to which governments were able to rely on the political support of opposition parties and trade unions.

Concertation as a condition for successful implementation of pension reforms

How much did the political support of parliamentary opposition parties and/or the trade unions enhance the political feasibility of pension reforms? As argued in the theoretical chapter, there is reason to believe that "concerted" reforms are easier to implement politically than unilateral governmental reforms. Empirical evidence seems to corroborate this (see table 9.1). A broad consensus between governing and opposition parties and/or between government and trade unions (or both social partners) seems to provide a sufficiently amount of stable political support for pension reforms. However, governments that lacked the political support of both the opposition and the trade unions often failed in their reform efforts. The reasons for failure vary: The Austrian SPÖ/ÖVP government had to withdraw its planned savings package in 1994, after it became clear that the bill wasn't going to receive a parliamentary majority without union support. In France (1995) and Italy (1994), mass demonstrations and lengthy strikes supported by the major trade unions (and to a lesser extent by the opposition) forced the governments to abandon planned pension cuts. Unilateral pension reforms in France ("Thomas Law") and Germany were passed in Parliament in 1997 but quickly suspended after the new government came to power a few months later. Within our sample of major pension reforms, we can only identify two instances (the most recent pension reforms in Austria in 2000 and 2003) where governments were able to implement substantial pension cuts without backing from the opposition and against the fierce resistance of trade unions. In the theoretical chapter, I have made a number of basic assumptions about the conditions under which opposition parties and trade unions are likely to oppose or accept a pension consensus with the government. In the following, I will dicuss these assumptions in the light of the empirical findings provided in the country chapters.

Conditions for a pension consensus between government and opposition

With respect to the conditions for a pension consensus between government and opposition, I began from the theoretical assumption that the willingness of the opposition to support the government's pension policies not only depended on the distance of policy positions but also on the intensity of positional conflict between the government and the opposition. More specifically, I expected that a high degree of positional conflict between government and opposition would impede a pension consensus even if the policy positions were actually quite similar. I also expected that an opposition party would block pension reform initiatives that were diametrically opposed to its policy interests, even in those cases where the intensity of positional conflict was low. These assumptions led to the hypothesis that a pension consensus between government and opposition could only be possible if both sides shared a common policy interest in a change of the pension status quo and if positional conflict did not prevent a policy-oriented bargaining process (see table 3.1).

My empirical findings largely corroborate this hypothesis. In all of the countries studied, both Social Democratic and bourgeois parties have come to accept the need for incisive cost containment measures. At the same time, even market-liberal parties have come to acknowledge that the double payment problem impedes a radical privatisation of public pay-as-you-go pension systems in a stage of full maturation. As a consequence, the pension policy positions between Social Democratic and bourgeois parties have increasingly converged in recent years. From a pure policy-perspective, this should facilitate consensual pension reforms in the partisan arena.

However, the (partial) congruence of policy positions is not a sufficient condition for a cross-party consensus. The empirical findings suggest that it is mainly political competition between left and right parties, and not unbridgeable policy positions, that impedes a party-based pension consensus. The instances of pension reform based on a broad cross-party consensus appear to be exceptions to the rule. More often than not opposition parties cannot resist the temptation to exploit the pension issue in the electoral arena even when their material policy goals do not deviate radically from the government's policy positions.

Among the countries studied, I found only two cases where the government and the major opposition parties arrived at a comprehensive consensus on pension policy: the German 1992 pension reform and the recent pension reform in Sweden. In these cases, situational factors reduced the degree of positional conflict and allowed for a relatively policy-oriented bargaining process. Most importantly, however, only in these two cases did the (Social Democratic) opposition expect to return to power and thus deemed it unnecessary to exploit the pension issue in the electoral arena. Interestingly, the Social Democratic party leaders in both countries were willing to strike a pension deal with the bourgeois government although they were forced to make a number of substantial concessions. This suggests that a pension consensus in the partisan arena requires a reduced level of positional conflict between government and opposition but not necessarily an approximate identity of their policy positions.

Both reforms imply comparatively large reductions of pension costs in the medium and long run and – in the Swedish case – comprehensive structural changes. In both cases, the trade unions exerted some influence on the reform process through party channels but they were not directly represented at the bargaining table. Thus, the main features of both reforms were primarily developed through cross-party negotiations rather than through negotiations between government and trade unions. Hence, the final result largely reflected the policy positions of the major political parties, which favoured more far-reaching changes to the status quo than the trade unions. This corroborates our theoretical assumption that a party-based pension consensus frequently allows for greater and faster adjustments than a consensus between government and trade unions.

This is why in a number of cases governments sought to reach a consensus in the partisan arena and only referred to the trade unions after they failed to organise a broad cross-party agreement. In Germany, for instance, the Schröder government first concentrated its efforts on bringing the Christian Democratic opposition on board in order to sidestep the resistance of the trade unions and leftist reform opponents within its own ranks. Only after this strategy failed was the red-green government prepared to offer far-reaching concessions to the trade unions. In a similar vein, the grand coalition between SPÖ/ÖVP, which governed Austria until January 2000, attempted on at least two occasions (1994 and 1997) to organise a pension consensus at the party leadership level without union approval. Only when it became clear that union approval was necessary to get pension legislation passed in Parliament did the government offer far-reaching concessions to the trade unions. In France and Italy, by contrast, a broad consensus on pension reform between the major parties on both sides of the political spectrum does not appear to provide a realistic alternative for governments that seek to organise a stable political support base for pension reform. In both countries, party systems are highly competitive and polarised, resulting in a high degree of positional conflict between the government and opposition parties thus rendering cross-party agreements as unlikely. In Italy, consensus building is further aggravated by the traditional fragmentation and instability of the party system. Thus, in both countries, governments primarily sought to achieve at least trade union acquiescence in order to create a politically feasible reform package.

As expected, the generation of a pension consensus between government and opposition proved to be almost impossible in those cases where opposition parties rejected pension cuts as a matter of principle (thus showing a great policy distance to the governing parties). This is especially true for Communist opposition parties, which have frequently opposed any efforts at pension retrenchment, even in those cases where Social Democratic governments were dependent on their parliamentary support. Here, the emergence of consensual solutions was not primarily impeded by fierce party competition but by more or less unbridgeable differences in pension policy positions. Among the instances of pension reform investigated in this study, we can only find one case, namely the 1997 amendments by the Prodi government, where a Communist party was willing to give its (grudging) acquiescence to pension cuts. However, even in this case the *Rifondazione Communista* (RC) initially rejected the cuts, which again precipitated a veritable government crisis. Only after the Prodi government offered more modest pension cuts combined with important concessions in other policy areas (such as the introduction of the 35-hour work week), were the Italian Communists prepared to support the reform. The fact that the RC finally accepted the pension cuts may also be attributed to the notion that the Communists would have caused the fall of a leftist government if they had continued to oppose the reforms. This also suggests that the strategy of an opposition party vis-à-vis governmental reform plans may also depend on whether or not the opposition party has formal veto power in the decision-making process. In general, however, Social Democratic governments relying on the parliamentary support by Communist parties were effectively restricted in their capacity to bring about substantial cost containment reforms in pension policy. Among the countries studied, this was the case for French centre-left governments and for the Swedish SAP government in the 1980s.

Conditions for a pension consensus between government and trade unions

While only a few of the numerous pension reforms examined in this study were based on a broad consensus between government and opposition parties, we find many instances of pension reforms based on concertation between the government and the trade unions. As expected, in all of the countries studied, the politics of pension reform was associated with more or less intense government and trade union conflicts. Nevertheless, in the majority of cases, the government and the unions finally settled their conflicts and at least came up with an implicit agreement over the pension reform package. This empirical finding is consistent with my theoretical expectations. As suggested in my theoretical framework, trade unions have basically no competitive incentives vis-à-vis the government and are primarily policy seekers. As long as they have no chance of blocking the adoption of the reform, they will maintain an interest in serious government negotiations even if they have to accept a reform outcome that is less attractive than the retention of the status quo. In this case, union agreement depends on whether the government is willing to reward their acquiescence with a reform package that is at least more attractive than the outcome would have been in the case of unilaterally imposed reform. Conversely, if the unions are able to prevent a reform that they consider as inferior to the status quo, it is the government that is forced to make the more far-reaching concessions. Thus, irrespective of the location of the non-agreement point (retention of the status quo or imposition of a reform outcome close to the government's ideal point), I began from the expectation that rational governments and rational trade unions will in principle arrive at an amicable agreement.

The problem is, however, that in practice, the location of the non-agreement point is not always clear-cut and may change. As the largely failed attempts of unilateral reform by Berlusconi (Italy 1994), Juppé (France 1995), and Vranitzky (Austria 1994) suggest, governments may overestimate unions' willingness to accept certain reform proposals and underestimate their capacity for blocking reform initiatives in the legislative arena or for mobilising their members and/or large sections of the public against those initiatives. There is strong reason to believe that the above-mentioned governments would have embarked on a more co-operative strategy vis-à-vis the unions if they had correctly judged the balance of power between themselves and the labour movements. On the other hand, we observe reforms where the unions underestimated the resolve and/or the power of governments to impose pension reforms despite their resistance. The recent pension reforms in Austria (2000 and 2003) and France (2003) could be interpreted in such a way.

However, my empirical findings also suggest that unions may – under certain conditions – refuse an agreement with the government over pension reform even if they cannot prevent the government from unilateral action. When confronting a presumed labour-hostile government, unions may be prepared to sacrifice minor (and perhaps temporary) policy gains that they could have achieved. Instead of stabilising a "labour-hostile" government through their co-operation, unions may decide to concentrate their efforts on replacing it with a more labour-friendly alternative. The relationship between government and trade unions during the last two years of the Kohl government is a case in point. The 1997 pension reform was adopted in a political climate that was not conducive to policy-oriented bargaining between government and trade unions. The Kohl government's earlier (and highly contested) cutbacks in sick pay continuation and employment protection, had triggered massive conflicts with the trade unions. These conflicts impeded a compromise solution, which might have been possible otherwise. The trade unions decided to embark on a confrontational strategy vis-à-vis the Kohl government. As part of this strategy, the trade unions supported the election campaign of the Social Democratic opposition en masse in the hopes that a Social Democratic government would rescind the social policy and labour market reforms of the Kohl government. This suggests that unions may be more likely to embark on a collision course in the case of a bourgeois government (whose replacement is basically in their long-term interest). To be sure, trade unions do not in general seek to avoid conflicts with a Social Democratic government. However, it is not in their interest to fuel conflicts with a left-wing government until a point where the survival of the government itself is put at stake. Hence, unions may – at least under certain circumstances – show a greater willingness to compromise vis-à-vis a left-wing government.

Factors determining union bargaining power

The fact that the government and trade unions reach a (formal or informal) agreement over pension reform still does not reveal any information about the scope and content of this specific agreement and about the extent of the government's concessions vis-à-vis the trade unions. As I have argued in the theoretical chapter, the bargaining outcome is likely to reflect the balance of power between government and trade unions and the relative distance between their ideal points in a given policy space.

The bargaining power of the trade unions vis-à-vis the government is contingent upon a multitude of factors on the part of both the unions and the government. In the theoretical section, I argued that trade unions can basically draw on at least three distinct strategies to influence the government's reform agenda in pension policy and prevent the adoption of unwanted measures. These strategies are lobbying, bargaining, and mobilising. By lobbying, unions organise political support for their demands within the government apparatus and within political parties, possibly preventing a political majority voting for governmental reform initiatives. By mobilising their members as well as the general public against these initiatives (through staging information campaigns, organising public demonstrations or, as a last resort, engaging in industrial actions), unions attempt to pressure the government from without, especially with respect to its electoral standing. The extent to which unions are able to make effective use of these strategies has a crucial impact on their bargaining position with the government. However, as we have seen in the country chapters, the availability and potential effectiveness of these strategies may differ considerably both within and between countries.

Lobbying appears to be a very effective union strategy in the context of ideologically fragmented multi-party governments, especially if they lack a strong parliamentary majority and if trade union functionaries control a sizeable share of key positions within the party apparatus, as is often (albeit to different degrees) true for left-wing parties. Under these conditions, union lobbying activities may lead to a situation in which a government is too weak to produce its own political majority in favour of its reform plans. However, governments can compensate for their own weaknesses if they can rely on the support of the parliamentary opposition. In this case, pension reform is based on a very strong parliamentary majority, against which the trade unions may be relatively powerless.

Mobilising protests against governmental pension reform plans seems to be a particularly powerful strategy if the union rank and file is able and willing to actively engage in protests against the government. As we have seen in the case of France and Italy, this may even lead to large-scale and long-lasting industrial actions, which may paralyse strategic sectors of the national economy. However, even milder forms of counter-mobilisation may prompt governments to water down or at least to withdraw their reform plans if union protests seem capable of damaging the electoral prospects of the governing parties. This is also true for governments whose institutional position would in principle be strong enough to pass pension legislation unilaterally.

In other words, the government's response to union protests depends both on its institutional power and its electoral vulnerability. If the next election is in the distant future or if the opposition stands no chance of winning the next election, the government may more readily ignore union protests. The same holds true for technocratic governments (like the Dini government in Italy), which are from the outset only nominated for a limited term of office. However, the governing parties can withstand union electoral pressure more easily if they have the support of the parliamentary opposition, which deprives trade unions the ability to exploit the pension issue in the electoral arena because union members no longer have partisan alternatives to turn to. Finally, a government may be less sensitive to trade union protests against its reform plans if the avoidance of reforms would be equally harmful to its electoral prospects. If benefit cuts remain undone and lead to sharply rising contribution rates and/or to an increasing budget deficit, which in turn may aggravate existing employment problems, the government may generate a policy result that will alienate potential voters to a similar degree than a harsh trade union confrontation over the issue of pension cuts. Given high or rising unemployment and tight budgetary pressures, this dilemma appeared fairly frequently in the countries studied. For instance, the pension cuts adopted by the Kohl government in 1996 and 1997 were needed to avoid a sharp increase in tax levels, which was considered as politically unacceptable in the context of rising unemployment and stagnating or even declining real wages. This scenario created a powerful countervailing pressure to union demands for the retention of pension benefits.

A union's mobilising capacity, like a government's electoral vulnerability, is by no means a constant. The country studies offered strong empirical evidence that union abilities to mobilise their members or the general public against governmental retrenchment plans varies considerably. As we have seen, union "militancy" may not only differ from country to country but also between sectors and between unions with different ideological tradi-

Table 9.2   Factors influencing union bargaining power vis-à-vis the government

Institutional strength and internal cohesion of government:

Share of seats in parliament
Ideological fragmentation
Number and significance of trade union functionaries within the government parties
Support of parliamentary opposition

Electoral vulnerability of government:

Temporal distance from next election
Presence of a technocratic government
Support by the parliamentary opposition

Mobilising capacity of trade unions:

Militancy and ideological tradition of the trade union
Rate of unionisation in the country or sector
United or internally split trade union front

tions. At the same time, however, union mobilising potentials also depend on the content of the proposed reform package itself and – related to that – on the degree to which unions are able to form a united front vis-à-vis the government. The government may seriously weaken union resistance by splitting them on important issues such as pension reform. Governments may, for instance, confine pension cuts to the less-unionised sectors or – through targeted concessions – attempt to arrive at a (tacit) agreement with the more moderate forces of the labour movement and thus isolate the more militant unions, which again may render it more difficult for them to obtain (or maintain) the support of the general public.

Table 9.2 summarises the most important factors that determine a union's bargaining position vis-à-vis the government in pension politics. Among the factors we see considerable empirical variations within our sample of pension reform efforts. Consequently, we observe instances of pension reform where the unions had a very strong bargaining position vis-à-vis the government and instances of pension reform where the unions had only limited bargaining power because they had little capacity for preventing the government from unilateral action.

The bargaining power of trade unions vis-à-vis the government is most pronounced in a constellation where an institutionally weak and internally fragmented government confronts a strong and united union movement. This was until very recently the case in Italian politics. Faced with a highly fragmented and polarised party system and lacking stable parliamentary majorities, Italian governments of all partisan stripes were unable to enact substantial pension reforms against the trade unions, which had repeatedly proven their capacity for provoking social unrest. Berlusconi's failed attempt to impose radical pension cuts unilaterally is a case in point. His internally divided and institutionally weak government proved unable to present a unified front to the unions, which for their part closed ranks and jointly launched a massive protest movement against the government's pension reform plans. Finally, Berlusconi's coalition partner *Lega Nord* broke ranks with the parliamentary majority, forcing the government to withdraw its reform plans. French left-wing governments seeking to reform public sector pensions found themselves in a comparable situation. Given their internal dissention over pension reform and their dependence on the parliamentary support of the Communist party, Socialist governments in France dissociated themselves from controversial pension reform plans, against which the militant public sector unions were likely to mobilise.

Even in cases where the trade unions largely lack the capacity for powerful counter-mobilisation (such as the trade unions in Austria, Germany and Sweden, which do not have a long-standing tradition of political strikes like their French and Italian counterparts), they may still be able to exploit their links to political parties in an effort to block the adoption of pension reforms in the legislative process. This avenue of union influence on the political process of pension reform is the most promising in cases where the government coalition consists in part of left-wing parties and where multiple office-holders between political mandates and mandates within the trade union organisation are frequent. This was the case under the SPÖ/ÖVP coalition government in Austria, which proved unable to assert itself against the resistance of numerous trade union functionaries within its own ranks. For instance, in 1994, the Austrian government sought to impose cuts in the pension system as part of a broader consolidation package against union resistance. However, the government had to withdraw these measures when it became clear that they did not have a parliamentary majority without the support of the many deputies affiliated with the trade unions. Furthermore, the SPÖ/ÖVP government was only able to adopt the 1997 pension reform after it had drastically watered-down the originally reform package in response to the internal pressures of trade union functionaries. Similarly, German trade unions took advantage of their "blackmail potential" vis-à-vis the red-green Schröder government which had not managed to bring the opposition parties on board. In alliance with representatives of the Social Democrats' left-wing, a group of trade union functionaries within the SPD's parliamentary group was able to form a critical mass of deputies, which threatened to block the adoption of the Riester reform unless the government made substantial modifications.

Conversely, we can also identify instances where unions found themselves in a comparatively weak bargaining position as they were neither able to engage in large-scale industrial actions against the government nor block controversial reform initiatives in the legislative arena. Under these conditions, governments were frequently able to enact relatively far-reaching reforms even without union support (given that they were willing to pay the electoral costs associated with unilateral pension reform). In Austria, the trade unions lost their traditional veto powers when the bourgeois ÖVP/FPÖ coalition assumed office, which could therefore adopt two pension reforms despite union disapproval. Similarly, German trade unions neither had the mobilising capacity nor the institutional powers to prevent the Kohl government from acting unilaterally on pension policy. As a consequence, the Kohl government was able to impose pension cuts even against the protests of both unions and the opposition, a move which, however, contributed to its defeat in the 1998 elections. The Swedish trade unions also found themselves in a relatively weak position during recent pension reforms, which had been developed and supported by a broad party coalition, meaning that Swedish unions could not block the reform and hence confined themselves to exerting an indirect influence on the reform process through their close links to the Social Democratic party. The French pension reform in 1993 also took place in a political context where trade unions were unable to obstruct the reforms. On the one hand, the bourgeois government was internally unified with an overwhelming parliamentary majority, which gave Balladur a strong institutional power base. On the other hand, Balladur confined the reform to the virtually non-unionised private sector. As a consequence, French unions did not even try to engage in large-scale industrial actions, which would probably not have been very effective. Instead, they signaled their (tacit) acquiescence to the overall reform package since the government had included a number of elements that were also palatable to the unions.

The balance of power between government and trade unions is less clear-cut in a situation where an institutionally strong government is able to present a unified front vis-à-vis a trade union movement that is in principle capable of effective counter-mobilisation. If, under such conditions, the government and the unions clash in a head-to-head confrontation, the outcome of this power struggle is always very uncertain. The withdrawal of the Juppé plan in 1995 shows that even an institutionally strong and ideologically cohesive government facing only limited electoral constraints[1] may finally cave in if it faces a united trade union camp engaging in long-lasting and large-scale industrial actions. Conversely, the successful reform attempt by Juppé's successor Pierre Raffarin suggests that governments can withstand union protests more easily if they can split the trade union movement on crucial issues. Arguably Raffarin's deal with the moderate CFDT increased the acceptance of pension cuts among the French public and thus weakened the position of those unions that continued to mobilise against the government.

Factors determining a union's preferences in pension policy

As I argued in the theoretical section, the bargaining outcome between the government and trade unions cannot be derived from the location of the non-agreement point alone. We also have to take into account the position of the actors' ideal points concerning pension reform and especially the distance between them. The country reviews provide ample empirical evidence for the assumption that union preferences with respect to pension cuts will always be closer to the status quo than those of the government. Otherwise, we would not see the frequent and often caustic conflicts between government and trade unions on this issue. For both, however, the location of the ideal point (reflecting the actors' reform-willingness) is a variable rather than a constant and the distance between their ideal points varies considerably.

Concerning the government, our empirical findings suggest that the sought-after pension cuts by and large correspond to the strength of fiscal and demographic pressures. By contrast, the general political orientation of the government appears to be of less importance concerning the aspired degree of pension retrenchment. Under strong budgetary and economic pressures governments of all partisan stripes sought to contain pension spending, whereas left-wing and right-wing governments alike were less determined in their savings efforts if acute pressures for adjustment were modest or absent. In several cases (such as Sweden and Germany), Social Democratic governments appeared to be even more ambitious in their efforts to control pension spending than their bourgeois predecessors.

While a majority of governments in the 1990s accepted the necessity of substantial cost containment reforms in pension policy, especially in the context of acute fiscal crisis, the same is not necessarily true for the trade unions. To be sure, trade union leaders might ignore or downplay the necessity of pension cuts in their official rhetoric, perhaps in order to present themselves as staunch defenders of their members' interests, while their actual positions are often more moderate. Nevertheless, from a comparative perspective, it appears that trade unions still differ greatly in the extent to which they consider pension cuts as necessary or even as desirable. While some trade unions, most notably in France, bluntly reject *any* cuts of pension benefits, others seem to acknowledge the necessity of benefit reductions under certain conditions or even welcome the curtailment of pension entitlements for certain groups of wage earners as a contribution to greater distributional justice.

The factors that affect trade union positions concerning pension policy are manifold. My empirical analysis reveals that the reform willingness of trade unions does not only reflect the strength of external pressures on the pension system but also the specific mechanisms of interest formation and interest aggregation within individual trade unions. In all of the countries studied, trade unions were eager to ensure the long-term sustainability of public pension schemes. When severe economic and fiscal pressures threatened to undermine the financial stability of the pension system, trade unions generally acknowledged the need for consolidation measures, especially in cases where the system was already in a state of acute fiscal crisis. Under certain conditions, trade unions will also accept that the consolidation of public pension schemes cannot be achieved on the revenue side alone but must also include cost-cutting measures. Since trade unions frequently face a trade-off between secure pensions and stable contribution rates they may accept at least modest pension cuts in order to avoid an excessive increase in contribution levels. For instance, without the 1992 pension reform, the German pension insurance contribution rate was predicted to reach a level between 36% and 41% in 2030. Even the trade unions considered this scenario as unacceptable, both for economic reasons and for reasons of intergenerational equity, and therefore acknowledged in principle the necessity of cost-containment measures.

In several cases, union support for pension curtailments was at least partly driven by the need to abide by the convergence criteria of the Maastricht Treaty. Various pension reforms in Italy (especially in 1995 and 1997) and the Austrian savings package adopted in 1996 are cases in point. The readiness of the population to make material sacrifices for EMU membership was most pronounced in Italy, which also profited most strongly from falling interest rates. A general blockage of any pension reform initiatives by the trade unions would not only have contradicted their own preferences but also caused confusion among the general public.

However, even massive economic crises, severe imbalances in the public pension system, and strong political pressure emerging from the Masstricht criteria were sometimes not enough to alter pension policy positions of unions and reconsider their rigid rejections of benefit cuts. In these cases, national trade union structures often impeded or at least hampered a reorientation of policy positions. In general, trade unions based on encompassing structures showed a greater ability to adopt more reform-oriented policy positions than highly fragmented and particularistic trade unions. This is because fragmented single trade unions may be tempted to improve the material position of their own members at the expense of collective wage earner interests (Olson 1982). Three organisational aspects appear to be particularly important with respect to their impact on the formation and aggregation of unions' interests in pension policy:

First, encompassing and highly centralised trade unions are, at least in principle, able to aggregate the multitude of heterogeneous and often divergent interests within their rank and file. This may influence their approach to pension reform in categorically fragmented pension schemes of the Bismarckian type, which often imply particularly favourable benefit rules for certain occupational groups (most notably in the public sector). The existence of an encompassing and highly centralised union confederation like the Austrian ÖGB facilitated the removal of such privileges. Assuming that large trade unions will primarily defend the interests of the working class as a whole, they are likely to approve the reduction of distributional inequalities within and across different public pension schemes.

In Italy, trade unions also pressed for a more equitable pension system, including a gradual harmonisation of pension benefits between the private and the (highly privileged) public sector. However, the mechanism of internal interest aggregation differed from the Austrian approach. In Austria, compliance of union rank and file with loss-imposing reforms was primarily achieved through a hierarchical and internally undemocratic organisational structure enabling the leaders of interest groups to impose reforms on their members to which they would not subscribe voluntarily. A similar mechanism failed in Italy where local unions questioned the democratic legitimacy of this procedure and launched strikes on their own. In the 1990s, however, Italian trade unions increasingly binding referenda among the workforce. This procedure was also applied to obtain union member acceptance of the Dini reform. In this case, the (potential) losers of the reform caved in, because they could not seriously deny the procedural justice of the vote.

In France, by contrast, union leaders have comparatively less control over their members, which often organise their own local strike committees. Hence French unions have a hard time aggregating particularistic interests.

Against this background, we note that French unions have more mobilising power in the public sector than in the private sector. While private sector employees saw cuts in their pension claims by the Balladur administration, public sector unions could successfully block comparable cost-cutting measures aspired by the Juppé government.

A second and interrelated factor concerns the degree of inter-union competition within a country. In Austria, Germany, and Sweden inter-union competition is very low as political divisions within the trade union movement are more or less absent. By contrast, the many ideologically divided French trade union federations find themselves permanently competing for members. As pointed out above, this structure is likely to create a situation where unions will end up blaming each other for selling out workers' interests and so they remain very reluctant to support unfavourable reforms. Traditionally, Italy's trade union movement has also been divided along ideological lines. However, in the context of permanent economic and political crises during the early- to mid-1990s, Italian unions settled their internal conflicts, at least temporarily, making it easier for individual union confederations to organise consent on controversial reforms among their members. They also, at least temporarily, assumed certain policymaking functions which the paralysed Italian party system was unable to fulfil.

Third, in a country where the share of union members among the population is high, trade unions will be less likely to externalise the costs of their actions. In this case, the membership structure of the national trade union movement is similar to the socio-economic composition of the population as a whole and thus union objectives are more in line with the general public interest. This again seems to enhance the willingness of trade unions to reform. Most importantly, unions with a high degree of organisation will display a more balanced age structure, which is roughly comparable to the age distribution of the general workforce. Among the countries studied, this is clearly the exception to the rule. In all of the countries but Sweden, union membership is more or less strongly biased towards older wage earners, while younger workers tend to be under-represented. As argued in the theoretical framework, this factor is likely to amplify union preferences for the maintenance of pension benefits. Against this background we should expect that trade unions would be more prone to accept pension cuts if current pensioners and elderly workers were (partly) exempted from these measures. By and large, our empirical findings confirm this expectation. Unions often pressed for protracted transition periods of reform plans that sought major changes in the calculation of benefits or a higher legal retirement age. The extremely slow phasing-in of new pension regimes in Italy is indicative of this. As in Sweden, Italy is about to gradually replace the existing defined-benefit with a defined-contribution scheme. In Italy, however, the transition phase is about 20 years longer than in Sweden.[2] Thus, the Italian reform largely imposes the demographic adjustment burden on younger generations, whereas in Sweden middle-aged workers and (to a lesser degree) older workers also bear a sizeable share of these costs. I argue that the overly long transition period in Italy can be traced more or less directly to the extraordinarily strong age bias of Italian trade unions, whose membership consists of about 50% of pensioners (Fargion 2000). It should be kept in mind, however, that the introduction of the new Italian pension system was preceded by a referendum amongst union rank and file members. Due to the preponderance of older members, a majority of the rank and file would probably have opposed the reform if the transition period had been shorter. By contrast, there is no comparable age bias within the Swedish trade unions because the net density rate is almost 90% among the gainfully employed (Ebbinghaus and Visser 2000). As a consequence, Swedish unions were able to accept a much shorter transition phase than their Italian counterparts.

The French case illustrates that a low degree of unionisation may also favour the particularistic interests of certain occupational groups at the expense of collective wage earner interests. The extremely low union density in the private sector did not facilitate French unions to press for harmonisation of private and public sector pensions, which would inevitably have entailed tangible pension cuts for the previously privileged employees in the public sector. Given their predominance within the French trade union movement, public sector workers were able to defend their privileges despite their minority status within the French workforce. By contrast, the representatives of public sector interests are much less dominant in the Austrian and Italian trade union movement and thus could not prevent the gradual removal of their pension privileges.

Irrespective of the issue of benefit cuts, the very low level of unionisation in France[3] also impedes the readiness of French unions to accept the development of private pension funds. Instead, the low unionisation rates in France reinforce the organisational self-interests of French trade unions in the retention of the institutional status quo of the pension system. Due to their extremely low degree of organisation, French unions can only finance a limited share of their activities from member fees. As a consequence, French unions mainly fund their functionaries through jobs in the management of social insurance bodies. By the same token, unions have a powerful incentive to defend the organisational set-up of the existing French pension system. A move towards private pension funds, as launched by the Juppé government, might over time have crowded out the pay-as-you-go based complementary pensions and thereby also endangered the management functions held by trade union functionaries within these schemes.

The national trade union structures therefore differ greatly in the extent to which they enhance or restrict both the interest and the strategic capacity of union leaders to organise consent to loss-imposing reforms among their rank and file. Most importantly, these structures determine the degrees of freedom of union leaders with respect to inter- and intra-generational redistribution among their constituencies. A highly fragmented and particularistic trade union movement like in France will make it particularly difficult for trade union leaders to accept reform-oriented pension policy positions and to legitimise them within their own organisation even if the need for adjustments is inevitable.

Quid pro quo strategies

Nevertheless, a number of empirical instances show that even weak governments confronting powerful and reform-resistant trade unions can use their agenda-setting powers to obtain union consent to cuts in pension spending if they offer them attractive compensation payments. While trade unions may be highly critical of pension cuts they may advocate a modification of the pension status quo in other respects. In particular, unions have developed a strong interest in measures that ensure and broaden the revenue bases of contribution-based pension schemes (such as an extension of the scope of contributors and a shift in the financing of non-contributory benefits from social contributions to taxes). In many cases, this has allowed pension policymakers in the Bismarckian countries to devise reform packages where unions accepted moderate pension cuts in return for measures that prevent the financial erosion of the social insurance system and shift part of the pension costs from wage earners to taxpayers.

Sometimes these reform packages also contain elements that are in the organisational self-interests of trade unions, such as their spheres of competence, their institutional channels of influence in the policymaking process and personal salaries of union officials. In France, the Balladur government combined pension cuts in the private sector with a clearer separation of contributory and non-contributory benefits by funding the latter out of the state budget. In doing so, the government implicitly acknowledged the social partners as the legitimate actors for the management of the contributory elements of the insurance schemes. In Germany, the recent pension reform adopted by the red-green government established the precedent of collective agreements in the area of fully funded old age provisions and thereby strengthened the co-determination of unions with respect to occupational pensions. In both cases, the unions remunerated the government for the consideration of union institutional self-interests and accepted or at least approved of the final reform package.

By contrast, the unions vociferously attacked any reform attempts that threatened to undermine their organisational or institutional power bases. The Juppé plan, for instance, sought not only cuts in public sector pensions but also intended to extend the government's grip on social security at the expense of trade unions by introducing a parliamentary vote on the social security budget. This measure clearly contributed to the bitter resistance of the French labour movement. Similarly, French unions opposed the establishment of privately managed pension funds established in the "Thomas Law", a reform that would have reduced the significance of the public pension schemes in the long term and thereby endangered the managerial positions held by union functionaries. Another example is the failed attempt by the Austrian government in 1994 to adopt a savings package without the prior agreement of the social partners, who defended their corporatist control over the economic and social-policy choices of the government. It is telling that the consolidation package adopted in the following year was from the outset intensely negotiated with the Austrian social partners and proved to be much more successful in its savings effects than its predecessor. Thus, the mere fact that a government recognises the trade unions as a bargaining partner in the realm of pension policy may make it easier for the latter to accept the reform outcomes. In short, governments may overcome union resistance by carefully designing a pension reform package that includes targeted concessions to the trade unions and takes into account their institutional self-interests.

Can the left cut more easily than the right?

As noted earlier, I found strong empirical evidence for the hypothesis that pension policy positions between Social-Democratic and bourgeois parties have strongly converged in recent years. It is another question, however, whether the political constraints to pension retrenchment are different for left-wing and right-wing governments. As mentioned in the theoretical chapter, some scholars have argued that left-wing governments can trim the welfare state more easily as disappointed voters would have no partisan alternative to which they could turn to. On the basis of our empirical evidence, this hypothesis is not confirmed, however, at least as far as pension reform is concerned. Most recently, for instance, the bourgeois heads of state in France and Austria – Raffarin and Schüssel – brought about major reforms of their respective pension systems, while their left-wing predecessors only achieved very incremental adjustments. This, I argue, can be at least partly attributed to the fact that leaders of left-wing parties have as a rule greater difficulties in organising support for welfare cutbacks within their own camp than their bourgeois counterparts.

Moreover, there is little empirical evidence for the hypothesis that the electoral costs of pension retrenchment are lower for Social Democratic parties. The reason is that their constituencies strongly support existing welfare arrangements and may therefore punish a left-wing government by not voting. Bourgeois opposition parties may have difficulties in absorbing these voters, as they may lack the capacity to present themselves as a trustworthy alternative. However, they may still be able to keep the pension issue in the electoral arena (for instance, by accusing a left-wing government of having breached an election promise) in order to fuel dissatisfaction among the Social Democratic constituency. This was the case in the German *Länder* elections in 1999, when the Christian Democrats owed their electoral success largely to the fact that many displeased Social Democratic voters stayed at home, a reaction that was at least partly triggered by Chancellor Schröder's breached promise to maintain the wage indexation of pensions.

Paradoxically, Social Democratic governments may, however, profit from the existence of a strong leftist competitor who may absorb the lion's share of dissatisfied Social Democratic voters. As the Swedish case shows, welfare cutbacks may led to extraordinarily painful electoral losses for a Social Democratic party but they do not necessarily alter its pivotal position within the party system as long as most of these swing voters turn to a partisan alternative farther left rather than to bourgeois parties or to the non-voter camp.

How does the sequence of negotiations influence the bargaining outcome?

In the theoretical framework, I pointed out that government leaders usually cannot muster a political majority for pension reform without the political support of their own party organisations and government factions even if they have the support of external actors like the opposition or trade unions. Hence, governmental pension policymakers typically find themselves in various bargaining arenas at the same time. This may offer them certain degrees of freedom concerning their bargaining strategies. I proposed that governments (or, more precisely, those government members put in charge of reforming the pension system) will try to achieve the *first* agreement with those actors whose policy position is closest to its own ideal point regardless of whether or not these actors are themselves part of the government or not. Empirically, we find instances where pension policymakers in the government initially sought a consensus with external actors (i.e., the opposition or trade unions) and only referred to their own parties at a later stage. There are also instances where leaders of the ruling party sought an agreement within their own party first and then negotiated with the other parties or the trade unions. There is also empirical evidence that the sequence of negotiations sometimes had a significant impact on the bargaining outcome and subsequently on the scope of the pension reforms. I will now highlight three empirical instances of pension reform in order to demonstrate how the bargaining sequence may influence the scope and content of pension reforms.

The Swedish pension reform is a paradigmatic reform case where a government deliberately deviated from the traditional pattern of consensus formation in order to give momentum to the reform process and to prepare the foundation for a major overhaul of the pension system. In contrast to its predecessors, the Bildt government established a pension reform commission consisting of a few high-ranking representatives from the bourgeois governing parties and the Social Democratic opposition, which worked secretively and out of the public eye to draft key guidelines for a new pension system. Both the unions and the individual party organisations could only influence the reform process at a stage when the main principles of the reform were already resolved. While they called for substantial changes of the reform concept, they could only manage some minor adjustments.

The Italian pension reforms of 1992 and 1995 display a very different negotiation sequence, which also deviated from traditional policymaking patterns. Considering Italian politics at the time, this particular bargaining sequence turned out to be the most promising strategy for organising political consent to gain substantial reform of Italy's pension system. The presence of a highly unstable, fragmented, and polarised party system made it extremely difficult for Italian governments to build a consensus for major pension reforms through party channels as had been the case in Sweden in the 1990s, and Germany in 1989. Italian governments consequently resorted to the social partners and the trade unions as alternative consensus-building channels. Both the Amato and Dini governments then presented their pension reform bills to Parliament and asked for a vote of confidence based on some evidence of union consent, which passed through Parliament with no major changes.

The case of the German 1999 pension reform illustrates that key political actors within the government can also choose for a bargaining sequence that makes more radical reforms unlikely. The planning of this reform lay predominantly in the hands of Labour Minister Blüm, a left-wing Christian Democrat, who, contrary to the Christian Democrats' business wing and the smaller coalition partner FDP, called for a rather modest pension system reform, which featured changes in the benefit formula over a very long period of time. Blüm was anxious to limit the impact of the market-liberal forces within the government coalition on the reform's outcome. Based on the recommendations of an expert commission, whose members were largely nominated by Blüm himself, the reform was basically approved by the party's own pension commission, in which the more radical reform proponents were in a minority position. On that basis, Blüm entered into negotiations with the smaller liberal coalition partner, which was able to manage only some marginal changes to his pension concept. A case can be made for the notion that a different negotiation sequence would have led to a different policy result. Had Blüm started the negation process within a joint coalition working group rather than within the pension commission of his own party, he probably would not have been as successful, since he was up against an alliance of the Christian Democratic business wing and the liberal coalition partner. This suggests, that the pension policy positions of bourgeois governments may be somewhat more flexible than was earlier assumed in the theoretical section, depending on the specific intra-governmental power constellation.

Final remarks

In general, the empirical analysis of the political processes surrounding pension reform in the Bismarckian countries corroborates the basic assumptions laid out in the theoretical framework about the underlying actor constellation in pension politics. As we have seen, we cannot simply derive pension policy outcomes from the mere presence of "functional imperatives" or from a government's policy preferences. The adoption (or non-adoption) of specific reforms in the area of pension policy will always reflect the rather complex interplay of numerous individual and corporate actors characterised by specific capabilities, perceptions and preferences. Moreover, we must take into account the specific internal structures of corporate actors in order to account for variations in pension policy outcomes. At the same time, however, the country sections have shown that some actors appear to play a more important role in the political process of pension reforms than others. In this work I have sought to concentrate my theoretical focus on a rather limited set of actors, analyzing primarily the various roles of the government, the parliamentary opposition, and the trade unions. This approach proved to be particularly suited to explaining the variations in pension reform outcomes. This is not to say, that the role of other actors in pension politics, such as employer associations, pensioner organisations, or the banking and insurance industries, must be ignored. However, they are at best of secondary importance when seeking to develop more systematic explanations for the (relative) success or failure of distinct pension reform efforts.

This study has also sought to address the question of whether a consensual approach is better suited to bringing about effective pension policy reforms than (attempted) unilateral impositions of pension policies by governments. In his analysis of pension reforms in the post-communist countries, Orenstein (2000) concluded that the inclusion of more – as well as a greater variety of – political actors early in the deliberations increases buy-in and compliance when pension reform is ultimately implemented, but at the expense of faster and larger changes. This suggests that pension policy-makers face a trade-off between the legitimacy and the effectiveness of pension reforms. In other words, governments are forced to lower their reform ambitions in order to broaden the political support bases for their reforms. While this argument is theoretically appealing and in many cases corroborated by empirical evidence, it needs to be modified in at least two respects. First, within the countries studied, most of the attempts at unilateral pension reform were ultimately doomed to fail. In some cases, the government parties proved unable to bring about a parliamentary majority in favour of the reform. In other cases, they withdrew their reform plans in the face of powerful trade union counter-mobilisations. In still other cases, some pension legislation was rescinded when elections saw the opposition come to power. Thus – at least in the Bismarckian countries – a broad political support base typically facilitates rather than impedes effective adjustments to pension policy, even in cases where governments seemingly had the formal power to impose major reforms unilaterally.

Second, as the Swedish experience has shown, a broad cross-party alliance may be able to implement very comprehensive changes to the pension status quo even if policy positions diverge significantly. If all the parties involved are not only convinced about the necessity of reform, but also share a common interest in arriving at an agreement, they will be able to strike mutually acceptable and welfare-increasing package deals even if the single components of this package would, by themselves, be unacceptable to at least one of the individual parties involved. At the same time, a broad consensus between the government and the opposition parties can keep the pension issue out of the electoral arena, making it possible to adopt very unpopular measures the government parties would be reluctant to push on their own. Thus, under these conditions the inclusion of more political actors not only facilitated the adoption of pension reform as such but even favoured the adoption of more comprehensive and far-reaching reforms.

Despite great political difficulties, the progress that has already been made regarding pension reform since the late 1980s is significant. All of the countries studied managed to substantially curb the projected growth of pension costs. Moreover, several reforms entailed important structural innovations, such as the establishment of a fully funded pension pillar (Germany and Sweden) or the harmonisation of pension arrangements between the private and the public sector in Austria and Italy. If major institutional change is possible in a highly path-dependent and politically salient policy area such as public pensions (most notably those of the Bismarckian type), we have reason to believe that welfare state arrangements in general (even those in Continental Europe) are not as rigid or resistant to reform as has often been suggested. Nevertheless, in most advanced welfare states, pension reform is still considered unfinished business. It remains to be seen whether these countries will also be able to ensure the fiscal sustainability of their pension arrangements in the context of a rapidly ageing society.

Appendix I
Summary Description of Retirement Systems (1986)

A.   AUSTRIA

Earnings-related schemes with almost universal coverage for the employed

Coverage and structure

General schemes for employees (wage and salary earners; institutionally distinct, but identical provisions), public employees (civil servants only), self-employed (small business and some liberal professions) and farmers. Special schemes for miners and notaries.

Uncovered self-employed or former employees can join a corresponding scheme on a voluntary basis.

Source of funds

Insured people: 10.25 % of gross earnings.
Employer: 12.45 % of payroll.
Government: Any deficit, also cost of income-tested allowance.
Contribution ceiling (25,800 Austrian schillings a month) is annually adjusted with earnings index.
Contributions are not taxed; deductible from income tax base.

Eligibility conditions
a) Old age pension

Standard pension: Age 65 (men), 60 (women); 15 years of contributions
Long-service pension: Age 60 (men), 55 (women); 35 years of contributions, including 24 months in the last three years.

Early pension for long-term unemployed: Age 60 (men), 55 (women), 15 years of contribution and in receipt of unemployment benefits unemployment insurance, or sickness benefits in preceding 52 weeks.

Further early retirement programmes for special branches or arduous occupations with links to employees' pension scheme.

b) Invalidity pension

Loss of 50% of normal earnings capacity; 5 years of contributions (6 months of contributions before age 27).

c) Survivor's pension

Insured must meet invalidity pension requirements (completion of qualifying period) or was pensioner at time of death.

Benefit structure

a) Old age pensions

Full pension at standard retirement age is 79.5% of assessed earnings after 45 years of contributions. Assessed earnings: average (partial wage) adjusted earnings of last 10 years, or, if higher 5 years before age 45. Accrual factor: 1.9% per annum for first 30 insurance years, and 1.5% for 31-45 insurance years.

No spouse supplement, but child supplement and attendance allowance.

b) Disability pension

In principle, same as old age pension. In case of invalidity before age 50, missing contribution years are added up to this age.

c) Survivor's pension

60% of basic pension of insured, payable to widow, and phased in over next years also to widower. 24% or 36% of basic pension of insured, payable to each orphan or full orphan, respectively. Maximum survivors pension, 110% of pension of insured.

d) General features

Income-tested allowances (for singles, couples, and children). Earnings-tested (different allowances for standard and other pensions). 14 payments annually; taxable, with special tax credit; automatic annual adjustment of benefits for changes in contribution earnings (special adjustments in calculation, since 1985 including unemployment rate).

Administration of pensions: manual Workers' Pension Insurance Institution and Salaried Employees' Pension Insurance Institution (separate institutions for public employees, railroads, mining, and agricultural and non-agricultural self-employed). Self-governing agencies, managed by elected representatives of insured people and employers.

Sick funds collect contributions, transmit them to pension insurance institutions, and maintain contribution records for individual workers.

Equalisation funds to equalise surpluses and deficits between various systems.

B.   FRANCE (1 January 1987)

Earnings-related schemes, and minimum old age pensions ("minimum-vieillesse") for pensioners with low incomes

Coverage and structure

Main system (concerns private sector employees; about 70% of all employees): includes two tiers called *"régime général"* and *"régimes complémentaires"*. Both are compulsory and on pay-as-you-go basis. Complementary schemes are of the defined-contribution type.

Special systems for public employees, miners, seamen, railroad workers, other public companies, agricultural self-employed, and various kinds of self-employed.

Source of funds

"Régime général": 6.4% (insured person) and 8.2% (employer) of earnings. Contribution basis ceiling: 116,820 FF/year.

"Régimes complémentaires": 1.88% (insured person) and 2.82% (employer) of gross-earnings (usual contribution rates for non-executive employees).

Government contribution: none for the main system; covers a large part of the cost of *"minimum-vieillesse"* and of some special systems (mainly agricultural self-employed, public employees, miners, and railroad workers).

Eligibility conditions

a) Old age pension

Age 60; 37.5 years insurance for full pension.

Deferred pension: increment every three months of insurance (maximum 37.5 years).

Reduced pension: (maximum 50% for under age 65 (unless disabled, deported or interned during the Resistance; former soldiers and war prisoners; working mothers of at least three children) or insurance gaps.

b) Disability pension

Under age 60 loss of two-thirds normal earnings capacity (total or partial invalidity); twelve months of insurance before incapacity, 800 hours of employment in last twelve months of which 200 hours in first three months.

c) Survivor's pension

Widow's/widower's invalidity pension: insured was entitled to invalidity or old age pension, survivor under age 55 and permanently incapacitated.

Widow's/widower's pension: deceased met insurance requirements or was old age pensioner, survivor aged 55 or over and married for at least two years (income-tested).

Benefit structure
a) Old age pensions
Full pension (for 37.5 years of insurance) in main system:
"*Régime général*": 50% of average earnings in ten highest paid years after 1947 (past earnings being revalued for wage changes); minimum 30 258 FF; maximum 57 780 FF/year.
"*Régimes complémentaires*": about 20% of average earnings (for non-executive), revalued as in the "*régime général*".[1]
Total of pensions: about 70% of average earnings for non-executive. Up to 100% for low income workers (because of minimum pension in the "régime général"). Only 60% down to 50% for executives.
Reduced pension: 1/150 of full pension times quarter of insurance (in "*régime général*"; about same rule as in "*régimes complémentaires*").
Means-tested spouse supplement: 400 FF/year at age 65 if the insured had 37.5 years of insurance; otherwise proportionally reduced.
Child's supplement: 10% of pension if insured had or reared at least 3 children (in both "*régime général*" and "*régimes complémentaires*").
"*Minimum-vieillesse*" (means-tested): 31,590 FF (single) or 56,670 (married couple)/year (1987) for old age (over 65) or invalidity pensioners with low income.
b) Invalidity pension
50% (total invalidity) or 30% (partial invalidity) of average earnings in ten highest paid years. Minimum pension: 13,470 FF/year (total invalidity) or 34,668 FF/year (partial invalidity).
Constant attendance supplement: 40% of pension for total disability; minimum supplement 52,747 FF/year.
Benefit for handicapped adults: Up to 29,640 FF/year.
c) Survivor's pension
52% of main pension which insured was receiving or entitled to, or 52% of husband's pension at death; Minimum pension 13,470 FF/year.
Child's supplement: 10% of pension if insured had or reared at least 3 children.
Orphan's allowance: Full orphan's allowance 6,060 FF/year, half orphan's 4,545 FF/year.
Death grant: lump sum of 90 days earnings' of deceased; minimum 1,156 FF., maximum 28,890 FF (1985).
d) General features
Automatic semi-annual adjustment for changes in national wages; no automatic adjustment for national solidarity fund allowances. Family allowances payable in addition; means-tested allowance of 13,470 FF/year for low-income aged workers ineligible for pension.

Administrative organisation

"Régime Général":

Organised by the state.

Ministry of Social Affairs and National Solidarity, general supervision and issuance of regulations.

National Old Age Pension Insurance Fund, administration of old age pensions and surviving spouse's allowance.

National Sickness Insurance Fund, administration of invalidity and survivor pensions.

Contributions collected by joint collection agencies.

"Régimes complémentaires" managed by the social partners (including assignment of contribution rates).

C.   GERMANY

Earnings-related schemes with almost universal coverage for employed

Coverage and structure

General scheme for employees (wage and salary earners; institutionally distinct, but identical provisions).

Special schemes for miners, public employees, self-employed and farmers.

Uncovered people such as housewives, aliens with long-term residency etc. can join corresponding scheme on a voluntary basis.

Source of funds

Insured person: 9.6% of gross earnings.

Employer: 9.6% of payroll.

State: Annual subsidies fixed according to variations in the average national earnings.

Contribution ceiling: 67,200 DM/year.

Contributions taxed, with general tax allowance.

Eligibility conditions

a) Old age pension

Age 65 with at least five years of contributions paid, or age 63 (or age 60 when disabled) with at least 35 insurance years of which 15 years of contributions paid (earnings limit 1,000 DM/month) or age 60 when unemployed one year in last 18 months and at least 8 years of contributions in last 10 years (earnings limit 425 DM/month) or age 60 for women with at least 15 insurance years and at least 10 years of contributions paid in last 20 years (earnings limit 425 DM/month). Retirement not necessary after age 65.

b) Disability pension

General invalidity, incapacity for any gainful activity; occupational invalidity, 50% reduction of earnings capacity in usual occupation. Five years of contributions.

c) Survivor's pension

Deceased had at least five insurance years or was pensioner at death.

Benefit structure

a) Old age pensions

1.5% of assessed earnings per insurance year; assessed earnings represent ratio of insured's earnings to national average of gross earnings multiplied by current computation base (27,885 DM/year). Deferred pension for ages 65 to age 67: increment of 0.6% per month. Family allowances payable in addition.

b) Disability pension

For general invalidity 1.5%, for occupational invalidity 1% of assessed earnings times years of insurance. In case of invalidity before 55, contribution years are calculated up to this age.

c) Survivor's pension

100% of insured's general invalidity pension payable to all widows for 3 months; thereafter, 60% if aged above 45, invalid, or caring for child. Otherwise, 25% of occupational invalidity pension. Also payable to widower. Widow/widower pension is suspended by 40% if the amount earned or own pension income exceeds an exempt amount which is indexed.

d) Orphan's pension

10% (half orphan) or 20% (full orphan) of general invalidity pension plus supplements for each dependent child.

e) General features

Pensions adjusted annually primarily according to wage changes; benefits partially taxable.

Administrative organisation

Self-governing bodies under state supervision.

Eighteen state and 2 special insurance institutes, administration of wage earners' programme; Federal Salaried Employees' Insurance Institute, administration of salaried employees' programme.

Sickness funds collect contributions.

D.   ITALY

Earnings-related schemes and means-tested programme with universal coverage

Coverage and structure
General scheme for private sector employees.
Special schemes for public employees, railway employees, liberal professions, self-employed people.
Means-tested social pension for people over 65 with insufficient resources and ineligible for other benefits.

Source of funds
Insured person (industry): 7.15% of gross earnings (1987).
Employer (industry): 17.66% of payroll (1987).
Government: part of cost of minimum pension plus costs of social pension
Contributions cover old age, invalidity, and survivor's pension; different contribution rates for other sectors.
Annual ceiling for benefit purposes 36,787,000 liras; minimum earnings for contribution purposes 29,805 liras/day (blue-collar workers), 31,560 liras/day (white-collar workers) (1987).
All contributions to compulsory system are tax deductible.

Eligibility conditions
a) Old age pension
Standard pension: Age 60 (men) or 55 (women); 15 years of contributions; retirement necessary for full pension (otherwise minimum pension).
Seniority pension: At any age after 35 years of contributions; retirement necessary.
Pre-retirement pension: Age 55 (men) or 50 (women); steel and iron industry workers, if unemployed due to economic crisis or industrial reorganisation.
b) Disability pension
Invalidity allowance: Under pensionable age, loss of at least two-thirds of working capacity; five years of contributions including three years in the five years preceding claim; allowance subject to three-yearly reviews (automatically renewed after third review).
Invalidity pension: Under pensionable age, permanent total incapacity to work; five years of contributions including three years in the five years preceding claim.

c) Survivor's pension

Insured had five years of insurance and at least 5 years of contributions paid or one year of insurance and 52 weekly contributions paid if death due to occupational causes or was eligible for old age or disability pension.

Benefit structure

a) Old age pensions

Two percent of average earnings in last five years multiplied by years of contribution (first four years are adjusted to changes in the cost of living) up to a maximum of 80% of revalued earnings (40 years of contribution); minimum pension 412,250 liras/month (1987).

b) Disability pension

Two percent of average earnings in last five years multiplied by years of contribution (maximum 40), plus number of contribution years intervening between date of invalidity pension and normal pensionable age (permanent total invalidity only); minimum pension: 309,800 liras/month (1987); earnings limit for benefits; constant attendance supplement payable in addition.

c) Survivor's pension

Widow's/widower's pension: 60% paid or payable to insured; minimum pension 412,250 liras/month. (1987).

Orphan's pension: 40% of pension paid or payable to insured for each full orphan, up to 100%; 20% for half-orphans, up to 40%.

Other survivor's pensions: 15% of pension paid or payable to insured for each parent or other dependent relative, up to 100%.

Lump sum death benefit when insured was not entitled to pension.

Means-tested *social pension*: 242,200 liras in 1987.

d) General features

Benefits paid 13 times annually; benefits from statutory and supplementary plans are subject to normal income tax, lump sum benefits are tax free with some exceptions.

Administrative organisation

Ministry of Labour and Social Welfare, and Treasury, general supervision.

National Social Insurance Institute, administration of programme through its branch offices; managed by tripartite governing body.

Separate institute or funds administer special systems.

E.   SWEDEN

Public two-tier scheme, consisting of universal flat-rate and earnings-related pension

Coverage and structure

Universal scheme covers all residents; earnings-related scheme all employees and self employed over "base amount".
Special scheme for public employees.
Virtually mandatory occupational scheme for private sector employees.

Source of funds

Insured person: No contribution from employees to universal, earnings-related, and partial pension. Contributions of self-employed equal to employer's share.
Employer: 9.45% of payroll for universal, 10.0% for earnings-related and 0.5% for partial pension.
Government: Universal pension about 12% of outlays, but no contributions to earnings-related and partial pensions.
Contributions of self-employed and employers are deductible from income tax base.

Eligibility conditions

a) Old age pension

Standard pension: Age 65 (men and women), universal pension, no contributions or income test, but required years of residence. Earnings-related pension, three years coverage with earnings above the base amount.
Actuarially reduced pension: From age 60 onward with decrement of 6% per annum, for both universal and earnings-related pensions
Partial pension: Between age 60 and 64, reduced work schedule (average of five hours per week reduction and minimum work schedule of 17 hours per week), employed at least five out of 12 months before entitlement, and ten years earnings-related coverage after age 45.

b) Disability pension

Both universal and earnings-related pension, five-sixths loss of earnings capacity for full pension. Special early provisions for unemployed 60 and over, out of work for 21 months.

c) Survivor's pension

Universal pension, widow and orphans of specific age. Earnings-related pension, deceased was pensioner or had three years of coverage.

Benefit structure

a) Universal pension

96% of current base amount for single adult, or 150% for aged couples. Fourtysix or 67% of base amount for orphan or full orphan, respectively (base amount for benefits in 1986: 23,300 krona per annum).

Various supplements, mostly expressed as percentage of base amount, for those ineligible for earnings-related pensions or without means.

b) Earnings-related pension

Old age: 60% of difference between assessed earnings and base amount, based on coverage since 1960 (full benefits, 20 years coverage till 1980, thereafter increasing year by year to 30; shorter coverage, pension reduced accordingly). Assessed earnings, average adjusted pensionable earnings of best 15 years; pensionable earnings, earnings between base amount and 7.5 times base amount. Deferred pension credit, 7.2% per annum until age 70.

Partial pension: 50% of gross earnings lost due to part time work.

Disability: 2% of assessed earnings times years of coverage, with calculated years till age 65. Maximum, 60% of covered earnings.

Survivor's: Widow, 40% of pension insured, or 35% with eligible children. 15% for first, 10% for each other orphan; 40% for full orphan.

c) General features

Benefits are taxable. Universal and earnings-related benefits without retirement test. Automatic adjustment of assessed earnings and pension for changes in consumer price index.

Administrative organisation

National Social Insurance Board, supervision.

Administration of programme: regional social insurance bodies.

Contributions of self-employed paid with income tax; those of employers collected by the National Social Insurance Board.

Earnings-related pension fund managed by four tripartite boards for public employment, for private employment by large firms, and for private employment by small firms and self-employment.

Sources: US Department of Health and Human Services 1986; OECD 1988; Gillion et al. 2000

Appendix II
Chronology of National Pension Reforms
(from 1989 until 2001)

A.   Austria

1992   *Verfassungsgesetz über die Angleichung des Pensionsalters der Frauen an das der Männer*

Retirement age for women aligned with those of men (to be phased in 2018 to 2034).

1993   *Sozialrechtsänderungsgesetz 1993 (Pension reform 1993)*

Switch from gross to net wage indexation.

Higher coefficient for those retiring later.

Basis for calculation of benefits extended to 15 best years.

Introduction of partial pension for workers accepting shorter working hours.

Introduction of pension credits for child rearing.

1995   *Strukturanpassungsgesetz 1995 (Consolidation package 1995)*

No notable measures in the area of pensions (despite proposals in the original savings package).

1996   *Strukturanpassungsgesetz 1996 (Consolidation package 1996/97)*

Tighter eligibility criteria for early retirement pensions.

General freeze of pensions for one year (two years for civil servants).

Lower credits for schooling.

Lower civil servant pensions for those retiring before 60.

1997   *Arbeits- und Sozialrechtsänderungsgesetz 1997 (Pension reform 1997)*

For early retirees, number of "best years" on which benefits are computed increased from 15 to 18 years (to be phased in 2003 to 2020)

Introduction of uniform accrual rate of 2% of the calculation base for each year of insurance (old law: 1.9% per annum for first 30 insurance years and 1.5% for 31-45 insurance years). For each year of early retirement the above mentioned percentage is reduced by 2% up to a maximum of 10% (valid from 2000 onwards).

Criteria for taking up a part-time pension relaxed with respect to the required reduction of hours of work. New form of part-time pension introduced, requiring a shorter contribution period.

Pension credits for child rearing increased.

Individuals nursing family members who give up employment can still be covered by the pension insurance under related favourable conditions.

Higher contributions for the self-employed and farmers.

The pension base for civil servants is changed from the last salary to 18 years (to be phased in 2003 and 2020).

Pensions for civil servants to be annually adjusted applying adjustment factor of the general pension system.

Pension coverage extended to casual jobs.

2000 *Sozialrechtsänderungsgesetz 2000 (Pension reform 2000)*

Rapid increase of 18 months to the minimum early retirement age in the general scheme (from 55 to 56.5 years for women and 60 to 61.5 years for men) and to the retirement age in the civil servants' scheme (from 60 to 61.5 years for both sexes).

Increase in the reduction of pension payments if early retirement is taken (from 2% to 3% per year).

Reduction in survivors' pensions (old widows' pension: 40% to 60%; new widows' pension: 0% to 60%).

2001 *Reform of the severance pay system*

Severance pay extended to all employees in the private sector.

Employers obliged to pay 1.5377% of employees' wage to a central fund.

6% income tax on contributions to severance pay abated if payments are invested into a pension fund.

Source: OECD, *Economic Surveys*, Austria, various years; Wöss (2000).

B. France

1991 Introduction of a new tax – the *contribution sociale généralisée* CSG at a flat rate of 1.1% on all incomes including pensions.

1993   *Reform of the régime général (Balladur reform; law no. 93-936)*
Introduction of a *Fonds de solidarité vieillesse* to finance non-contributory
benefits and to repay social security debt. Financed through an increase of
the CSG by 1.3% and by duties on alcoholic or non alcoholic drinks.
Reference period for calculation of benefits extended from 10 to 25 best
years (to be phased in until 2008).
Qualifying period for full pension increased from 37.5 to 40 years (phased
in until 2002).
Government authorised to stipulate the amount of indexation by decree.
Decree that for a five-year period pensions will be indexed to consumer
prices.
*Agreement between social partners on balancing the complementary pen-
sion scheme ARRCO*
Increase in minimum contribution from 4% to 6% of pay in 1999.

1995 Constitutional amendment allows Parliament to vote on social security budget (as part of the Juppé plan).

1996   *Agreement between the social partners on balancing the comple-
mentary schemes ARRCO and AGIRC until 2005*
Increases in the purchasing price of points.
Less generous indexation in the nominal value of these points.

1997   *Loi Thomas ("Thomas Law")*
Framework for optional retirement savings funds managed by private in-
surance agencies.
Up to a certain ceiling payments by both employees and employers will be
exempted from income taxation and social security contributions.
The law was never implemented by Jospin government.
1998 Decree by government that pensions will continue to be indexed to
consumer prices.
Creation of the Fonds de reserve des retraites (Pension Reserve Fund)
Part of the public pay-as-you-go pension system invested in financial markets.
Managed by the government.

Source: Blanchet and Legros 2000; Bonoli 2000; OECD, *Economic
Surveys*, France, various years

C.   Germany

1989   *Rentenreformgesetz 1992 (Pension Reform Act 1992)*
Pension indexation changed from gross to net wage growth.
Gradual increase of early retirement age (*Renten für langjährig Versicherte*) from 63 to 65 years (as of 2001).
Gradual increase of retirement age for women and unemployed from 60 to 65 years (as of 2001).
Maximum non-contributable years for education reduced from 13 to seven.
Future pensions for immigrants from Eastern Europe with German ancestors (*Fremdrenten*) who have moved to Germany after 1990 will be reduced by 30%.
Expansion of pension credits for child-rearing.
Introduction of actuarial deductions for early retirement.
Federal grant increased to 20% of expenditures and linked to developments of the contribution rate.

1990   *German Reunification*
Existing pensions in former GDR were converted from East German marks to DM and indexed to wage increases in former East Germany.

1991   *Rentenüberleitungsgesetz (effective as of 1992)*
West German pension system extended to East Germany.

1996   *Wachstums- und Beschäftigungsförderungsgesetz (Growth and Employment Promotion Act)*
Increase of retirement ages stipulated in the Pension reform act 1992 will be phased in earlier.
Maximum non-contributable years for education reduced from seven to three.
Abolition of student privileges in statutory pension insurance.
Future pensions for immigrants from Eastern Europe with German ancestors (*Fremdrenten*) reduced by 40%.

1997   *Rentenreformgesetz 1999 (Pension Reform Act 1999)*
Introduction of the demographic factor into the pension formula (leading to a lowering of standard pension from 70% to 64%).
Increased and additional crediting of child-rearing.
Tighter eligibility criteria for disability pensions.

Dienstrechtsreformgesetz 1997 (for civil servants' pensions)
Increase in retirement age upon application (*Antragsaltersgrenze*) from 62
to 63 years and actuarial reductions in cases of early retirement already
phased in as of 1998.
Reduced credits for schooling.

1998   Increase value-added tax by 1% to avoid an increase in pension
        contribution rate.
Versorgungsreformgesetz (for civil servants' pensions)
Increase in retirement age upon application (Antragsaltersgrenze) from 60
to 61 years in the police, fire brigades and judiciary fields.
Establishment of a public reserve fund financed through reduced increases
in salaries and pensions (reduction of 0.2% per years accumulated from
2001 to 2015).

1999   *Rentenkorrekturgesetz*
Retraction of the demographic factor.
Suspension of new regulations for disability pensions.
Reimbursement of expenditures caused by unification by federal govern-
ment in addition to federal grant.
Gesetz zur Neuregelung der geringfügigen Beschäftigungsverhältnisse
Expanding social insurance coverage to people in minor employment
(income less than 630 DM/320 euros per month).
Gesetz zur Förderung der Selbständigkeit
Bogus self-employed included into social insurance coverage.
Haushaltssanierungsgesetz
Indexing of pensions to inflation rate for 2000 and 2001.
Reduced pension entitlements for periods of military service and receipt of
unemployment assistance.
Earmarking of revenues from eco-tax for statutory pension insurance.
Reductions in the federal grant.
Reduction of contribution rate to 19.3%.

2001   *Altersvermögensergänzungsgesetz (Old Age Provisions Extension
        Act)*
Lowered pension level by modified pension formula, retraction of indexa-
tion to inflation in 2001.
Increased credits for child-rearing.
Tighter income-test criteria for survivors' pensions.
New widow pension (including child-component).

Option of splitting pension rights between spouses.
Closing legal loopholes at the beginning of the insurance history.

2001   *Altersvermögensgesetz (Old Age Provisions Act)*
Creation of an additional funded pension promoted by tax breaks and sub-
sidies.
Individual right to an occupational remuneration-conversion pension
(*Anspruch auf betriebliche Entgeltumwandlung*).
*Altersvorsorgeverträge-Zertifizierungsgesetz (Old Age Pension Agree-
ment Certification Act)*
Regulations concerning the award of subsidies to old age pension products.
Improved information service to be provided by statutory pension insur-
ance.
Need-based entitlement to social assistance for elderly people without re-
course to their children.

Sources: Färber 1998; Arbeiterkammer Bremen 2000; VDR 2001

D.   Italy

**1992   *Amato Reform (legge delega 421/1992, legge 438/1992, decreto
legge 503/1992)***
Indexing of pensions to consumer prices rather than minimum wages (plus
temporary suspension of indexation).
For those with more than 15 years of contributions in 1992: salary for private (public) employees changed from last five years' (last month's) to 10
last years' salary.
For those with less than 16 years of contributions in 1992: Shift to lifetime
earnings.
Years of contributions for eligibility raised from 15 to 20 years.
Granting of new seniority pensions suspended for one year.
Minimum years of contributions for eligibility for public employee seniori-
ty pensions gradually raised to 35 years (old rule: between 15 and 25
years); alignment with private employees.
Gradual increase in the statutory retirement age from 60 (man) and 55
years (women) to 65 and 60 years, respectively (from 2002 onwards).
Tighter means-testing for minimum pensions.
Improved credits for child rearing.
Private pension funds introduced with 15% withholding tax on funds de-
posited.

1994 *Ciampi Budget Law*
Cuts in seniority pensions for public sector workers retiring with less than 35 years of contributions.

1995 *Berlusconi Budget Law*
Increase in the statutory retirement age by 2000 (rather than 2002).
1995 indexation delayed until January 1996.
15% withholding tax suspended.

1995 *Dini reform (legge 335/1995)*[2]
Switch from a defined-benefit to a notional defined-contribution system.
Introduction of flexible retirement age 57 to 65 years for younger workers
Years of contributions for eligibility lowered from twenty to five years for younger workers.
Seniority pensions abolished for younger workers (Middle-aged and older workers: 57 years of age plus 35 years of contributions *or* 40 years of contributions).
Graduation of survivors' pensions according to income.
Abolition of minimum pension within social insurance system – minimum security for those age 65 and over henceforth only granted by the *pensione sociale*.
Improved credits for child rearing.
Broadening of contribution base (extending compulsory pension insurance to special categories of self-employed workers + higher social security payments).
Earnings-ceiling for participation in public system, to favour the creation of private funds.
Introduction of a framework for the establishment of voluntary supplementary pension funds.
Tax relief on contributions to supplementary pension funds up to an annual ceiling of 2.5 million Lira (about 13,000 euros).

1997 *Prodi amendments (legge 449/1997, provvedimento collegata alla legge finanziaria 1998)*
Lowered indexation for high pensions.
Acceleration of the harmonisation of the public and private pension regimes.
Gradual increase in contribution rates for the self-employed to 19%.
Tightening of the conditions governing access to seniority pensions.
Harmonisation of rules for special schemes with those for private

employees in terms of contribution rates, yield coefficients, and eligibility criteria on seniority pensions.

Financing of assistance benefits shifted from contribution to taxes.

2000 *Improved tax incentives for supplementary pension funds (Legislative decree no. 47, 18 February 2000)*

Tax rate on pension fund returns set at 11% (compared to a rate of 12.5% for other financial yields).

12% (hitherto 6%) of income tax deductible for pension funds contributions up to an annual ceiling of 10 million Lira (about 5000 Euro; hitherto 2.5 million Lira/1,250 euros).

Only applicable for workers who allocate parts of severance pay allowance to funds established on the basis of collective agreements.

Workers' relatives are also entitled to the 12% tax-deduction on contributions.

Tax incentives for employers to recover the loss of financial liquidity resulting from the allocation of severance pay allowances to the pension funds.

2001 Minimum pensions raised from about 360 to 516 euros

Sources: Klammer and Rolf 1998; OECD, *Economic Surveys*, Italy, various years; Eiroline 2000a; Paparella 2001

E.   Sweden

1990 *Reform of widows pensions*

Lifetime widows' pension abolished (except for those whose spouse died before 1990 and for women born before 1930).

New widows pension only limited in time (one year for widows without children), means-tested and only for those under age 65.

1992 *September Crisis package*

Retirement age raised from 65 to 66 (later postponed).

Base amount used to calculate ATP and basic pension (as well as other social benefits) reduced by 2% (as of 1993).

1993 *Reform of basic pension*

Full basic pension only available after 40 years of residence or 30 contribution years in the ATP system (previously: 5 years of residence).

1994   The age limit for part-time retirement is raised from 60 to 61 years. Replacement rate lowered from 65 to 55%.

Major principles of the new pension system adopted by the Riksdag

Sift from best 15 years to life-time income as base for pension entitlements. Pensions linked to income developments.

Introduction of flexible pension age based on actuarial principles.

Pensions linked to life expectancy at the age of retirement.

Employee contributions to the old age pension system to be introduced as of 1995.

2% is to be diverted into fully funded individual accounts, with the contributor deciding how it will be managed (later increased to 2.5%).

1995   For calculation of the base amount only 60% or 80%, respectively, of changes in consumer prices taken into account, as long as the budget deficit is higher than 100 billion or between 50 and 100 billion Swedish crowns, respectively.[3]

Introduction of 1% employees contribution.

1996   Reduced basic pension for all married pensioners from 96% to 78.5% of base amount.

1997   *Cuts in survivors pensions*

Pensions for widows below regular retirement age for only 6 rather than 12 months after spouse's death and corresponding to 90% rather than 96% of basic pension. Means-tested pension supplement increased from 55.5 to 61.5%.

Introduction of means-test even for widows' pensions according to the pre-1990 rule.

1998   *Major legislation concerning the new pension system adopted*

Pension contributions split between employers and employees (9.25% each).

Employees compensated by abolition of employees' sickness insurance contributions and reduced income taxes.

Contribution to premium reserve system stipulated at 2.5%.

Minimum age for old age pension increased from 60 to 61 years.

1999 2% reduction of base amount discontinued.

2001 Final legislation concerning the new pension system settled.

2002 Old age pensions indexed to wage growth.

Sources: OECD, *Economic Surveys*, Sweden, various years; Socialdepartementet 1999; http://www.rfv.se/social/forandr/index.html

Appendix III
Glossary of Terms

Accrual rate The percentage of assessed income that enters into the pension formula (usually 1% to 2%).

Actuarial neutrality Used here to indicate pension arrangements which neither penalise nor unduly benefit those who retire earlier or later than the standard retirement age.

Advance-funding In an advance-funded scheme, current contributions are set aside and invested in order to finance the pensions of current contributors. Many company plans are advance-funded as are individual retirement accounts. Public pay-as-you-go pensions may be partly pre-funded when the government raises the contribution rate above what is necessary to finance current benefits, in order to accumulate a fund to help pay future benefits.

Average effective retirement age The actual average retirement age, taking into account early re-tirement and special regimes.

Basic pension The single person's flat rate state pension paid to all who have met the minimum national insurance contribution requirement.

Beneficiary A person entitled to benefit under a pension scheme or who becomes entitled because of a specified event.

Benefit rate The ratio of the average pension to the average economy-wide wage or covered wage.

Beveridgian pension system Public pension arrangement based on means-tested or universal flat-rate benefits, either contribution- or tax-financed.

Bismarckian pension system Public pension arrangement based on earnings-related social insurance, typically financed out of wage-based contributions.

Consolidation A fiscal policy that aims to reduce public-sector deficits, or increase public-sector surpluses, by increasing taxes or reducing public-sector expenditures, or both.

Defined-benefit plan A pension plan where benefits are prescribed by a formula. It is the converse of a defined-contribution plan.

Defined-contribution plan A pension plan in which a periodic contribution is prescribed and the benefit depends on the contribution plus the investment return.

Demographic transition The historical process of changing demographic structure that takes place as fertility and mortality rates decline, resulting in an increasing ratio of older to younger people.

Equivalence principle Principle according to which monthly pension payments correspond to the individual contribution record.

Final pensionable earnings The pensionable earnings, at or near retirement or leaving service, on which the pension is calculated in a final salary scheme. The earnings may be based on the average over a number of consecutive years prior to retirement.

Flat-rate benefits These are benefits, such as pension benefits, that are related only to age and citizenship, not prior to earnings. These usually have an anti-poverty objective and are sometimes means-tested or partially recaptured through the tax system.

Full funding Same as advance funding.

Funding level The relationship at a specified date between the actuarial value of assets and the actuarial liability.

Hybrid pension plan Plan that combines some features of the defined-benefit approach and some aspect of the defined-contribution method.

Implicit contribution rate Contribution rate required when there is no state subsidy.

Implicit public pension debt The value of outstanding pension claims on the public sector minus accumulated pension reserves.

Indexation A system whereby pensions in payment and/or preserved benefits are automatically increased at regular intervals by reference to a specified index of prices or earnings.

Inter-generational distribution Income transfers between different age groups of people.

Intra-generational distribution Income transfers within a certain age group of people.

Legal retirement age The normal retirement age written into pension statutes.

Liabilities Amounts which a pension scheme has an obligation to pay now or in the future.

Means-tested benefit A benefit that is paid only if the recipient's income falls below a certain level.

Minimum pension guarantee A guarantee provided by the government to bring pensions to some minimum level.

Mixed contribution rate Weighted average of contribution rates across different pension schemes.

Notional accounts A centrally managed, pay-as-you-go, notional contribution plan. In this model, each worker has an account in the central pension system institution, which is credited with the contributions made by or on behalf of the worker. Account balances are also credited with the analogue of interest payments, but typically at a rate tied to the growth of wages – either the rate of increase in the average wage or the rate of increase in total wages. At retirement, the balance in the account is converted into a life annuity based on estimates of the group's expected life-span. The promises under notional accounts are similar to those under the defined-contribution model.

Occupational pension scheme An arrangement organised by an employer or on behalf of a group of employers to provide pensions for one or more employees upon leaving service or upon death or retirement.

Old age dependency ratio The population aged 65 and over expressed as a percentage of the working age population, usually defined as aged 15 to 64.

Pay-as-you-go An arrangement under which benefits are paid out of current revenues and no funding is made for future liabilities.

Pre-funding Same as advance-funding.

Qualifying period Number of contribution years required to be entitled to a full pen-sion.

Reference salary Salary on which the calculation of pension benefits is based. The reference salary generally varies between career earnings and earnings of a number of "best years".

Replacement rate The value of a pension as a proportion of a worker's wages during some base period, such as the last year or two before retirement or the entire lifetime average wage.

System dependency ratio The ratio of people receiving pensions from a certain pension scheme divided by the number of workers contributing to the same scheme in the same period.

System maturation The process in which young people eligible for pensions in a new system, gradually grow old and retire, thereby raising the system dependency ratio to the demographic dependency ratio. In a fully mature system, all old people in the covered group are eligible for full pensions.

Vesting period The minimum of time required to qualify for full ownership of pension benefits.

Sources: World Bank (1994); OECD (1998); and Bonoli (2000)

Notes

Notes Introduction

1 The most important technical terms used to describe the design of various pension systems are explained in the glossary (appendix 3).

Notes Chapter 1

1 An arrangement under which benefits are paid out of current revenues and no funding is made for future liabilities.
2 It should be kept in mind that this does not apply to the complementary schemes in the French pension regime that are typically based on a defined-contribution design.
3 This is illustrated by the recent developments on international capital markets. For instance, pension funds within the EU have on average lost more than 25% of their value in 2000 and 2001 (Towers Perrin 2002: Global Capital Market Update 2001).
4 These differences are by no means negligible. In the Netherlands, for example, it has been calculated that only 1.2% of revenues are needed to finance the administrative expenses of the public pension system. By contrast, these costs amount to 4.4% in the case of occupational pension funds, 7.2% in the case of private group insurance and 21.1% in the case of private individual pension plans (Schmähl 1999).
5 According to a simulation study by Müller (1996) the introduction of a general basic pension as suggested by Miegel (1999) would increase costs by 12%. The costs of the contributory system will only begin to surpass those of the basic system after twenty years. Twenty years onward, the costs of the basic pension are calculated to be about 15% lower than they would have been if the contributory system had been retained. By contrast, Miegel himself argues that a *gradual* changeover towards a tax-financed basic pension could avoid these additional costs.

6 Depending on the respective opinion poll, only between 20 to 37% of German citizens would welcome a tax-financed basic pension as an alternative to contributory pension insurance (FORSA 1997a; FORSA 1997b; FORSA 1997c).

7 The repertoire of measures discussed below is explicitly confined to the area of pension policy. To be sure, legal steps taken in other policy areas such as immigration policy, family policy or employment policy may be important or even necessary in order to alleviate the demographic and economic pressure on national pension systems. However, I will not address these aspects within the scope of this study which aims to analyse the politics of *pensions*.

8 Following Hinrichs (2000) this move is probably not only inspired by a notion of gender equity according to which women should not suffer from reduced pension entitlements resulting from their overwhelming contribution to unpaid family work. It may also be driven by an implicitly pronatalist impetus considering the raise of children as an essential prerequisite to maintain a pay-as-you-go based pension system in the long run.

9 The following description draws mainly on Bonoli (2000), Myles and Quadagno (1997) and OECD (1988).

10 In effect, this measure boils down to a lowering of the accrual rate.

11 In principle, a lower average accrual rate (and thus a reduction in overall pension outlays) might also be realised by a *stronger* differentiation of accrual rates according to income rather than their harmonisation at a single level. Typically, this would imply that higher incomes are revaluated at a lower rate than low incomes. In Italy, for instance, the indexation of those parts of the pension income exceeding the eightfold amount of the minimum pension was suspended in 1998 (Hohnerlein 2001).

12 The reinforcement of work incentives was also an important criterion behind the recent pension reform in Sweden, although employment ratios are still very high by international standards. As Wadensjö (2002) points out, a tighter link between contributions and benefits is expected to increase the number of years of employment (by fewer interruptions and later exiting from the labour market) and to encourage full-time rather than part-time employment.

13 The German pension scheme for civil servants is a case in point. According to model calculations carried out in 1995 expenditures for civil servants pension will increase from 1.46% of GDP in 1990 to 3.18% in 2040 (Färber 1998). Thus, the imminent increase in pension outlays for civil servants is, at least in relative terms, far more pronounced than in the general statutory pension insurance programmes.

14 The World Bank (1994) recommends a publicly managed and tax-financed first pillar providing for basic security needs. This is to be supplemented by a mandatory, privately managed, and fully funded second pillar, which again might be

topped off by voluntary occupational or individual savings plans as the third pillar.

15 This problem has emerged in Germany, where the federal state of *Schleswig-Holstein* recently set up a reserve fund designed to cover a certain share of expenditures for civil servants pensions during the demographic peak. Shortly thereafter this reserve fund was dissolved again in order to cover the general deficit in the public budget (Färber 1998).

16 For instance, such a legal framework may stipulate that only a certain share of the investment capital be placed within one company.

17 Occupational pensions may also be encouraged through labour law measures in order to enhance the attractiveness of these schemes for both employers and employees. For instance, a shortening of vesting periods for occupational pensions will enhance the portability of claims and hence increase the coverage among people with high rates of job turnover. For a more detailed analysis see Griebeling (1998). Moreover, the institutional framework for an expansion of occupational old age provisions may be improved through a change in accounting regulations. For instance, the recent German pension reform has newly introduced the legal option to set up occupational pension funds. As compared to the traditional forms of occupational pensions in Germany, the pension funds model is particularly suited to utilising the full potential of the capital market, in particular with respect to its potentially higher yields and its ample possibilities for diversification (Bank 1999).

18 Limitations on individual choice amount to an implicit tax and may generate welfare losses. Hence, there is a trade off between economies of scale in uniform pension plans and attuning pensions to the specific needs through product differentiation (CPB 1997).

19 In France, the deficit in the *régime général* increased from 4.6 to 39.5 billion francs between 1989 and 1993, which corresponds to about 0.56% of GDP (Bonoli 2000). In Italy, the accumulated deficit at the largest single pension scheme FPLD was 57,358 billion Lira in 1991, corresponding to roughly 4% (!) of GDP (Klammer 1997:195).

20 Share of people aged 65 and older relative to the population between 15 and 64 years.

21 Please note, that in the German figures the huge savings effects resulting from the *Pension Reform Act 1992* (legislated in 1989) have not yet been taken into account.

22 In Sweden, the high level of labour market participation of older people can be attributed to a number of different factors. First, until the early 1990s, the labour market situation was characterised by a high demand for labour contributing to high employment levels in general. Second, in Sweden, social securi-

ty programmes have been less geared towards early labour market exiting than in most other countries. For instance, part-time employment has been (and to some extent still is) relatively widespread among elderly workers due to the existence of a relatively attractive part-time pension scheme for those aged 60 to 65. Plus, in contrast to the situation in other countries, older workers in Sweden are also covered by active labour market programmes, in particular by programmes for disabled workers. Finally, Sweden is the only country studied where the retirement age for men and women has been traditionally the same (Wadensjö 2002).

Notes Chapter 2

1 EPC figures on public pension expenditures are based on a less encompassing definition than the EUROSTAT data presented above. Hence, the expenditure ratios displayed in tables 2.1 and 2.2 are not comparable.
2 Technically speaking, the accrual rate as applied to the pension formula does not fully take into account changes in the development of wages and of average life expectancy and thus does not ensure a stable pension contribution. While the most recent pension reform law envisages a maximum contribution rate of 22% until 2030, it also states, that the replacement rate for a standard pensioner must not fall below 67% of previous wages. A very vaguely formulated clause has been incorporated into the law stating that the government has to take *appropriate* measures if compliance with one of these criteria is jeopardised.
3 Until recently, Austrian pensioners were credited an accrual rate of 1.9% per contribution year for the first 30 years and 1.5% for insurance years 31 to 45. With the 1997 pension reform, a uniform accrual rate of 2% for all contribution years has been established leading to a full pension of 80% after 40 rather than 45 contribution years.
4 For a more detailed description of the changes in retirement ages see appendix two.
5 As already noted, this problem is of no relevance for Sweden with its universal pension system.
6 Between 2001 and 2015, 0.2% of every annual increase in salaries and pensions for civil servants will be deposited in a public reserve fund. From 2020 onwards, the accumulated capital reserves will be used to keep the burden for the public budget lower than it would have been otherwise.

Notes Chapter 3

1 This section draws heavily on Green-Pedersen and Haverland (2002).
2 A useful and critical overview on quantitative studies about welfare state retrenchment is provided by Kittel and Obinger (2001).
3 As Kitschelt (2001) puts it, "an anti-communist Republican like Nixon with a hawkish reputation in foreign policy could initiate reconciliation with communist China more easily without raising suspicions of "selling out" America than a liberal Democrat in the presidency".
4 Interestingly, Kittel and Obinger (2001) discovered contrary empirical evidence which indicates that countries that rely largely on a contribution-based revenue structure display a smaller growth rate in social expenditures. The authors' somewhat speculative explanation for this counter-intuitive finding is that financial problems within social insurance funds (rather than within the government budget) are likely to appear at a fairly early stage through the need to formulate demands on the government budget for additional funding in public.
5 It should be noted that veto points may also have an informal character. For instance, a number of countries have – irrespective of their constitutional provisions – established systems of social corporatism in which legislation in economic and social policy is negotiated with or even by the social partners in advance. Such arrangements of social partnership allow trade unions to articulate their claims on national policymakers. More importantly, the government may also consider unions approval of social policy legislation as indispensable, in which case unions will have a de facto veto power to block welfare retrenchment (Bonoli 2000; Swank 2000; Obinger 2001).
6 According to Tsebelis (1995; 1999), a veto player is defined as an individual or collective actor whose agreement (by majority rule for collective actors) is required for a change in policy.
7 The French majoritarian electoral system is a case in point. During the 1993 elections, for instance, the bourgeois UDF and the Gaullists collectively garnered 39.5% of votes, but 79.7% of the mandates. By contrast, in the 1988 elections their common vote share was only somewhat lower (37.7%), while their share of parliamentary seats was only 44.9% (Nohlen 2000).
8 One example is a recent publication by Katharina Müller (1999), where the theoretical approach of actor-centred institutionalism is used to explore the political conditions under which countries in central and Eastern Europe have been able to privatise their public pay-as-you-go schemes.
9 The figure is supposed to display a one-dimensional policy space indicating policy positions with respect to the aspired degree of benefit retrenchment or expansion. It is not aimed at making statements about the extent to which various ac-

tors prefer an expansion of fully funded old age provisions or a shift from contribution- to tax-financing.

10 Green parties are a clear exception to the rule. For instance, about 10% of voters between 18 and 44 years voted for the Green party in the 1998 federal elections in Germany as opposed to only 2.3% of voters above age 59 (Klein and Ohr 2001).

11 In Germany, for instance, it has been estimated that the average voter age is currently about 47 years (Weizsäcker 2000).

12 These difficulties will be most pronounced for Social Democratic party leaders, who have to move the pension policy position of their party to the right in order to move it closer to their own ideal point. By contrast, the ideal point of Christian Democratic party leaders in social policy issues is less likely to deviate substantially from the ideological centre of gravity of the party as a whole. Thus, the leadership of Christian Democratic parties may often confine itself to hammer out a compromise between the left and the right wing of the party. This compromise may again be relatively close to the leaders' own ideal point. Hence, intraparty conflicts over the party's pension policy goals will be somewhat more easily solved for Christian Democratic than for Social Democratic parties.

13 The German system of civil servants' pensions is a case in point. While benefits are concentrated on the relatively small group of civil servants, the costs accrue the general mass of taxpayers.

14 This argument may be less valid in the case of social service programmes such as health insurance. Here, the groups of beneficiaries and contributors are largely identical. Nevertheless, there seems to be a greater willingness to pay higher health insurance contributions than to accept cuts in health care benefits.

15 One important qualification has to be made, however. While a vast majority of citizens rejects both higher contributions and lower pensions as a means of securing old age provisions in the future, there is a considerable readiness to pursue supplementary old age provisions, especially among younger age groups. While most citizens do not want additional mandatory private pension provisions, they welcome the promotion of private and occupational pensions through favourable tax treatment or direct state subsidies. Thus, the large-scale subsidies for supplementary old age provisions are relatively popular and may also facilitate the acceptance of benefit cuts in the public system.

16 In recent years, the readiness of German citizens to accept pension cuts seems to have increased somewhat, although the level is still lower than in other social policy areas. In a 1998 opinion survey, 16% of respondents stated that they would accept pension cuts, whereas 25% would accept cuts in unemployment compensation (FORSA 1998).

17 In the UK, for instance, the median age of *active* voters is estimated to be around 55 years (*Handelsblatt*, 27 June 2002)

18 By contrast, in an era of high economic growth, governments were able to design pension reform packages that offered substantial benefit increases to current and future pensioners while wage earners still saw their post-tax wages rising. Under these conditions, expansionary pension reforms clearly favoured the electoral prospects of governing parties. In Germany, for instance, two major expansionary pension reforms were adopted in the post-war period, the first under a government led by Christian Democrats (1957), the second under a government led by Social Democrats (1972). In both cases the ruling parties achieved their best election results ever.

19 The opposition may also criticise the lack of initiatives for containing rising pension costs by arguing that the government has done nothing to prevent higher pension contributions rates.

20 Many changes in pension legislation only become fully effective after very long transition periods. As a consequence, the full implementation of pension reform will only be guaranteed if subsequent governments are willing to retain these measures.

21 These conditions are not self-evident. In a consociational democracy like Switzerland, for instance, all of the relevant parties are represented in government regardless of their vote shares. Another possibility is a party system, in which the governing parties can rely on a strong structural majority within the electorate and thus do not have to fear that they will be voted out of office.

22 This is in accordance with the general assumption in the theoretical organisation literature that self-interests usually take precedence over normative aspirations.

23 In principle, the members of a coalition government have similar (or even stronger) incentives for finding compromises as they share a common interest in retaining office. For a small coalition partner this may even imply the reluctant acquiescence in a reform that runs contrary to its policy interests.

24 According to a German opinion poll (DIA 2000), about two-thirds of those aged 18 to 24 were willing to retire later in order to keep pension contribution rates stable. By contrast, barely more than one fifth of those aged 45 to 64 would accept this.

25 In the German metal workers union (*IG Metall*), for instance, the median age is about 53 (Streeck 2002).

Notes Chapter 4

1 The introductory descriptions of the national pension systems refer to the legal situation in the late 1980s in order to pinpoint the status quo in pension policy at

the beginning of the period under investigation (see also the summary synopsis in appendix 1).

2 Until 1993, everyone with at least 5 years residency in Sweden was entitled to a full basic pension. Thereafter this was changed to 40 years of residence or 30 contribution years in the ATP system.

3 The base amount (*basbelopp*) is an accounting unit used to calculate qualifying income and benefits in all social insurance schemes (Anderson 1998).

4 Until 1989, the financing share covered by state grants had fallen to about 12% of total outlays.

5 Among the politicians involved, some have even argued that without this promise the election victory of the Social Democrats in 1982 would have been in danger (Lundberg 2001).

6 For instance, a governmental initiative to replace widows' pensions with a means-tested benefit was withdrawn before it came to a vote in Parliament (Pierson and Weaver 1993).

7 Although yearly ATP expenditures rose from about 27 billion Swedish kronas in 1982 to almost 70 billion in 1989, employer contributions were only raised from 9.4% to 11% of the wage sum during the same period. At the same time, the strength of AP funds (expressed as the value of funds divided by expenditures for the year) diminished from 7.4% to 5.5% (Anderson 1998).

8 The SAP was in office until 1991 and again from 1994 onwards (interrupted by a minority government consisting of four bourgeois parties).

9 The latter measure was postponed, however, when presented to Parliament in spring 1993 in the face of continued rising labour market slack. Hence, it was instead scheduled to be implemented as part of the new pension system (OECD 1994).

10 In absolute terms even the Moderates suffered tangible losses.

11 In 1998, Sweden again displayed a budget surplus of more than 2% of GDP (OECD Economic Outlook).

12 Given the multitude and complexity of changes and given the paradigmatic character of this reform for other Bismarckian countries, I will describe the contents of this reform in somewhat more detail.

13 For an in-depth analysis of the Swedish pension reform process see Anderson (1998), Haag (2000) and Wadensjö (2000).

14 During that period, various societal interest groups had the possibility to submit official statements on the bill.

15 One reason why trade unions were highly critical of the fee swap was the recent breakdown of centralised wage bargaining, which would have been the only way to ensure that wage earners could be compensated through an increase in gross wages (Haag 2000).

16 The largest part of the compensation had been realised already by a commensurate reduction in employees' sickness insurance contributions.

Notes Chapter 5

1 In Italy, it is only workers hired since 1996 to which the new rules are fully applied. In Sweden, by contrast, all people born after 1953 receive their pensions
entirely from the new system (Lißner and Wöss 1999).
2 The Amato government was composed of four parties of the political centre albeit a sizeable share of ministers was not affiliated to political parties.
3 In the early 1990s, Italy's party system was shaken by a political turmoil triggered by the "clean hands" (*mani pulite*) investigations against the old party
establishment. As a consequence, the core parties of the First Republic (the
Christian Democrats, Socialists, Social Democrats, Republicans, and Liberals)
virtually vanished from the political scene after the 1994 election.
4 In Italy, three major trade union confederations exist side by side: The CISL with
a formerly Christian Democratic orientation, covering about 3.5 million members (in 1990), the formerly Socialist-oriented UIL representing about 1.5 million members and the formerly Communist-oriented CGIL with more than five
million members (Rosanelli and Wolf 1994).
5 The agreement states that employers and employees should each divert 2% of
salary into these funds, with another 2% made up of money hitherto used for
severance pay (*trattamento di fine rapporto*, or TFR). Under this arrangement,
employers are legally obligated to pay around 7% of gross salary into a fund designed to finance a lump sum for each employee after the termination of his/her
job (EIRR 1996).
6 It should be noted, however, that the reduction in replacement rates resulting
from the Dini reform only concerns workers who opt to retire early. Therefore,
the Dini reform created a strong incentive to stay longer in work than hitherto.
For instance, an industrial worker retiring at the age of 57 with 35 years of contributions will – under the rules applied by the Dini reform – draw a pension that
is 12% lower than under the previous Amato regime. By contrast, if the same
worker decides to postpone retirement until the age of 65, his pension will be
27% higher (Baccaro 2002).
7 Part of the parliamentary group of the *Forza Italia* voted against, whereas others
abstained from voting (personal communication from David Natali).
8 E-mail communication from Matteo Jessoula.
9 In 1992, the level of long-term interest rates in Italy was still 13.3% – 3.3% higher than the average for the Euro zone and 5.4% higher than in Germany. In the

mean time, the Euro zone (including Italy) displayed a long-term interest rate of approximately only 5%. This decline had a very positive impact on Italy's outlays for public debt service, which fell from 11.8% of GDP in 1993 to less than 6% in 2001 (as compared to a more or less stable level in countries such as Austria, France, and Germany) (OECD 2001).

10 Personal communication from Antonia Gohr.

11 In Sweden, by contrast, where the new pension system is to be phased-in over a much shorter time period, trade unions display a much more balanced age structure. For instance, only 12% of LO members are pensioners (Kjellberg 1999).

12 For a more detailed analysis of strengths and shortcomings, see Franco (2000).

Notes Chapter 6

1 The standard pensioner (*Eckrentner*) refers to a person with a contribution record of 45 years and an average earnings level.

2 *Verband Deutscher Rentenversicherungsträger.*

3 Note that the reform was legislated before German reunification. Opinion polls at the time suggested an election victory for the Social Democrats and their imminent return to power. Although the Social Democrats' expectations were thwarted by German reunification, my interviews with German pension policymakers clearly confirmed my assumption about the strategic reasoning of the then-Social Democratic leadership.

4 Only one commission member (Meinhard Miegel) dissented and pleaded for the introduction of a universal tax-financed basic pension as a substitute to earnings-related social insurance.

5 Among the 20 members of the party commission, 10 approved the proposals of the expert commission, six voted against and four abstained (Richter 2001:88).

6 Note, however, that the Schröder government did not undo the pension cuts enacted in 1996, such as the advanced increase of the retirement age for women (although this step had been fiercely criticised by the then-Social Democratic opposition).

7 The following analysis largely draws on newspaper coverage in the *Handelsblatt* and on Dünn and Fasshauer (2001).

8 For periods of military/civilian service the assessment base was reduced from 80% to 60% of average gross wages. For recipients of unemployment assistance the basis is reduced from 80% of last *gross* wages up to 50% of last *net* wages.

9 Later, this measure was limited to one year.

10 Social Democratic Labour Minister Walter Riester himself was fully aware of this fact, as the following quotation illustrates: "*Durch die Beschränkung der*

Rentensteigerungen auf den Inflationsausgleich in diesem und nächstem Jahr entlasten wir die Rentenkasse stärker, als es die Opposition mit ihrem demographischen Faktor getan hätte" (By restricting pension increases to the rate of inflation this year and next year, we will achieve a greater relief of pension finances than would have been possible through the demographic factor proposed by the opposition. Translation by the author) (Reuber 2000).

11 In the parliamentary debate, Friedrich Merz, the deputy chairman of the Christian Democrats' parliamentary group, quoted Rudolf Dreßler, the former social policy spokesmen of the SPD, with the vitriolic remark: "*Wenn die alte Koalition solche Vorschläge gemacht hätte, wie es jetzt die rot-grüne Regierung getan hat, dann hätten wir den Dritten Weltkrieg ausgerufen*" (CDU-Bundesgeschäftsstelle 1999). (If the old [bourgeois, the author] coalition had made proposals like the red-green government has made now, then we would have declared the third world war. Translation by the author).

12 One interview partner even claimed: "I have never seen a reform that was prepared as badly as this one".

13 The VdK represents the interests of pensioners and disabled people.

14 Under the new regime, workers are entitled to convert parts of their remuneration to an occupational pension (*Entgeltumwandlung*), as long as there is a corresponding provision by a collective agreement between the employer and the union (*Tarifvorbehalt*). In the first years, tax incentives for these occupational pension schemes will be much more favourable than for private pension plans. From 2002 onwards, 4% of the income limit for chargeable contributions by wage and salary earners (currently about 55,000 euros per annum) can be converted tax- and contribution-free (the exemption from payroll taxes, however, will only be possible until the end of 2008). By contrast, tax breaks and allowances in favour of private old age provision will be phased in gradually and reach their full effect only in 2008. Moreover, contributions to these schemes will not be exempted from social insurance contributions (BMAS 2001). Thus, the majority of wage earners are likely to make use of the right to remuneration conversion, which again will promote the expansion of occupational pension schemes.

15 At the last minute, trade unions threatened to withdraw their support unless the reform was changed to commit the government to ensure that the standard pension level would not fall below 67% ("*Niveausicherungsklausel*"). Contrary to previous agreements with the trade unions, this bill only stipulated 64% rather than 67%. In order to prevent SPD deputies associated with the trade unions from voting against the bill, this clause was changed through a separate amendment ("*Entschließungsantrag*").

16 Effectively, however, this 67% correspond to 64% according to the previous

pension formulae due to a changed definition of the net wage. The "modified net adjustment formula" ensures that changes in income taxes, child benefits and contribution rates to unemployment insurance will no longer affect the pension level. Henceforth, only contributions to the statutory pension insurance and (notional) contributions to private old age provisions will be taken into account. As the latter will increase to 4%, the *calculated* net wage will be correspondingly lower (Fehr and Jess 2001).

17 According to a simulation study by Fehr/Jess the necessary contribution rate – in the medium- and long-term – would have been more than one percentage point higher if the demographic factor had been retained (Fehr and Jess 2001). According to a study by Hain and Tautz (2001), the corresponding difference would be smaller and vary between 0% and 0.5% between 2010 and 2030.

18 By and large, however, the measures adopted within the statutory pension insurance were – often with some time lag – also applied to the civil servants' scheme (Battis 1998; Färber 1998).

Notes Chapter 7

1 While Tálos and Wörister (1998) correctly argue that the process of pension retrenchment has gained momentum since the mid-1990s due to tighter fiscal constraints, pension cuts in Austria are rather modest if compared to the pension reforms in other countries (Alber 1998; Mantel 2001).

2 Between 1987 and 2000, Austria was ruled by a "grand coalition" between the Socialist SPÖ and the bourgeois Austrian People's Party (ÖVP).

3 For instance, until recently the Ministry of Social Affairs was basically controlled by the Austrian Trade Union Confederation ÖGB (Obinger 2001).

4 The final savings package also included a suspension of yearly pension adjustments for 1997. Civil servants' pensions were even frozen for two years (1996 and 1997). Moreover, civil servants' pensions are reduced for those retiring before 60 years of age by 2% per year – up to a maximum of 18%.

5 In the past, pension reforms were typically preceded by expert reports issued by the social partners (Tálos and Kittel 2001).

6 Weighted average of contribution rates across different pension schemes.

7 Contribution rate required if there was no state subsidy.

8 In 1992, the Austrian constitutional court declared the different retirement age for men and women unconstitutional. Shortly thereafter, the government adopted a constitutional law according to which the retirement ages for women were to be aligned with to those of men. However, this would only be phased in from 2018 to 2034.

9 It needs to be noted that the saving effects would amount to 1.5% of GDP in 2030 if increasing life expectancies were taken into account in the annual adjustment formula. This had been agreed upon in principle, but has yet to be implemented (Buczolich et al. 2002).

10 The statement of a pension policy actor within the Austrian People's Party ÖVP is telling: "*I've often said in interviews that for me the biggest disappointment ever was the pension reform of 1997*" (cited from Linnerooth-Bayer 2001:30).

11 It is an open question, however, of whether the quarrels over pension reform were the real reason or only a pretext for Schüssel to abandon his coalition with the SPÖ.

12 It needs to be noted, however, that the government would still have had a slight parliamentary majority vis-à-vis the opposition parties if all of the ÖAAB deputies abstained from voting (this was more likely than all of the ÖAAB deputies voting against their own government).

13 Austrian employment legislation states that severance pay must be granted to private sector employees if the employment relationship is terminated by the employer.

14 The German government adopted a very similar law in 1996. However, in sharp contrast to the corresponding law in Austria, this measure has been phased-in from 2000 to 2004.

15 It needs to be remembered that a country like Sweden will implement a full changeover to lifetime earnings within about the same time period.

Notes Chapter 8

1 In France, the labour movement is traditionally divided along ideological lines. There are five major national federations operating independently from each other. The *Confédération Générale du Travail* (CGT) represents about 23% of all union members (in 1995) and is closely allied to the Communist party through personal ties and by ideology. The *Force Ouvrière* (FO), representing some 17% of unions rank and file, originated from a division within the CGT in 1947 and is not related to any party in particular, but still belongs to the more radical elements of the French labour movement. The *Confédération Française des Travailleurs Chrétiens* (CFTC) is a federation of Catholic unions, which is, however, only of minor importance, as it represents less than 5% of total union members. The *Confédération Française Démocratique des Travailleurs* (CFDT), is situated close to the Socialists, and emerged from a division of the CFTC and covers about 25% of all union members. In recent years, it has been more reform-oriented and co-operative vis-à-vis the government than its counterparts.

Finally, the CFE-CGC (*Confédération Française de l'Encadrement – Confédération Générale des Cadres*) represents the interests of managers (Visser 2000). Apart from the CGT, all of the trade union federations typically interdict the simultaneous pursuance of political mandates and mandates within the trade union organisation.

2 The following citation of a French Old Age Insurance Fund official underscores the importance of this motive: "*The introduction of the Fonds de Solidarité Vieillesse was a skilful move, because it reduced the deficit of the old age insurance budget in a way that was acceptable to the trade unions. It showed that the State was making an effort. In fact the FSV had been carefully designed in order to be able to attract the approval of the social partners*" (cited in Bonoli 2000:148).

3 According to a high civil servant involved in preparing the reform, this temporal limitation was crucial to obtain CFDT's implicit support (Bruno Palier, personal communication).

4 A frequently applied strategy of French governments is to let journalists publish information on extremely controversial proposals (such as an increase in the legal retirement age from 60 to 65 years) and then present a softer reform proposal which appears more acceptable to potential reform opponents (Bruno Palier, personal communication).

5 Figures compiled by Visser (2000) indicate a unionisation rate of 19.2% in the public sector but only 3.4% in the private sector (1993).

6 In 1998, the Socialist government decided to continue with price indexation (OECD 1999).

7 Although the French President lacks any formal competencies in the realm of pension policy, he has the legal power to dismiss the government and to dissolve the Parliament. Hence, the political risks of French governments retrenching the welfare state are higher if the President belongs to the opposite political camp.

8 For instance, Bernard Kouchner, a former health care minister, commented that: "*it is an ambitious and courageous plan, which picks up many of our proposals*" (*Le Monde* 17 November 1995, p.12).

9 In all of the major trade union confederations – except the CGD – more than 60% of members come from the public sector. Within the FO this share is more than 73% (Visser 2000:272).

10 Various estimates range from 600,000 to more than 2,000,000 participants (Vail 1999:328).

11 In addition, students took to the streets demanding higher spending for education.

12 The ARRCO agreement in February 1993, the ARGIRC agreement of February 1994, and the ARGIRC and ARRCO agreements of April 1996.

13 In order to encourage the investment in shares, the law stipulates that no more than 65% of the funds should be invested in bonds.

14 The small CFTC took an intermediate position. It criticised the CFDT for its "premature" deal with the government, but did not support the industrial actions launched by the other union confederations. Instead, it sought to achieve further improvements to the bill (such as an increase of minimum pensions to 100% of the minimum wage) through lobbying various parliamentary groups (Jolivet 2003b).

Notes Chapter 9

1 At the time of the Juppé plan presentation, the next regular elections were still some three years away.

2 In Italy, people with more than 18 years of contributions at the end of 1995, will receive pension benefits that are to a great extent still based on the old system, whereas only people who started working in 1996 are entirely covered by the new system (with a "pro-rata" system applying for the intermediate age groups, OECD 2000). In Sweden, by contrast, only those born in 1937 or earlier are subject to the old law, while the new system fully applies to all people born in 1954 or after (with transition rules for those born between 1938 and 1953, Lißner and Wöss 1999).

3 With a net density rate below 10%, the level of unionisation is much lower than in other Bismarckian countries (Figures for 1995: Austria: 38.9%, Germany: 26.5%, Italy: 32.4%, Sweden: 87.5% of all gainfully employed; Ebbinghaus and Visser 2000).

Notes Appendix

1 As these schemes are defined-contribution schemes, there is no fixed target in terms of benefits.

2 Old pension formula applying to workers with more than 18 years of contributions at the end of 1995 and a weighted average of the two formulae applicable to those with less than 18 years.

3 This means that social benefits will only be partly adjusted to inflation, as long as the public budget deficit surpasses certain thresholds.

Bibliography

1   Periodicals and Newspapers

Der Spiegel
Der Standard
Die Zeit
Economist
European Industrial Relations Review
Från Riksdag och Departement
Handelsblatt
Le Monde
OECD, *Economic Surveys*
Süddeutsche Zeitung

2   Other Documents

Abramovici, G. (2002). *Der Sozialschutz: Rentenausgaben, Statistik kurz gefasst: Bevölkerung und soziale Bedingungen. Thema 3 – 6/2002,* EUROSTAT.

Adam, G. (2002). "Parliament passes reform of severance pay". Eiroline, European industrial relations observatory on-line (http://www.eiro.eurofound.ie/).

Alber, J. (1987). "Germany". *Growth to Limits: The Western European Welfare States since World War II.* Vol. 4. Appendix (Synopses, Bibliographies, Tables). P. Flora. Berlin: Walter de Gruyter, 247-353.

Alber, J. (1998). *Recent developments in continental European welfare states: Do Austria, Germany, and the Netherlands prove to be birds of a feather?* World Congress of Sociology, Montreal.

Anderson, K. M. (1998). The Welfare State in the Global Economy: The Politics of Social Insurance Retrenchment in Sweden, 1990-1998. Dissertation. Washington, DC.

Anderson, K. M. (2001). The Politics of Retrenchment in a Social Democratic Welfare State. Reform of Swedish Pensions and Unemployment Insurance, *Com-*

parative Political Studies, Vol. 34, No. 9, 1063-1091.

Anderson, K. M. and T. Meyer (2003). "Social Democracy, Unions, and Pension Politics in Germany and Sweden". *Journal of Public Policy*, vol. 23, no. 1, 23-55.

Antichi, M. and F. R. Pizutti (2000). "The public pension system in Italy: Observations on the recent reforms, Methods of control and their application". *Social dialogue and pension reform*. E. Reynaud (ed.). Geneva: International Labour Office, 81-96.

Arbeiterkammer Österreich (2002). Alles rund um die "Abfertigung neu".

Arbeiterkammer Bremen (2000). Sozialpolitische Chronik. Die wesentlichen Änderungen im Bereich der Arbeitslosenversicherung, Rentenversicherung, Krankenversicherung, Pflegeversicherung und Sozialhilfe (HLU) in den vergangenen Jahren.

Arter, D. (1999). "The Swedish general election of 20 September 1998: A victory for values over policies?" *Electoral Studies* 18, pp. 296-300.

Baccaro, L. (2000). *Negotiating Pension Reform with the Unions: The Italian Experience in European Perspective*. International Conference of Europeanists, Chicago.

Baccaro, L. (2001). The Construction of "Democratic" Corporatism in Italy. Paper prepared for presentation at the Max Planck Institute for the Study of Societies. Cologne: Germany.

Baccaro, L. (2002). "Negotiating the Italian pension reform with the unions: lessons for corporatist theory". *Industrial and Labour Relations Review* 55 (3): 413-430.

Bank, M. (1999). "Betriebliche Pensionsfonds". *Wirtschaftswissenschaftliches Studium* 28 (7).

Barr, N. (2000). *The Welfare State as a Piggy Bank: Information, Risk, Uncertainty, and the Role of the State*. Oxford: Oxford University Press.

Battis, U. (1998). *Beamtenversorgung. Handbuch zur Altersversorgung. Gesetzliche, betriebliche und private Vorsorge in Deutschland*. J.-E. Cramer, W. Förster and F. Ruland (eds.). Frankfurt am Main: Fritz Knapp Verlag, 117-127.

Bergmann, T. (1999). "Trade-offs in Swedish Constitutional Design: The Monarchy under Challenge". *Policy, Office or Votes?: How Political Parties in Western Europe Make Hard Decisions*. W. C. Müller and S. Kaare (eds.). Cambridge: Cambridge University Press, 237-257.

Blanchet, D. and F. Legros (2000). *France: The difficult path to a consensual reform*. NBER-Kiel Institute Conference on "Coping with the Pension Crisis – Where does Europe Stand?", Berlin.

Blöndal, S. and S. Scarpetta (1998). *The Retirement Decision in OECD Countries*.

OECD Economics Department Working Papers no 202. Paris: OECD.

BMAS, Bundesministerium für Arbeit und Sozialordnung (1997). Vorschläge der Kommission "Fortentwicklung der Rentenversicherung", Bonn.

BMAS (2001). Key points of the pension reform, Berlin.

Bönker, F. and H. Wollmann (2001). Stumbling Towards Reform. The German Welfare State in the 1990s. *Welfare States under Pressure*. P. Taylor-Gooby (ed.). London: Sage, 75-99.

Bonoli, G. (2000). *The Politics of Pension Reform: Institutions and Policy Change in Western Europe*. Cambridge: Cambridge University Press.

Bonoli, G. and B. Palier (2000). "How do welfare states change? Institutions and their impact on the politics of welfare state reform in Western Europe". *European Review* 8 (3): 333-352.

Bouget, D. (1998). "The Juppé Plan and the Future of the French Social Welfare System". *Journal of European Social Policy* 8 (2): 155-172.

Bovenberg, A. L. and A.S.M. van den Linden (1996). *Can we afford to grow old? Adjusting pension policies to a more aged society*. OECD. Paper presented at the conference "Beyond 2000: The New Social Policy Agenda", Paris.

Bovens, M. and P. 't Hart, et al. (2001). *Success and Failure in Public Governance: A Comparative Analysis*. Cheltenham: Edward Elgar.

Bozec, G. and C. Mays (2001). Pension Reform in France (http://www.iccr-international.org/pen-ref/).

Brugiavini, A. et al. (2001). "What Do Unions Do to the Welfare State?" *The Role of Unions in the Twenty-first Century: A Study for the Fondazione Rodolfo Debenedetti*. T. Boeri, A. Brugiavini and L. Calmfors (eds.). New York: Oxford University Press: 157-253.

Buczolich, G., B. Felderer, et al. (2002). Pension Reform in Austria (Manuscript).

Castles, F. G. (2001). "On the Political Economy of Recent Public Sector Development". *Journal of European Social Policy* 11 (3): 195-211.

CDU-Bundesgeschäftsstelle (1999). Redebeitrag von Friedrich Merz in der Debatte über das rot-grüne "Spar"-Programm (http://www.cdu-rg.de/pm/pr0008.htm).

CFDT (2003a), Jean-Marie Toulisse dans *Syndicalisme Hebdo*: "*À aucun moment, la CGT ou fo n'ont soutenu la CFDT dans les négociations*" (http://www.cfdt.fr/actu/presse/media/actumedia122.html).

CFDT (2003b), François Chérèque dans *La Croix*: "*Maintenant, il faut se mobiliser pour l'emploi*", http://www.cfdt.fr/actu/presse/media/actumedia121.html

Charpin, J.-M. (1999). *L'avenir de nos retraites. Rapport au premier ministre*. Paris: Commissariat général du plan.

Cioccia, A. et al. (2001). The Italian Pension System and Pension Reform Pathways (http://www.iccr-international.org/pen-ref/).

Council of the European Union (2001), *Objectives and working methods in the area of pensions: applying the open method of co-ordination*. Joint Report of the Social Protection Committee and the Economic Policy Committee. November 2001, Brussels (http://europa.eu.int/comm/employment_social/news/2002/jan/laeken_en.pdf).

Council of the European Union (2001a). *Adequate and Sustainable Pensions*. A report by the Social Protection Committee on the future evolution of social protection. Brussels.

CPB, Centraal Planbureau (1997). *Challenging Neighbours: Rethinking German and Dutch Economic Institutions*. Berlin.

Culpepper, P. D. (2000). *The Sources of Policy Innovation: Sub-National Constraints on Negotiated Reform*. Annual Meeting of the American Political Science Association, Washington, D.C.

D'Ercole, M. and F. Terribile (1998). Pension Spending: Developments in 1996 and 1997. *Italian Politics: Mapping the Future*. L. Bardi and M. Rhodes (eds.). Bologna: Westview Press, 187-207.

Deuscher Bundestag (2000). Ausschußdrucksache 14/1080. *Ausschuss für Arbeit und Sozialordnung*. Berlin: Deutscher Bundestag.

Deutsch-Französisches Institut (2001). *Standortpolitik und Globalisierung: deutsch-französische Perspektiven*. Opladen: Leske & Budrich.

DIA (Deutsches Institut für Altersvorsorge) (1999). *Reformvorschläge zur gesetzlichen Alterssicherung in Deutschland. Ein systematischer Überblick*. Cologne.

DIA (Deutsches Institut für Altersvorsorge) (2000). Rentenreform und Eigenvorsorge. Mehrländerumfrage – die Ergebnisse für Deutschland. Cologne.

Downs, A. (1957). *An Economic Theory of Democracy,* New York: Harper & Row.

Ds, Departementserien (1992:89). Ett reformerat pensionssystem – Bakgrund, principier och skiss. Promemoria av Pensionsarbetsgruppen. Stockholm: Socialdepartementet.

Dünn, S. and S. Fasshauer (2001). "Die Rentenreform 2000/2001 – Ein Rückblick". *Deutsche Rentenversicherung* 5: 266-275.

Ebbinghaus, B. (2001). *Reform Blockage or Self-Regulation? The Ambigious Role of Social Partnership in European Welfare States*. Paper presented at the SASE 13th Annual Meeting on Socio-Economics (Workshop on Re-thinking the Welfare State: Pension Reform in the Three Europes – II), University of Amsterdam, June 28-July 1.

Ebbinghaus, B. and J. Visser (2000). *Trade Unions in Western Europe since 1945*. London: Macmillan.

Economic Policy Committee (2000). Progress Report to the Ecofin Council on the impact of ageing populations on public pension systems. Brussels: European Commission.

Economic Policy Committee (2001). Budgetary challenges posed by ageing populations: the impact on public spending on pensions, health and long-term care for the elderly and possible indicators of the long-term sustainability of public finances. Brussels: European Commission.

Economist, The (2002). "The politics of pensions. We know what's best for your old age, why can't you see it?" 27 February 2002.

Eiroline (2000). Le financement du syndicalisme en débat. (http://www.eiro.eurofound.ie/).

Eiroline, (1997a). The government crisis and the reaction of the social partners (http://www.eiro.eurofound.ie/).

Eiroline, (1997b). Law on the financing of the social security system (http://www.eiro.eurofound.ie/).

Eiroline, (1997c). Sweeping changes in social insurance contributions (http://www.eiro.eurofound.ie/).

Eiroline, (2000a). New tax rules aim to foster supplementary pensions (http://www.eiro.eurofound.ie/).

Eiroline (2000b). New pension reform plans heavily disputed (http://www.eiro.eurofound.ie/).

Eiroline (2003a). Major industrial action planned over pensions reform (http://www.eiro.eurofound.ie/).

Eiroline (2003b). Further strikes as pension talks fail (http://www.eiro.eurofound.ie/).

EIRR, (1993). "France. Agreement on pensions". *European Industrial Relations Review* 230: 7.

EIRR (1994). "General strike over pension reforms". *European Industrial Relations Review* 250: 17.

EIRR (1995a). "Italy: Parliament adopts pension reform". *European Industrial Relations Review* 260: 8.

EIRR (1995b). "France. Trade unions respond in disarray to Juppé plan". *European Industrial Relations Review* 263: 6.

EIRR (1996a). "Italy. Pension reform in force". *European Industrial Relations Review* 264: 31-34.

EIRR (1996b). "France. France racked by massive crisis over social security reforms". *European Industrial Relations Review* 264: 6.

EIRR (1996c). "France. Major agreements on financing of supplementary pensions". *European Industrial Relations Review* 269: 5.

EIRR (1997a). "Austria. Pension proposals unveiled". *European Industrial Relations Review* 285: 3.

EIRR (1997b). "France. Bill on private pension schemes". *European Industrial Relations Review* 279: 6.

EIRR (1998). "Austria. Reform of state pension system". *European Industrial Relations Review* 289: 30-32.

EIRR (2002). "Italy. 2002 Budget law". *European Industrial Relations Review* 336: 9.

Emmert, T. et al. (2001). "Das Ende einer Ära – Die Bundestagswahl vom 27. September 1998". *Analysen aus Anlass der Bundestagswahl 1998*. H.-D. Klingemann and M. Kaase (eds.). Wiesbaden: Westdeutscher Verlag, 17-56.

Esping-Andersen, G. (1990). *The Three Worlds of Welfare Capitalism*. London: Polity Press.

Esping-Andersen, G. (1996). "Welfare States without Work: The Impasse of Labour Shedding and Familialism in Continental European Social Policy". *Welfare States in Transition: National Adaptations in Global Economics*. G. Esping-Andersen (ed.). London: Sage: 66-87.

Färber, G. (1998). "Mittel- und langfristige Entwicklung der Beamtenversorgung". *Handbuch zur Altersversorgung. Gesetzliche, betriebliche und private Vorsorge in Deutschland*. J.-E. Cramer, W. Förster and F. Ruland (eds.). Frankfurt am Main: Fritz Knapp Verlag, 973-994.

Fargion, V. (2000). *Italian Reforms: Towards more Equality?* Paper presented at the conference "Comparer les systemes de protection sociale en Europe". Ministère de L'Emploi et de la Solidarité, Paris.

Featherstone, K. (2001). *The Political Dynamics of External Empowerment: the emergence of EMU and the challenge to the European social model*. Paper prepared for the 5th Biennial Conference of the European Community Studies Association, Madison, Wisconsin, May 31-June 2.

Fehr, H. and H. Jess (2001). "Gewinner und Verlierer der aktuellen Rentenreform". *Zeitschrift der Bundesversicherungsanstalt für Angestellte* 48: 165-175.

Ferrera, M. (1987). "Italy". *Growth to Limits: The Western European Welfare States since World War II*. Volume 4. Appendix (Synopses, Bibliographies, Tables). P. Flora (ed.). Berlin: Walter de Gruyter, 475-528.

Ferrera, M. and E. Gualmini (2000a). "Italy: Rescue from without?" *Diverse Responses to Common Challenges*. F. W. Scharpf and V. A. Schmidt (eds.), Oxford: Oxford University Press, 351-398.

Ferrera, M. and E. Gualmini (2000b). "Reforms Guided by Consensus: The Welfare State in the Italian Transition". *West European Politics* 23 (2): 189-208.

Finansdepartement (1998). AP-fonden och det reformerade ålderspensionssystemet. Stockholm.

FORSA, Gesellschaft für Sozialforschung und statistische Analyse (1996). Meinungsumfrage zur Altersversorgung (unpublished).

FORSA (1997a). Die Zukunft der Altersversorgung. Meinungen der Deutschen (unpublished).

FORSA (1997b). Einheitliche Grundrente für alle Bürger? (unpublished).

FORSA (1997c). Meinungen der Bürger zum Rentensystem (unpublished).

FORSA (1998). Meinungen der Bürger zur Sozialpolitik (unpublished).

FORSA (1999a). Meinungen der Bürger zur Rentendiskussion (unpublished).

FORSA (1999b). Meinungsumfrage zur Akzeptanz einer privaten Zusatzversicherung (unpublished).

FORSA (2000). Meinungsumfrage zur Altersvorsorge (unpublished).

Forschungsgruppe Wahlen (various years). "Politbarometer".

Franco, D. (2000). *Italy: a never-ending pension reform.* NBER-Kiel Institute conference on "Coping with the Pension Crisis – Where Does Europe Stand?", Kiel.

Gächter, A. (1998). Social partners discuss severance pay and holiday entitlements, Eiroline, European industrial relations observatory on-line. 1998.

Geissler, H. (1998). *Zeit, das Visier zu öffnen.* Cologne: Kiepenheuer & Witsch.

Gern, K.-J. (1998). "Recent Developments in old age pension systems – an international overview". Kieler Arbeitspapiere, no. 863. Kieler Institut für Weltwirtschaft.

Gillion, C. et al. (2000). *Social Security Pensions: Development and Reform.* Geneva: International Labour Office.

Gilmour, J. B. (1995). *Strategic Disagreement: Stalemate in American Politics,* Pittsburgh: University of Pittsburgh Press.

Gohr, A. (2001a). "Der italienische Wohlfahrtsstaat: Entwicklungen, Probleme und die europäische Herausforderung". *Sozialstaat in Europa. Geschichte, Entwicklung, Perspektiven.* K. Kraus and T. Geisen (eds.). Wiesbaden: Westdeutscher Verlag: 143-169.

Gohr, A. (2001b). Maastricht als Herausforderung und Chance. Die Auswirkungen der europäischen Integration auf den italienischen Wohlfahrtsstaat. ZeS Arbeitspapier 8/01. Bremen, Zentrum für Sozialpolitik.

Green-Pedersen, C. and M. Haverland (2002). "The New Politics of the Welfare State and the New Scholarship of the Welfare State". *Journal of European Social Policy* 12 (1): 43-52.

Griebeling, G. (1998). "Arbeitsrechtliches Umfeld und Tendenzen". *Handbuch zur Altersversorgung. Gesetzliche, betriebliche und private Vorsorge in Deutschland.* J.-E. Cramer, W. Förster and F. Ruland (eds.). Frankfurt am Main: Fritz Knapp Verlag, 347-362.

Haag, D. (2000). Die schwedische Rentenreform 1998 – Analyse eines Gesetzgebungsprozesses, Diplomarbeit, Universität Konstanz.

Hain, W. and R. Tautz (2001). "Finanzielle Auswirkungen der Rentenreform". *Deutsche Rentenversicherung* 6-7: 359-377.

Haverland, M. (2000). *Constrained choices? Reforming pension systems in advanced European welfare states.* XVIIIth IPSA World Congress, Quebec City.

Hering, M. (2002). *The Politics of Privatizing Public Pensions: Lessons from a Frozen Welfare State.* Paper prepared for delivery at the 2001 Annual Meeting of the American Political Science Association, San Francisco, August 30-September 2, 2001.

Hicks, A. (1999). *Social Democracy and Welfare Capitalism.* Ithaca: Cornell University Press.

Hinrichs, K. (1998). *Reforming the Public Pension Scheme in Germany: The End of the Traditional Consensus?,* ZeS Arbeitspapier Nov. 1998, Bremen .

Hinrichs, K. (2000a). Elephants on the move. Patterns of public pension reform in OECD countries. *European Review* 8: 353-378.

Hinrichs, K. (2000b). "Von der Rentenversicherungs- zur Alterssicherungspolitik. Reformen und Reformprobleme". *Kontingenz und Krise. Institutionenpolitik in kapitalistischen und postsozialistischen Gesellschaften.* K. Hinrichs, H. Kitschelt, and H. Wiesenthal (eds.). Frankfurt am Main and New York. 291-317.

Hohnerlein, E.-M. (2001). Alterssicherung und demographische Entwicklung in Italien. *Demographischer Wandel und Alterssicherung. Rentenpolitik in neun europäischen Ländern und den USA im Vergleich.* H.-J. Reinhard (ed.). Baden-Baden: Nomos Verlagsgesellschaft: 93-133.

Huber, E. and J. D. Stephens (2001). *Development and Crisis of the Welfare State: Parties and Policies in Global Markets,* Chicago: University of Chicago Press.

Immergut, E. M. (1990). "Institutions, veto points, and policy results: a comparative analysis of health care". *Journal of Public Policy* 10 (4): 391-416.

Immergut, E. M. (1992). "The Rules of the Game: The Logic of Health Policymaking in France, Switzerland, and Sweden". *Structuring Politics.* S. Steinmo et al. (eds.). Cambridge: Cambridge University Press: 57-89.

Jackson, R. (2002). *The Global Retirement Crisis: The Threat to World Stability and What to Do About.* Washington, DC: Centre for Strategic and International Studies.

Jackson, R. and N. Howe (2002). *Preliminary Results from the CSIS Ageing Vulnerability Index.* Washington, DC: Centre for Strategic and International Studies.

Jolivet, A. (2002). "Active strategies for older workers in France". *Active strategies for older workers in the European Union.* M. Jepsen, D. Foden and M. Hutsebaut (eds.). Brussels: European Trade Union Institute: 245-275.

Jolivet, A. (2003a). Le projet gouvernemental de réforme des retraites se précise, 21 May 2003
(http://www.eiro.eurofound.eu.int/2003/05/word/FR0305103FFR.doc).

Jolivet, A. (2003b). Retraites : Le projet de réforme arrive au Parlement, 26 June 2003, (http://www.eiro.eurofound.eu.int/2003/06/word/FR0306104FFR.doc).

Jolivet, A. (2003c). La réforme des retraites est officiellement lancée. 7 March 2003, (http://www.eiro.eurofound.eu.int/2003/02/word/FR0302108FFR.doc).

Kitschelt, H. (1994). *The transformation of European Social Democracy*. Cambridge: Cambridge University Press.

Kitschelt, H. (2001). Partisan Competition and Welfare State Retrenchment. When Do Politicans Choose Unpopular policies? *The New Politics of the Welfare State*. P. Pierson (ed.), Cambridge: Oxford University Press: 265-302.

Kitschelt, H. (2003). "Political-economic context and partisan strategies in the German federal elections, 1990-2002". *West European Politics* 26 (4): 125-152.

Kittel, B. and H. Obinger (2001). Political Parties, Institutions, and the Dynamics of Social Expenditure in Times of Austerity. MPIfG Discussion Paper 02/01. Cologne: Max-Planck-Institut für Gesellschaftsforschung.

Kjellberg, A. (1999). "Sweden". *The Societies of Europe: Trade Unions in Western Europe since 1945*. B. Ebbinghaus and J. Visser (eds.). London: Macmillan: 605-655.

Klammer, U. (1997). *Alterssicherung in der Europäischen Union II. Alterssicherung in Italien. Eine institutionelle, theoretische und empirische Analyse.* Sozialpolitische Schriften, 70-II. Berlin: Duncker & Humbolt.

Klammer, U. and G. Rolf (1998). "Auf dem Weg zu einer gerechten Alterssicherung? Rentenreformpolitik in Deutschland und Italien im Vergleich". *Zeitschrift für Sozialreform* 44 (11/12): 793-817.

Klein, M. and D. Ohr (2001). Die Wahrnehmung der politischen und persönlichen Eigenschaften von Helmut Kohl und Gerhard Schröder und ihr Einfluß auf die Wahlentscheidung bei der Bundestagswahl 1998. *Analysen aus Anlass der Bundestagswahl 1998*. H.-D. Klingemann and M. Kaase. Wiesbaden: Westdeutscher Verlag: 91-132.

Korpi, W. (1983). *The Democratic Class Struggle*. London: Routledge and Kegan Paul.

Krupp, H.-J. (1997). "Pro und Kontra Grundrente – Eine Analyse aus volkswirtschaftlicher Sicht". *Deutsche Rentenversicherung* 3-4/97: 204-219.

Levy, J. D. (2000). "France: directing adjustment?" *Welfare and work in the open economy (Vol. II): Diverse responses to common challenges*. F. W. Scharpf and V. A. Schmidt (eds.). Oxford: Oxford University Press: 308-350.

Lijphart, A. (1984). *Democracies: Patterns of Majoritarian and Consensus Government in Twenty-One Countries.* New Haven: Yale University Press.

Lindbom, A. (2001). "De borgerliga partierna och pensionsreformen". *Hur blev den stora kompromissen möjlig? Politiken bakom den svenska pensionsreformen.* J. Palme (ed.). Stockholm: Pensionsforum: 50-87.

Linnerooth-Bayer, J. (2001). Pension Reform in Austria. Laxenburg: International Institute for Applied System Analysis.

Lipset, S. M. and S. Rokkan (1967). *Party Systems and Voter Alignments: Cross-National Perspectives.* New York: Free Press.

Lißner, L. and J. Wöss (1999). *Umbau statt Abbau: Sozialstaaten im Vergleich. Deutschland – Österreich – Schweden.* Cologne: Bund-Verlag/ÖGB-Verlag.

Livre Blanc sur les retraites (1991). Rapports officiels. Paris: La documentation Français.

LO, Landsorganisationen (1994). LOs yttrande över pensionsarbetsgruppens betänkande Reformerat pensionssystem (SOU 1994:20).

Lundberg, U. (2001). "Socialdemokratin och 1990-talets pensionsreform". *Hur blev den stora kompromissen möjlig? Politiken bakom den svenska pensionsreformen.* J. Palme (ed.). Stockholm: Pensionsforum: 8-49.

Madeley, J. T. S. (1999). "The 1998 Riksdag Election: Hobson's Choice and Sweden's Voice". *West European Politics* 22 (1): 187-194.

Mantel, J. (2001). Progress Report European Pension Reforms, Merill Lynch.

Marhold, F. (1997). "Die Pensionsreform 1997. Ziele, Maßnahmen, Ergebnisse – eine kritische Würdigung". *Österreichisches Jahrbuch für Politik.* A. Khol, G. Ofner and A. Stirnemann (eds.): 505-514.

Math, A. (2001). Le nouveau projet de loi sur le fonds de réserve des retraites accueilli avec le plus grand scepticisme par les partenaires sociaux, European Industrial Relations Observatory (http://www.eiro.eurofound.ie/).

Maydell, B. v. (1998). Sachgerechte Finanzierungs- und Alterssicherung (insbesondere Beitrags- und/oder Steuerfinanzierung). *Handbuch zur Altersversorgung: Gesetzliche, betriebliche und private Vorsorge in Deutschland.* J.-E. Cramer, W. Förster and F. Ruland (eds.). Frankfurt am Main: Fritz Knapp Verlag, 891-908.

Meinhardt, V. (1997). Vereinigungsfolgen belasten Sozialversicherung, DIW-Wochenbericht 40/97.

Merten, D. (1999). "Einbeziehung aller Selbständigen in die gesetzliche Rentenversicherung". *Deutsche Rentenversicherung* 10-11/99: 609-615.

Miegel, M. and S. Wahl (1999). Solidarische Grundsicherung – private Vorsorge. Der Weg aus der Rentenkrise.

Ministry of Health and Social Affairs (1998). Pension reform in Sweden (http://social.regeringen.se/pressinfo/pdf/pensioner/pensionsreform_en.pdf).

Möller, T. (1999). "The Swedish election 1998: A Protest vote and the birth of a new political landscape?" *Scandinavian Political Studies* 22 (3): 261-276.

Mulé, R. (2000). *Political Parties, Games and Redistribution*. Cambridge: Cambridge University Press.

Müller, H.-W. and R. Tautz (1996). "Ein Grundrentensystem ist teuer!" *Deutsche Rentenversicherung* 12: 770-783.

Müller, K. (1999). *The Political Economy of Pension Reform in Central-Eastern Europe*. Cheltenham: Elgar.

Myles, J. and P. Pierson (2001). "The comparative political economy of pension reform". *The New Politics of the Welfare State*. P. Pierson (ed.). Oxford: Oxford University Press, 305-333.

Myles, J. and J. Quadagno (1997). "Recent trends in public pension reform. A comparative view". *Reform of Retirement Income Policy – International and Canadian Perspectives*. K. G. Banting and R. Boadway (eds.). Kingston: Quenn's University, 247-272.

Nahles, A. (2001). Rentendiskussion endet mit Erfolg für die SPD (http://home.t-online.de/home/detlev.larcher/).

Neumann, W. (1999). *Die Zukunft unserer Renten. Reformdebatten in Frankreich und Deutschland*. Ludwigsburg: Deutsch-Französisches Institut.

Ney, S. (2001a). The Rediscovery of Politics: Democracy and Structural Pension Reform in Continental Europe. Vienna: Interdisciplinary Centre for Comparative Research in the Social Sciences (http://www.dsv.su.se/~mab/mcp/Ney2.doc).

Ney, S. (2001b). Pension Reform in Germany. Vienna: Interdisciplinary Centre for Comparative Research in the Social Sciences (ftp://ftp.iccr.co.at/penref/d2-germany.pdf).

Niemeyer, W. (1990). "Die politisch wichtigen Stationen". *Bundesarbeitsblatt* 1: 21-24.

Niemeyer, W. (1998). "Die Rentenreform 1999". *Neue Zeitschrift für Sozialrecht*, Heft 3: 103-109.

Nohlen, D. (2000). *Wahlrecht und Parteiensystem*. Opladen: Leske + Budrich.

Nullmeier, F. (1996). "Der Rentenkonsens- Eine Stütze des Sozialstaates in Gefahr?" *Gegenwartskunde* 45 (3): 337-350.

Nullmeier, F. and F. W. Rüb (1993). *Die Transformation der Sozialpolitik: Vom Sozialstaat zum Sicherungsstaat*. Frankfurt am Main: Campus Verlag.

Obinger, H. (2001). Vetospieler und Staatstätigkeit in Österreich. Sozial- und wirtschaftspolitische Reformchancen für die neue Mitte-Rechts-Regierung, ZeS-Arbeitspapier Nr. 5/01. Bremen: Zentrum für Sozialpolitik.

OECD (1988). Reforming Public Pensions. Paris.

OECD (1994). OECD Economic Surveys. Sweden. Paris.

OECD (1996). OECD Economic Surveys, 1996-1997: Austria. Paris.

OECD (1998). Maintaining Prosperity in an Ageing Society. Paris.

OECD (1999). OECD Economic Surveys: France. Paris.

OECD (2000a). Statistical and Analytical Information on Ageing. Paris.

OECD (2000b). OECD Economic Surveys 1999-2000: Italy. Paris.

OECD (2001). Economic Outlook. Paris.

Office for Official Publication of the European Communities (1996). Ageing and Pension Expenditure Prospects in the Western World, Luxembourg.

Olson, M. (1982). The Rise and Decline of Nations: Economic Growth, Stagflation, and Social Rigidities. New Haven: Yale University Press.

Olsson, S. (1987). Sweden. Growth to Limits: The Western European Welfare States since World War II vol. 4. Appendix (Synopses, Bibliographies, Tables). P. Flora (ed.). Berlin: Walter de Gruyter: 1-64.

Orenstein, M. A. (2000). How Politics and Institutions Affect Pension Reform in Three Postcommunist Countries, World Bank Policy Research Working Paper, Syracuse University.

Orszag, P. R. and J. E. Stiglitz (1999). Rethinking Pension Reform: Ten Myths about Social Security Systems. Conference on "New Ideas About Old Age Security", Washington, DC.

Palier, B. (2000). "'Defrosting' the French Welfare State". West European Politics 23 (2): 113-136.

Palier, B. (2002). "Beyond Retrenchment: Four problems in current welfare state research and one suggestion how to overcome them". What Future for Social Security? Debates and Reforms in National and Cross-National Perspective. J. Clasen (ed.). London: Kluwer Law International, 105-120.

Palme, J. and I. Wennemo (1997). Swedish Social Security in the 1990s: Reform and Retrenchment (manuscript).

Palmer, E. (2000). "Swedish pension reform – How did it evolve and what does it mean for the future?" NBER-Kiel Institute conference on "Coping with the Pension Crisis – where does Europe stand?", Kiel.

Paparella, D. (2001). Supplementary pension funds under debate, Eiroline (http://www.eiro.eurofound.ie/).

Pedersini, R. (2002). Government initiatives spark major confrontation with trade unions, Eiroline (http://www.eiro.eurofound.ie/).

Pernicka, S. (2001a). Future role of social partnership under dispute, Eiroline (http://www.eiro.eurofound.ie/).

Pernicka, S. (2001b). Social partners agree far-reaching reform of severance pay, Eiroline (http://www.eiro.eurofound.ie/).

Pierson, P. (1994). *Dismantling of the Welfare State? Reagan, Thatcher, and the Politics of Retrenchment*. Cambridge: Cambridge University Press.

Pierson, P. (1996). "The new politics of the welfare state". *World Politics* 48, January 1996: 143-79.

Pierson, P. (1997). The politics of pension reform. *Reform of Retirement Income Policy – International and Canadian Perspectives*. K. G. Banting and R. Boadway (eds.). Kingston: Queen's University, 273-294.

Pierson, P. (1998). "Irresistible forces, immovable objects: post-industrial welfare states confront permanent austerity". *Journal of European Public Policy* 5 (4): 539-560.

Pierson, P. and R. K. Weaver (1993). "Imposing Losses in Pension Policy". *Do Institutions matter? Government capabilities in the United States and Abroad*. R. K. Weaver and B. A. Rockmann (ed.). Washington, DC: The Brookings Institution, 110-150.

Pitruzello, S. (1997). "Social Policy and the Implementation of the Maastricht Fiscal Convergence Criteria: The Italian and French Attempts at Welfare and Pension Reforms". *Social Research* 64(4): 1589-1642.

Pontusson, J. (1997). *The limits of Social Democracy. Investment politics in Sweden*. Ithaca: Cornell University Press.

Prinz, C. and B. Marin (1999). *Pensionsreformen. Nachhaltiger Sozialumbau am Beispiel Österreichs*. Frankfurt am Main: Campus Verlag.

Rahn, M. (1999). Reform der gesetzlichen Rentenversicherung in Deutschland aus rechtsvergleichender Sicht. *Rentenversicherung im internationalen Vergleich*. Verband Deutscher Rentenversicherungsträger. Frankfurt am Main: 377-410.

Regini, M. (1997). "Still engaging in corporatism? Einige Lehren aus jüngsten italienischen Erfahrungen mit der Konzertierung". *Politische Vierteljahresschrift* 38 (2): 298-318.

Reuber, L. (2000). *Politik im Medienzirkus*. Frankfurt am Main: Verlag der Universitätsbuchhandlung Blazek und Bergmann seit 1891 GmbH.

Reynaud, E. (1997). Des fonds d'épargne retraite créés par la loi, Eiroline (http://www.eiro.eurofound.ie/).

Richter, S. (2001). *Ideen, Interessen und Institutionen. Bestimmungsfaktoren des rentenpolitischen Entscheidungsprozesses*. Diplomarbeit, Universität Konstanz.

Roller, E. (1999). "Shrinking the Welfare State: Citizens' Attitudes Toward Cuts in Social Spending in Germany in the 1990s". *German Politics* 8 (1): 21-39.

Rosanelli, M. and J. Wolf (1994). Exkurs I: Die italienischen Rentnergewerkschaften. *Alter und gewerkschaftliche Politik*. J. Wolf, M. Kohli and H. Künemund (eds.), Cologne: Bund Verlag, 97-121.

Ross, F. (2000). "'Beyond Left and Right': The New Partisan Politics of Welfare". *Governance* 13 (2): 155-183.

Ruland, F. (1999). "Contra: Bedürftigkeitsorientierte Mindestsicherung". *Deutsche Rentenversicherung* 8-9: 480-493.

Rürup, B. (2000). "Die Pensionsreform 1997". *Versicherungsgeschichte Österreichs* 6: 353-379.

Rürup, B. and I. Schröter (1997). Perspektiven der Pensionsversicherung in Österreich. *Gutachten im Auftrag des Bundesministeriums für Arbeit, Gesundheit und Soziales*, Darmstadt.

SACO, Sveriges Akademikers Centralorganisation (1994). Remissvar: Reformerat Pensionssystem (SOU 1994:20).

Sauviat, C. (1998). Réforme des retraites: un premier pas du gouvernement Jospin vers une forme de capitalisation, Eiroline (http://www.eiro.eurofound.ie).

Sauviat, C. (1999). Réforme des retraites: réactions des partenaires sociaux, Eiroline (http://www.eiro.eurofound.ie).

Sauviat, C. (2000). Nouvel épisode du débat sur la réforme des retraites, Eiroline (http://www.eiro.eurofound.ie).

Scarbrough, E. (2000). "West European welfare states: The old politics of retrenchment". *European Journal of Political Research* 38: 225-259.

Scharpf, F. W. (1997a). Balancing Sustainability and Security in Social Policy. Paris: OECD.

Scharpf, F. W. (1997b). *Games Real Actors Play: Actor-Centred Institutionalism in Policy Research*. Boulder, CO: Westview Press

Scharpf, F. W. (2000a). "Economic Changes, Vulnerabilities, and Institutional Capabilities". *From Vulnerability to Competitiveness* (vol. 1). F. W. Scharpf and V. A. Schmidt (eds.). Oxford: Oxford University Press, 21-124.

Scharpf, F. W. (2000b). "Institutions in comparative policy research". *Comparative Political Studies* 33 (6/7): 762-789.

Scharpf, F. W. and V. A. Schmidt (2000). Conclusions. *From Vulnerability to Competitiveness* (vol. 1). F. W. Scharpf and V. A. Schmidt (eds.). Oxford: Oxford University Press, 310-336.

Schäuble, W. (2001). *Mitten im Leben*. Gengenbach/Berlin: Goldmann.

Schludi, M. (1997). Kürzungspolitik im Wohlfahrtsstaat – Deutschland und Schweden im Vergleich. Diplomarbeit, Universität Konstanz.

Schmähl, W. (1999). "Arbeit – Basis für die soziale Sicherung der Zukunft". *Wandel der Arbeitswelt – Folgerungen für die Sozialpolitik*. W. Schmähl and H. Rische (eds.). Baden-Baden: Nomos, 189-226.

Schmähl, W. (2001). "Finanzverflechtung der gesetzlichen Rentenversicherung. Interner Finanzausgleich und Finanzbeziehungen mit dem Bund sowie anderen Sozialversicherungsträgern – Elemente einer Bestandsaufnahme und einige Reformüberlegungen". *Finanzierungsverflechtung in der Sozialen Sicherung.*

Analyse der Finanzierungsströme und -strukturen. K.-D. Henke and W. Schmähl (eds.). Baden-Baden: Nomos, 9-37.

Schmitter, P. C. and G. Lehmbruch (1979). *Trends Toward Corporatist Intermediation.* Beverly Hills: Sage.

Sebald, M. (1998). "Die 'Sparpakete' Mitte der neunziger Jahre". *Sozialpartnerschaft und Entscheidungsprozesse.* E. Tálos and B. Kittel (eds.). Vienna: Hochschuljubiläumsstiftung der Stadt Wien, 5-105.

Settergren, O. (2001). "The automatic balance mechanism of the Swedish pension system – a non technical introduction". *Wirtschaftspolitische Blätter* 4: 339-349.

Siebert, H. (1998). "Pay-as-You-Go versus Capital-Funded Pension Systems: The Issues". *Redesigning Social Security.* H. Siebert. Kiel, Mohr Siebeck (eds.). Tübingen: Mohr-Siebeck, 3-33.

Siegel, N. A. (2002). *Baustelle Sozialpolitik. Konsolidierung und Rückbau im internationalen Vergleich.* Frankfurt am Main: Campus Verlag.

Sinn, H.-W. (1999). "The crisis of Germany´s pension insurance system and how it can be resolved. CESifo Working Paper no. 191, Munich.

Socialdepartementet (1996). Välfärdsprojektet. Pensionärerna och den ekonomiska krisen. Stockholm.

Socialdepartementet (1999). Sämre för mig Bättre för oss. En analys av pensionärernas ekonomiska situation under 1990-talet. Stockholm.

SOU (1990:76). Allmän pension. Huvudbetänkande av pensionsberedningen. Socialdepartementet. Stockholm.

SOU (1994:20). Reformerat pensionssystem. Betänkande av Pensionsarbets-gruppen. Socialdepartementet. Stockholm.

SPD, Sozialdemokratische Partei Deutschlands (1997). Strukturreform statt Leistungskürzungen. Vorschläge der Alterssicherungskommission der SPD zur Zukunft der Renten. Bonn.

Standfest, E. (1999). "Zur aktuellen Lage der Rentenversicherung". *Deutsche Rentenversicherung,* Heft 6-7: 325-334.

Stephens, J. D. (1979). *The Transition from Capitalism to Socialism.* Atlantic Highlands, NJ: Humanities Press.

Streeck, W. (1994). "Pay Restraint Without Incomes Policy: Institutionalised Monetarism and Industrial Unionism in Germany". *The Return to Incomes Policy.* R. Dore, R. Boyer and Z. Mars (eds.). London: Pinter, 118-140.

Streeck, W. (2002). "Weniger ist für viele mehr". *Financial Times Deutschland, 20 February 2002*

Strøm, K. and W. C. Müller (1999). Political Parties and Hard Choices. *Policy, Office, or Votes?* K. Strøm and W. C. Müller (eds.). Cambridge: Cambridge University Press, 1-35.

Sully, M. (1996). "The 1995 Austrian Election: Winter of Discontent". *West European Politics* 19 (3): 633-640.

Swank, D. (2000). "Political Institutions and Welfare State Restructuring: The Impact of Institutions on Social Policy Change in Developed Democracies". *The New Politics of the Welfare State*. P. Pierson (ed.). New York: Oxford University Press: 197-237.

Szarka, J. (1997). "Snatching defeat from the Jaws of Victory: The French Parliamentary Elections of 25 May and 1 June 1997". *West European Politics* 20 (4): 192-199.

Tálos, E. (2001). "Sozialpolitik zwischen konservativer Tradition und neoliberaler Orientierung. Eine Einjahresbilanz der ÖVP/FPÖ-Regierung". *Kurswechsel* 1: 17-29

Tálos, E. and B. Kittel (1999). "Sozialpartnerschaft und Sozialpolitik". *Zukunft der Sozialpartnerschaft*. F. Karlhofer and E. Tálos (eds.). Vienna: Signum Verlag, 137-164.

Tálos, E. and B. Kittel (2001). *Gesetzgebung in Österreich. Netzwerke, Akteure und Interaktionen in politischen Entscheidungsprozessen*. Vienna: Universitätsverlag.

Tálos, E. and K. Wörister (1998). "Soziale Sicherung in Österreich". *Soziale Sicherung im Wandel – Österreich und seine Nachbarstaaten. Ein Vergleich*. E. Tálos (eds.). Vienna: Böhlau Verlag, 209-288.

Taverne, D. (2000). *Can Europe Pay for its Pensions?* London: Cogan Page.

Taylor-Gooby, P. (2001). "Sustaining state welfare in hard times: who will foot the bill". *Journal of European Social Policy* 11 (2): 133-147.

TCO, Tjänstemannens Centralorganisation (1994). Yttrande. Reformerat Pensionssystem. Betänkande av Pensionsarbetsgruppen (SOU 1994:20).

Traxler, F. (2001). Reform of severance pay under discussion, Eiroline (http://www.eiro.eurofound.ie).

Trentini, M. (1997). Welfare reform results from negotiations between government and trade unions, Eiroline (http://www.eiro.eurofound.ie).

Tsebelis, G. (1995). "Decision making in political systems: veto players in presidentialism, parliamentarianism, multicameralism and multipartism". *British Journal of Political Science* 25 (3): 289-325.

Tsebelis, G. (1999). "Veto Players and Law Production in Parliamentary Democracies: An Empirical Analysis". *The American Political Science Review* 93 (3): 591-608.

Universität Kassel (2002). Bilanz der Europawahl und der Landtagswahlen 1999 (http://www.uni-kassel.de/fb5/politikwissenschaft/Demokratietheorie/wahlen99.html).

US Department of Health and Human Services (1986). *Social Security Programmes Throughout the World*. Washington, DC.

Vail, M. I. (1999). "The better part of valour: The politics of French welfare reform". *Journal of European Social Policy* 9 (4): 311-329.

VDR, Verband Deutscher Rentenversicherungsträger (2001). *Rentenversicherung in Zeitreihen. Juli 2001*. Frankfurt am Main.

Veil, M. (2000a). "Konfrontation oder Konsens? Rentensystem und Rentenreformen in Frankreich". *Frankreich-Jahrbuch*. Deutsch-Französisches Institut: 205-223.

Veil, M. (2000b). "Reform der Alterssicherung in Frankreich – Thematisierungschancen für die Diskussion in Deutschland". *WSI Mitteilungen* 11/2000: 726-734.

Visser, J. (2000). "France". *Trade Unions in Western Europe since 1945*. B. Ebbinghaus and J. Visser (eds.). London: Macmillan, 237-277.

Wadensjö, E. (2000). Sweden: Reform of the public pension system. *Social dialogue and pension reform*. E. Reynaud (ed.). Geneva: International Labour Office: 67-80.

Wadensjö, E. (2002). "Active strategies for older workers in Sweden". *Active strategies for older workers in the European Union*. M. Jepsen, D. Foden and M. Hutsebaut (eds.). Brussels: European Trade Union Institute: 381-402.

Wagschal, U. (2000). Schub- und Bremskräfte sozialstaatlicher Anstrengungen. *Der gezügelte Wohlfahrtsstaat. Sozialpolitik in reichen Industrienationen*. H. Obinger and U. Wagschal (eds.). Frankfurt am Main: Campus Verlag, 73-94.

Weaver, R. K. (1998). "The Politics of Pensions: Lessons from Abroad". *Framing the Social Security Debate: Values, Politics, and Economics*. R. D. Arnold, M. J. Graetz and A. H. Munnell (eds.). Washington, DC: Brookings Institution Press, 183-228.

Weigel, W. and A. Amann (1987). *Growth to Limits: The Western European Welfare States since World War II*. Volume 4. Appendix (Synopses, Bibliographies, Tables). P. Flora (ed.). Berlin: Walter de Gruyter, 529-609.

Weizsäcker, J. v. (2000). "Alle Macht den Rentnern?" *Generationengerechtigkeit. Leitbild für das 21. Jahrhundert*. W. Homolka (ed.). Frankfurt am Main: Alfred-Herrhausen-Gesellschaft für Internationalen Dialog, 39-47.

Werding, M. (2001). *Auswirkungen des demographischen Wandels auf die öffentlichen Finanzen: Modellrechnungen für die staatlichen Alterssicherungssysteme – im Auftrag des Bundesministeriums der Finanzen*. München: Institut für Wirtschaftsforschung.

Wijnbergen, C. v. (2000). *Co-opting the Opposition: The Role of Party Competi-*

tion and Coalition-Making in Curing the Dutch Welfare State. Paper prepared for presentation at the Second Graduate Student Training Retreat in Comparative Research, Yale University.

Wischeropp, D. (1999). Das französische Sozialleistungssystem. Leistungen, Finanzierungsprobleme und Lösungsansätze. *Soziale Leistungen und ihre Finanzierung. Länderstudien zu Frankreich, Italien und den Niederlanden.* D. Döring, R. Hauser, and W. Schmähl (eds.). Berlin: Duncker & Humblot: 39-188.

World Bank (1994). *Averting the Old Age Crisis.* Oxford: Oxford University Press

Wöss, J. (2000). "Gesetzliche Pensionsversicherung – Rückblick auf die letzten 30 Jahre" (http://www.netzwerkinnovation.at/downloads/themen/balance/09GV_G_Woess.pdf).

Index

tary regimes/schemes) 191, 192, 204-206, 207, 213, 251-253

regimes spéciaux (special regimes/ schemes) 191, 192, 200, 209, 215, 217

replacement rates 17, 30, 109, 112, 132, 159, 192, 205, 267, 271

Riester, Walter 131, 146, 148, 152, 154, 158, 235

saco (Sveriges Akademikers Centralorganisation / Confederation of Academics) 103

sap (Socialdemokratiska Arbetarepartiet) 92-97, 100-102, 104,106-108, 224, 229

Schmoldt, Hubertus 136

Schröder, Gerhard 145-148, 152, 154, 156-159, 161, 227, 234

Schüssel, Wolfgang 177, 188, 189, 243

seniority pensions (Italy) 46, 112-114, 116-121, 127, 264-266

severance pay 56, 118, 121, 127, 181, 182, 260, 266

Single European Market 13

social partnership ("Sozialpartnerschaft") 167, 168, 180, 182-184, 188, 189

spd (Sozialdemokratische Partei Deutschlands) 132-156, 224, 235

spö (Sozialdemokratische Partei Österreichs) 168-189, 224, 225, 228, 234

strategic disagreement 79

Sweden / Swedish 10, 11, 16, 17, 28, 44-48, 50-57, 72, 89-108, 110, 126, 131, 161, 166, 212,

219, 224, 227, 234-236, 239, 240, 243, 244, 246, 247, 257-258, 266-267

Switzerland 41

system maturation 62, 63, 271

targeting 26, 27

tax resistance 21, 24

tax wedge 33, 36, 39, 40, 132

tco (Tjänstemännens Centralorganisation / Confederation of White Collar Employees) 95, 103

technocratic government (see also caretaker government) 125, 126, 208, 232, 233

transition costs (see also double payment problem) 26, 38, 108

vdk (Sozialverband VdK Deutschland) 154

vdr (Verband Deutscher Rentenversicherer) 133, 149, 152, 154, 162

Vermittlungsausschuß (Mediating Committee) 143, 156

veto players 64, 65, 77, 105, 162

veto points 63, 64

Vranitzky, Franz 169, 229

wkö (Wirtschaftskammer Österreichs / Federal Economic Chamber) 168, 171, 187

World Bank 39, 39, 56